A Reluctant Heretic

T0369153

Let us soar like an Eagle for eternal truth!

A Reluctant
Heretic

2010
Aquila Press, Inc.

Request for permission should be addressed to Aquila Press, Inc., 1350 South Ninth Street, Noblesville, Indiana, 46060.

This first edition printed by Trafford Publishing.

Co-published by **Aquila Press, Inc.** and **Trafford Publishing.**

Order this book online at www.trafford.com
or email orders@trafford.com

Most Trafford titles are also available at major online book retailers.

Printed in Victoria, BC, Canada.

ISBN: 978-1-4269-2969-4 (sc)
ISBN: 978-1-4269-2970-0 (eb)

Our mission is to efficiently provide the world's finest, most comprehensive book publishing service, enabling every author to experience success. To find out how to publish your book, your way, and have it available worldwide, visit us online at www.trafford.com

Trafford rev. 6/30/2010

 www.trafford.com

North America & international
toll-free: 1 888 232 4444 (USA & Canada)
phone: 250 383 6864 ♦ fax: 812 355 4082

Preface

ON NOVEMBER 11, 2005, Adelaide Pelley Pearson graduated to a Higher Dimension of Spirit. She was ninety-two years old at the time. During a most unique and challenging life, being the daughter of William Dudley Pelley, she experienced both private and public challenges that resulted in constant evaluations as to the worth and purpose of what she lived through.

During the last twenty-five years of her life she dealt with two bouts of cancer, a stomach aneurism, a partially blocked aorta valve and two heart attacks. Her mortal body had great difficulty in keeping up with her indomitable spirit. However, she wanted no heroics. She was always uncomfortable in having her aches and ill health recited. She referred to such voiced list as an "organ recital."

However, despite her personal reluctance to have her ills publicized, they are stated here to cover the circumstance that while she always looked forward to ultimately organizing into publishable form her ponderings and observations, her failing health never allowed her to do so. She had the will but lacked sufficient physical vitality.

For sixty-two years, Adelaide and I were mortal partners. We researched together, wrote together, printed together, published together and played together. We functioned as one person. And, while we have been separated physically, we have not been separated spiritually. We are eternally bonded.

It has now fallen upon me to organize and make available to the public some of her timely and pertinent insights. I know I am doing so with her help from a higher perspective.

"Reluctant Heretic"? This is a self-identification that she applied to herself over the years.

Here is how she expressed it in one short piece of writing. It will serve as the "introduction" to this book.

(It should be noted that I will italicize and put within parentheses all editorial comments in this book.)

Mel Pearson

March 25, 2009

Introduction

ALLOW me to present my credentials. I was born a "wasp" of the first water. This means, as I suspect you know, that I was born (9/1/1914) into a white, Anglo Saxon Protestant family two days before the guns began firing in Europe in World War I. I had the very good excuse to be born in Vermont, a very exclusive club because there are so few of us. Further, anyone from Vermont is dubbed an eccentric before a word is spoken, so I speak with greater freedom than other areas might permit me.

My forebears, for what it is worth, were so far as I can ascertain, completely British, English, Scottish, Irish and Welsh in goodly mixture. My grandmother once remarked that she'd always thought there had been an Indian wife, way back somewhere, but my maternal grandmother was noted for speaking outrageous things that were promptly shushed by the rest of the family. I always hoped she was right, and she frequently was, but I never found evidence.

I heard the family discuss such possibility and also that the ancestors were hardworking, thrifty, honest, and spoke with brash voices. A U.S. President turned out something less than upright but had the grace to die before the spotlight reached him. Graft and corruption were there but in spots and places where the public mop could be applied. Evil, public and private, was in short, controllable, or so we thought.

And the thought, as well as the reality, created a different atmosphere in which we lived and breathed and had our being.

7

Trust in leaders, institutions, in each other, were greater than our suspicions. Whenever trust proved ill lodged we coped, felt disappointment, but not despair. We could handle anything. In later years my children were delighted to note an association in name with the eastern bird, the pelican, from which emerged the phrase of confidence "Pelley can!"

This feeling of competence has been lost since the days at the other end of the bridge. Everything is too long, too complex, too powerful, even for groups to cope with, let alone individual citizens. Evil, that is forces that work against our security and our contentment, is out of hand and we are, as a people, scared, confused, and not a little angry.

How can we cope today? There are ways, but it is going to take courage, perseverance and imagination to get it back under control again. Can we do it? I think so, but I am going to have to get a little self-centered in order for you to understand how I arrived at my conclusions.

The following hypothetical story was always a jumping off point for me to launch my thinking as to the state of the nation. It seemed to have real impact and emotional content as to what we faced in this nation.

I used it in frequent written articles or when I was a participant on public panels discussing social issues.

Who's pushing them into the water?

TWO FISHERMEN were approaching a stream to fish. When they arrived at the stream they stopped in horror and bewilderment. The stream was filled with children trying to reach the safety of the shore. They dropped their fishing gear and sprang into the water to save as many struggling children as they could.

Some they were able to bring to the shore but the vast majority was beyond their reach and helplessly sinking beneath the waves. As the waters became more turbulent their efforts became more futile.

Looking up stream they saw that there was an endless flow of children in the life-and-death struggle to keep from drowning.

Reacting spontaneously, and urgently, one of the fishermen made his way to the shore and headed up stream. The other fisherman shouted, "Where are you going? Stay here and help me save these children!"

The other fisherman responded, "I am going up stream to see who is pushing these children into the water!"

Who is pushing these children into the water? Who was causing this drowning environment in which an endless number of children were desperately seeking the safety of the shore? There had to be an answer!

This hypothetical story is most relevant to our nation's serious problems. We are a people, a society and a government blindly dealing with the serious problems threatening life without confronting the underlying causes of the national dilemma. And, all the while the victims, both children and adults, are being created faster than they can be helped.

This simple parable illustrates the futility of our action today. People of good will and dedication are devoting their lives and energies to hauling the dead and dying out of the water. Few persons have the courage or the imagination to strike up stream to find out where the bodies are coming from, who or what is really responsible, and try to stop the tragedy at its source.

We are trying to cope with the problems of pervasive hunger, crime, pollution of air, water and soil, not to mention endemic political pollution, by treating the symptoms and not the diseases. We underwrite massive relief programs so that no one shall die of starvation. We demand law and order by passing a few laws that are spasmodically enforced against small offenders while the large ones go unpunished.

The national picture is so grim, so heart-rending, so tragic, while the threats to life are needless and preventable! Along with my husband, Mel, and his brother, Walt, we were determined to research and find answers. We weren't ordained to safe the world, but we wanted a voice to speak for the victims of the drowning environment. We wanted to help them to the safety of a secure shore!

On August 11, 1961, the three of us incorporated Aquila Press in order to research, document and identify what were the economic, financial and political entities that exercised abusive and monopolistic power. We wanted to identify and make known to the public those who were destroying constitutional rights and making everyone dependent on the whims of incumbent administrations.

Most seriously, how were these entities preventing the nation from utilizing its full working capacity to meet the needs of the total citizenry?

Since my father, William Dudley Pelley, had been denied the right to engage in political writings of any kind while under parole in 1950, he had turned over to our corporation the copyright to his book **No More Hunger** so we could promote its proposals. Within its pages are outlined the steps to incorporate the entire working capacity of the nation, making each citizen a voting and dividend-receiving shareholder.

With full implementation of human rights we would truly have a participatory democracy!

We had a dual approach: First, to identify the monopolistic entities who exercised economic, financial and political control in the society, and, secondly, to present the proposals that would bring about an equitable and peaceful solution to our major problems.

The Eagle's Eye, a monthly magazine, was born to fulfill both objectives.

Walter did most of the investigative research. He commenced obtaining all the independent reports he could from individuals and groups doing similar inquiry. He checked congressional committee reports, which focused on corporate abuse and monopolistic control and he scrutinized the actual reports of the transnational corporations.

We were a recipient of the Congressional Record and exchanged thinking with all organizations mutually concerned with what was happening to the nation.

My husband and I were co-editors. We did most of the writing. However, we did have outstanding guest writers such as Gen. Hugh B. Hester who traveled the nation lecturing against U. S. policies and embroilment in the Vietnam War. Another writer was Willis Overholzer, one of the founders of the "Overholzer-Wilson Library," and several times a candidate for the United States Congress.

We were the fortunate recipients of that Library and it was of much help as background material in writing articles for **The Eagle's Eye.** The Library was most comprehensive as an historical coverage of private banking and its abusive role in both our nation and the world.

Our subscribers were very diverse. On our mailing list were struggling farmers, workmen in industrial plants, businessmen and citizens in all walks of life who were distressed as to what was happening to their society. Also, we had contributors who did special research and were equally concerned about the state of the nation. This included writers like Gerald Piel, publisher of the Scientific American, who along with others authored the unique report called "The Triple Revolution."

For seven years, 1963 to 1970, we published our monthly magazine. We also wrote and published booklets focusing on specific areas of the economy and the bureaucracy in Washington. We promoted the features of a "National Cooperative Commonwealth," proposed in **No More Hunger,** and we published and promoted a companion book called **Challenge to Crisis,** which my husband wrote in 1969, which updated the proposals in light of advancing technology.

(The following editorials are ones that Adelaide wrote for the Eagle's Eye.)

The Challenge Is Ours --- 17

Inherent Right to Make Decisions --- 21

One In A Thousand --- 29

Giants In The Earth --- 33

Voices of Change --- 39

Collision Courses! --- 45

Look Behind All Labels ---51

Road to Utopia. . . --- 57

The Three B's --- 63

Hypocrisy and Sham --- 69

Whence Came They? ---73

Harbingers of Change --- 79

Yes, They'll Listen --- 83

Debacle Ahead! . . . --- 87

There Is An Alternative --- 91

"Social Planners" --- 95

Importance of Man ---101

The Roots Lie Deep ---107

How About Specifics? --- 113

The Great Election --- 119

Christmas Renewed --- 125

Participants --- 131

"Charity is Criminal" --- 135

Search for Bedrock --- 141

Ladder of Time --- 147

What Price Security? --- 153

"Eye Troubles" --- 159

What Makes Sense? --- 165

Our Day of Infamy! --- 169

The Most Precious Gift ---175

The Uncommitted --- 183

A Rational Religion --- 189

Proliferation of Change --- 193

The Uncommon Man --- 201

Easter . . .1966 --- 207

The Priceless Ounce --- 213

White Hats vs. Black --- 219

Chasm --- 223

Utopia, Really? --- 229

Brotherhood of Man --- 235

Realities --- 239

The New Reformation --- 243

A Design for All --- 249

Permanent Moratorium --- 255

Greater Love . . . --- 259

Woman Power --- 263

Who Shall It Profit? --- 267

Old Glory --- 275

The Thread --- 279

The Corporate Structure --- 283

A Higher Law --- 289

"We the People!" --- 295

Participation --- 299

The Real Obstacles --- 305

Tragic Stupidity --- 311

Upsetting Applecarts --- 317

The Generation Gap --- 323

Right to be Different --- 329

Welcoming Change --- 335

How to Answer --- 341

Imperatives --- 345

On with the New --- 349

A Question of Who Plans --- 353

A Relevant Religion --- 359

An Eye to the Future --- 363

Nowhere to Go but Up! --- 369

Are You With It? --- 375

A Bridge to Tomorrow --- 381

Impact of Television --- 385

For Alternatives --- 389

What We Seek --- 393

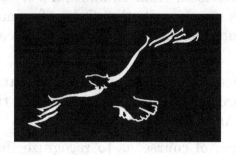

Vol. I, No. 1, January 1963:

I say ye are majestic and know not your kingship.

I come to bring it into you, to tell you of your grandeur,

To fell the croakers who defile man as dust.

(*Golden Scripts*, Chapter 198)

The Challenge Is Ours

IF THERE is one thing we should get firmly engrained in our thinking as we commence this new year of 1963, it is that the problems we face as a nation do not have to be tolerated one moment beyond a people's determined desire intelligently to solve them.

Let us with candor and honesty dispel from our thinking that we are hopelessly slated for perpetual suffering. Despair and futility can have no room in the hearts and souls of those who can catch even the merest glimpse of humans as the potential arbiters of their own destiny.

What should be our starting point? It should be simply this: The problems we face and the suffering endured are human made. They are not the result of directives, or power exercised, from inhabitants of some distant planet. They are not the fiats of some Celestial Potentate engaged in the dark arts of sorcery or black magic.

The injustices, the inequities, the hardships, all problems, are mortal created. As such, they can be uncreated. As such, they can be solved.

The first step, of course, is to recognize that we have problems. Too many Americans are unaware that they are the victims of any wrongdoing through the circumstance of a few taking advantage of the many. In a state of trance they strive from one day to another trying to eke out a living, all the while parroting "equal opportunity" and extolling the "American way of life."

On the other hand, a growing segment of Americans is commencing to realize that much is wrong with our ways of producing, distributing and rewarding and that both economic and political adjustments grow daily more imperative. Further, that only by making such adjustments can we truly begin to approach the American ideal.

The second step is to understand the problems. This means that we cannot remove the causes of our problems unless, and until, we thoroughly, deliberately and honestly examine the bedrock facts. Moreover, we must be willing to bring to such study fresh outlooks, devoid of prejudice or crystallized habits of thinking. Solutions, in short, cannot be forthcoming by accepting distortions, half-truths and faulty concepts of economics and government.

Solutions become surprisingly obvious when all facts are weighed in logical perspectives.

The third step is to endorse and install the arrived at solutions. This means positive action through the literal mechanics of constructive reform.

The foregoing three steps are indeed an over-simplification of the tremendous task of renovating a nation that had permitted itself to be burdened down with a two trillion dollar indebtedness, that denies employment to five to six millions of able-bodied and willing workers, and that tolerates the deplorable spectre of thirty-two million Americans living in poverty in the past year of 1961!

Yet, they do outline the fundamental steps that must be pursued consecutively to their successful conclusion. Any other approach is unrealistic and offers only increased frustration and despair.

The Eagle's Eye is dedicating itself to the over-all program of vividly presenting the problems that exist, analyzing their causes, and propounding those adjust-ments or reforms that bring about the good and abundant life for every American. It has not undertaken this role lightly or without the deepest conviction that a new era of constructive human relationships looms fast on yonder horizon.

The first issue of this magazine marks the beginning of an open, public pleading to gain support for our goals. Henceforth, **The Eagle's Eye** will be the official voice of Aquila Press, Inc. It was organized in August of 1961 and has as its central program the dynamic recommendations contained in the book **No More Hunger** written by William Dudley Pelley, one of the nation's outstanding researchers in philosophy, economics and government.

Along with this main program, Aquila has already published a number of booklets on allied subjects and will continue to make new ones available.

In one sense our chief undertaking is one of education. However, beside the graphic, factual portrayal of existing conditions, coupled with the propounding of workable solutions, there is the challenging need to highlight the prime importance of humans themselves in the tremendous drama of life.

In the final analysis, it is not an attainable, abundant society in itself that is the highest goal we seek, but an arena wherein ordinary, two-legged humans can perform to the utmost of each individual's spiritual and cultural capacity.

As we start this New Year together, let us be firm in our faith and conviction that we possess all the ingredients for the building of the kind of America where our hopes and aspirations for little children can be fulfilled.

And where human relationships are so arranged throughout the economy and government that the quality of life underscores all of our dealing with each other!

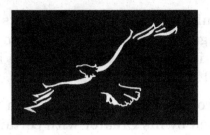

Vol. 1, No. 2, February 1963

Where is the oak that hath not its acorn?

Where is the acorn that contains not its oak?

All things I tell you transpire in time.

All promises mature. All expectations realize.

There is no defeat for the watchers in eternity!

(Golden Scripts, Chapter 219)

Inherent Right to Make Decisions

THE LARGER part of this issue is deliberately being devoted to a clearer grasp of why we seek constructive change, and what the basic premise is upon which such change is predicated. There is much more at stake than exposing wrongs and propounding remedial measures for the material comforts of all the people.

Our ultimate goal is immeasurably greater in scope and dynamic in meaning. Once we grasp its essence we will be motivated by a will to achievement that cannot be stayed.

What has become of man as Man?

Here is the real challenge of our times. Here is the bedrock problem that underlies all other problems.

When, and only when, we face up to its implications and deeper significance, can we determine and pursue a course of action for constructive change in our society that fulfills all needs.

It is in the context of considering man as a human being, "endowed by his Creator with certain inalienable rights," that we can best advance proposals for his betterment.

Unfortunately, few organizations that have risen in this nation have focused their attention on Man as a divine creature working out his destiny and growth in a purposeful Universe. The majority is genuinely seeking honesty in government and a more equitable sharing of production but they fail to consider the inherent rights of the individual.

As a consequence, the yardstick employed to determine his progress has been solely materialistic and not spiritual.

This by no means implies that the materialistic well-being of man is not important. It is of vital importance. At the same time, it must be grasped that such well-being is but a means to an end.

Of ultimate, and paramount, importance is that all human relationships worked out in the economic, political and cultural life of a society must serve to enhance the true worth of each individual. When his life's role has been played it is not the number of cars he has owned, it is not the luxurious home he possessed, it is not the ease with which his material comforts were provided that will determine what society has done for the individual.

The true measure is whether or not the character attainment and self-development of each person has been in direct ratio to his or her utmost capacity.

Imbed this cardinal goal in all your thinking and real perspective is yours for considering all contemplated changes in society!

FROM THE TIME this nation was founded up to well into the Twentieth Century, the struggle to meet the material needs of man has been the chief obstacle in his development. Opening new territory, cultivating larger and larger crops, the introduction of group endeavor with the advent of the factory, the advancements in both communication and transportation, all these have been steps toward perfecting the means of more easily meeting material needs.

It would be unfair to conclude that such historical struggles have not contributed to the character building of the individual. It would be equally unfair not to recognize that as society became more complex and more interrelated the individual commenced to lose identity and has increasingly become the pawn of voracious and unscrupulous forces that appreciate neither the material nor spiritual well being of the individual.

The tragedy, and the irony, of our times is that whereas we as a nation have developed a potential through science and the technology of mass production whereby no citizen would have to be denied any of his material needs to surfeit, tens of millions of our citizens live in want, endure physical hardships and futilely strive to acquire material necessities.

Instead of being given work, the unemployed are doled out subsistence checks and relief commodities; instead of a market for the farmer's produce, he is paid subsidies to let his productive land lie idle; instead of utilizing our best technological know-how for the most efficient production for the nation's needs, we stumble along with obsolete methods and refuse to lift the stress and strain from the backs of the tens of millions of producers.

The material challenge no longer exists as to capability. Potentially, no longer does the meeting of the material needs of the people have to be a problem. The challenge that does exist and must be met is the modifying or correcting of our methods of producing, rewarding and distributing so our material capability can benefit all of the people.

However, the foregoing challenge is but half of the picture, although complemented by the first, that constitutes the real goal of Man. This is man's full and absolute exercise of his own sovereignty, his right to make decisions!

AN ENTIRE new psychology and understanding must underlie our thinking in working out the economic and political problems that confront all people. No longer can we tolerate any conditioning of mind or superficial prejudice, which prevents us from facing our problems realistically, honestly and with open minds and open hearts.

Too many sincere and honest people, properly concerned over the problems we face, refuse to differentiate between certain ideals they attach to conventional methods of doing business and the un-

24

workability of such methods as to result. They cannot seem to grasp that it is immaterial whether a system is called "capitalistic," "free enterprise" or a "cooperative commonwealth" or some other name.

What is relevant and of prime concern is whether or not a structure of human relationships, both materially and spiritually, serves the true purpose of man, individually and collectively.

Let us accept the fact that we now have the physical tools by which we can meet all material needs to abundance for all. Let us recognize that labels and slogans are no substitute for existing wrongs that permeate our entire society. Above all, let us focus our attention on the importance of the individual in working for the well-being of, and a purposeful life for, all peoples.

It might be stated that in working out the material needs of the people, the group, is paramount. In working out the spiritual and cultural needs of the people, the individual is paramount.

Let us consider first how the group approach has now become the only rational solution to the economic problems of the nation. In so doing we must clearly grasp that we have developed, and possess, a productive capacity, of both goods and services, to provide to abundance all the basic needs of a people with a minimum of human effort.

We must grasp that the technology developed in mass production requires that all operations of extracting raw stock, manufacturing and the multiple services be done on a big scale to realize maximum efficiency.

Translated into realistic terms, we as a nation must accept that the role of the small factory, the small retailer, and the individual enterprise is irreconcilable with the explosive advances in technology. No longer is it efficient to do things on a small scale. No longer can small enterprises compete or exist in an age when science and invention dictate the close correlation of all operations.

Naturally there are those who are reluctant to accept major change in our way of doing business and desire to retain old methods however obsolete. Not only must they realize that the evolutionary process cannot be circumvented, but more importantly they must envision the tremendous benefits from constructively using all tools for the maximum benefit of all the people.

There is one specific distinction that must be recognized in considering the workability of the present state of automated machinery and billion-dollar corporations that largely make up our economy. The problems of unemployment, vast storehouses of surpluses, and exorbitant prices are not the basic result of too efficient methods of utilizing tools of production. These problems are the result of such tools not being used constructively and intelligently.

In short, there is nothing wrong with tools as tools. There is much wrong with the control and administration of our vast capacity for producing.

IT IS NOW within the realm of realistic, imaginative thinking to comprehend one giant interrelated, coordinated machine that would take all raw stock, refine it and distribute all finished products of every

26

description that are in use today. Bear in mind that less than 5% of the large corporations already supply over 90% of all products. The question is not the possibility of setting up such a machine. The real question should be obvious: Who owns that machine?

It in light of the foregoing that the recommendations contained in **No More Hunger** can best be understood. But they go further than providing for security of job, inviolate possession of home and insuring rightful share of the nation's goods and services. They make as the cornerstone of the whole national social structure, including all levels of government, the inherent right of the people to make all final decisions.

Under such Cooperative Commonwealth absolute power would be reserved to the people. Freed from the unjust controls of monopolistic and monied forces, liberated from all illegal claims and liens against their future earnings, for the first time the people themselves would be direct arbiters of their destiny.

Man is on the threshold of being an active participant and renderer of all decisions affecting his own well-being and that of his family. His right to act, live, decide and perform cannot be denied him. An unshakable faith in the essential honesty, judgment and purpose of man as a human being must permeate all aspects of a new order of human relationships.

NEVER in the history of the world has a nation had better opportunity to set an example for oppressed peoples everywhere to emulate and follow than the United States has now. But first we must put our own house in order.

The spirit of change and sought-for-freedom unsettles the world as nationalities and races over the entire globe are in the throes of adopting new ways and new ideas. One by one despotic rulers and oppressive controls are being discarded.

With increasing cynicism and fear the emerging nations view both Communism and Capitalism as enemies of the dignity of man and his happiness. Too long have these two dominating economies of the world greedily siphoned off the wealth of these countries with no thought given to their well-being and progress.

Into this economic chaos a vital and renovated America must move, with the caliber of inspired leadership which has put into actual practice "man's right to make decisions."

The first decision is yours.

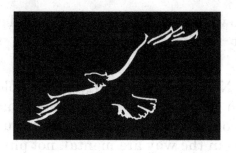

Volume 1, No. 3, March 1963

Receive ye my presence, all ye who are worldly.

Rise up and rejoice with me! For behold

I say unto you that I am Man as he shall be.

(*Golden Scripts*, Chapter 233)

One in a Thousand!

DREAM ALONG with me. Just for a moment, forget the problems that are hounding you. Relax. Picture yourself in a world where you would always be sure of the next meal for yourself and for your children, a world your home is perpetually safe from foreclosure, and on which you would not be paying double in value, a world in which a college education was assured for all your children, a world in which the fear of impossible medical bills and not of being laid off from job was forever gone, a world in which your lone voice in government really had meaning, and in which you could afford to take the time and money to do that thing you've always wanted; to go to Siam or Yellowstone, to study electronics or take banjo lessons, to build that boat or that cabin by the lake . . . Let your mind play around with it for a while. . . .

Do you know that such a world could be? Do you realize that in these fast-moving times, it could be much closer than you think?

Fantastic? Not at all! Barring atomic holocaust, it is inevitable in a world where technology has made an abundant economy possible. Easy? Of course not, but the obstacles in the way are mental, not physical.

Unworkable? Not at all! By basing it on the corporate form, proven a highly efficient means of doing business for private gain, the economy of the nation can be geared to conducting public business for public gain, with every citizen a shareholder in such business.

Unconstitutional? Not at all! The Constitution of the United States does not touch on economic matters in any way, beyond specifying that Congress should have the power to coin and regulate the value of money (not usurped by private banks for private gain), so that a single Constitutional amendment could, without disrupting the provisions of the document in any way, provide the economic safeguards now being wantonly flouted.

COMMUNISTIC? No! Indeed, it is the direct antithesis. Communism, aiming its appeal to the downtrodden, the underprivileged, the poverty-stricken of the earth, endeavors to achieve its ends by binding individuals into collective masses, easily controllable from a central power-directorate at the top, in which the single individual becomes subordinate to the State and is forever lost. The Christian Commonwealth conversely makes its appeal to all persons, ascribing to each individual the traits of dignity, self respect and difference. And guaranteeing to each person equal

30

opportunity to advance in the esteem of his fellowmen according to his merit and his genuine contribution to the physical, mental or spiritual betterment of his fellows.

Welfare state? No, not at all in the sense that a remote and monstrous government, secretly manipulated by financial power-concentrates and industrial monopolies, in which the people themselves wield small influence, makes the decisions that control welfare and progress. Only in the sense that all citizens must recognize that the welfare of each is important to the welfare of all, could it be so considered.

Planned economy? Frankly, yes. And high time, too! By what insane scheme of reasoning have we been taught from the cradle upward that the only proper way to accomplish any goal with ease, efficiency and thrift is to plan ahead in every single aspect of human life, except the national economy?

Why, are we propagandized into thinking a planned economy is a criminal procedure, to be practiced only by dictators and similar regimenters of human ideas and human freedom?

The fact is, the question lies in who does the planning!

In a truly free economy, where human needs were determined in their entirety, where resources and technology were reorganized to meet those needs, where financial manipulation behind the scenes became impossible, where private gain from human misery was abolished, and industrial, political financial secrecy became anathema, economic planning for the common good would become the responsibility, the privilege and pleasure of every thoughtful citizen.

31

THERE would be purpose in life instead of aimless pursuit of distraction, there would be enthusiasm instead of apathy, and material, mental and spiritual progress such as has been only dreamed of, instead of fear, suspicion and weak-kneed shilly-shallying in the face of national and world problems.

Are we constructing an impossible dream? No! If a one in a thousand persons educates himself in the fundamentals of what can be, he will provide sufficient leaven in the loaf. With us, he will work to educate others in the splendor of that goal. With us, he could be ready in the event of great social disruption caused by conflict, by financial collapse, by depression, or other national calamity to lead others back up out of the morass toward a better world here on earth. . . .

Are you that one in a thousand?

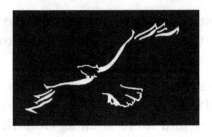

Volume 2, March 1964

We are laborers together in the worlds: That

Is your premise for radiant achievement.

(Golden Scripts, Chapter 10*)*

Giants in the Earth

IN THE sixth Chapter of Genesis, tucked in between Noah's family tree and the story of the construction of the Ark, appears a small paragraph that may be much meatier, more significant and worthy of consideration than the whole fabulous legend of the Deluge itself.

There were giants in the earth in those days, and also after that, when the sons of God came in unto the daughters of men, and they have children to them, the same became mighty men, which were of old, men of renown.

It is not our intention to enter into a theological exposition or metaphysical discussion of what this paragraph is supposed to treat historically, allegorically or symbolically. It just happens to fit our particular view of the present unhappy state of affairs very closely.

Mr. Webster, Unabridged expresses the definition we want in his very first line: "A mythical, manlike or monstrous being of huge stature and strength, and of more than mortal, but less than godlike, power and endowment."

It appears that around the time of the Flood giants went out of style, as a specie anyway, except for lone individuals here and there such as Goliath and Wilt the Stilt who must be considered as human beings who just forgot to stop growing till they got up somewhat above the crowd.

Now, however, there are giants in the earth once more.

We are not going to speculate on what the ancient giants were, literally or symbolically, but we do intend to identify as closely as possible today's mythical manlike, or monstrous, beings which are extremely real indeed.

THESE BEINGS are of more than mortal power and endowment because although they are made by men and of men, they have the strength of many men rolled into one. The lack of godlike qualities, alas, shows up with all too alarming frequency.

The general term for these giants is Organization, and the American people stand head and shoulders above the rest of the world in the art of creating the biggest, the strongest and the most effective of these organizational giants now in existence.

There are many kinds of Organization Giants these days. Financial cartels. Corporations. Associations. Foundations. Political parties. Unions. Racial minorities. Religious bodies. The names are many. The form is identical.

All these giants were formed when individuals, well known to each other, banded together for the sole purpose of creating a collective strength that was impossible to the single individual. In the beginning this strength is self-protective, but there is a point in all organizations where self-protective strength becomes the power to control. The giant begins to move with a life of its own beyond the original plan of its protection-desiring creators.

This has happened within the last century in all so-called civilized nations. Civilization means organization but the situation has gotten out of hand.

Man has lost his own individuality in the impersonality of each giant with whom he has chosen to identify. Man has lost his own soul in the soullessness of the giants among which he moves. He takes his life from them while they eat upon his substance.

Control of the giants is the short-cut to control of the earth, and the fruits thereof. Rugged individualism, what remains of it, has become a war between the strongest for the direction of these collective Franken-stein monsters.

ALL MODERN giants, whether they are economic, political or sociological in nature are pyramid-shaped, with the head of each pyramid composed of the few who by inheritance, by strategy or by shrewdness endeavor to guide the performance of those below them.

All those below turn their faces upward and dream and scheme in their own fashions as to how they them-selves can gain the space. In America today, the chief goal in life, almost the only goal, is to sit at the topmost point of one pyramidal giant or another. Few indeed are those who look back and down to see the depths and the darkness engulfing the base of each giant-pyramid.

The lifeblood of these giants is money. The more money that flows into them, the greater they grow. Money is magnetic. It sticks together after the critical mass has been reached, and the giants of today have long since passed that point.

Here lies the weakness that all the giants have. This weakness is visible only to a few who stand apart from the giants and view them without partisanship, oddballs who display no human desire to climb to the top of any of them. Daily this weakness grows more serious. Most of mankind moves either in the substance or the shadow of the giants, unaware of the danger which threatens, unaware that the giants could come crashing down, crushing all those who stand too near, shaking the earth in the devastation of their fall.

We have said the bloodstream of the giants is money. The giant-directors have forgotten or ignored the fact that money is only a representation of wealth, not wealth itself. Instead of letting the blood-money circulate throughout the entire bodies of the giants, permitting the people who compose it, like cells in a human body, to keep healthy and strong, they have made of money itself a thing to be bought and sold, a thing desirable to itself, a commodity.

They are drawing it ever upward into solider, more concentrated coagulations in the heads. Day by day the bases of the giant-pyramids grow weaker as buying power decreases. When enough blood-money is drawn up from the feet and legs of the giants, the day of mass depression and panic will arrive.

The giants will crash---those who are highest will fall farthest.

Such are the wages of greed and shortsightedness!

ACCORDING to Genesis, a hard time followed the giants in the earth. God repented Himself of having made a man-creature who permitted himself to become so wicked, and He decided to destroy him. Except for Noah, of course. Can we be wiser this time?

Have we, as a nation of supposedly civilized people, the wit to recognize that our giants of today are indeed rooted in the earth from which come most of our blessings? Can we recognize that all giants are man-made, of men, and for men?

Have we arrived at a point of spiritual wisdom where all of us, including the giant-directors, can see that the incredible strength of these giants should be a magnificent benefit to all mankind instead of just to the few?

Is there as yet a sufficient number of giant-directors who have the sense to connect their own well-being with that of the nation as a whole; who can see that the strangulation of the nation's buying power will eventually result in their own financially ruin; who are aware that coercion and regimentation result eventually and inevitably in explosion; and who are willing to listen to the clear, cool voice of Reason before it is too late?

It would be too bad if God should be forced to repent Himself again!

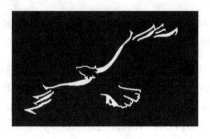

Vol. 1, No. 6, January 1963

Changes arrive, ordeal hath a surfeit. What is that

to you who have knowledge in your foreheads?

(Golden Scripts, Chapter 24)

Voice of Change

DID YOU ever stop to think that the only way we have of telling time, of noting the passage of time, is by change. If the sun did not appear to cross the heavens every day from east to west, if the seasons did not change, if silver hair and character lines did not appear upon our faces, we should have no way of telling that time had passed. Time, then, is change, and change is eternal.

Without trying to go too deeply into the fascinating and unending riddle of time and its illusions, we simply want to make the point that we move, breathe, and live in an atmosphere of perpetual change. Nothing is static; nothing endures in the same form forever. "You cannot," said the Greek philosopher, "put your foot in the same river twice."

Awareness of, and adaptability to, this constant flow and flux is what marks the continuing growth of man's mind. The moment he begins to resist or resent change, in that moment he ceases to grow.

Have you not admired the person of any age who seems ageless, who is at home equally with little children and old folks, who "keeps up" with the times, who looks forward to tomorrow with curiosity and enthusiasm? Such a person, consciously or unconsciously, is not resisting change, nor resenting it. He is truly accepting life as a long winding road, full of shadows but sunlight as well, with uplands to scale but from which the view is magnificent, and the unexpected lies tantalizing beyond each bend.

Such a person knows, consciously or unconsciously, that there is no static condition that is desirable, no absolute goal within our reach, no end to our development and growth. He faces conditions as they are at any given moment, leaves alone those of which he approves, and works to change for the better any which he finds should be altered.

He has as a dynamic factor in his character, awareness that as all things change so must his evaluations. He is wise in knowing that he cannot stop change, but he can to a greater or lesser degree guide it. This measures his worth.

He sets as the least changeable ideas in his consciousness certain fundamental principles of conduct. He is concerned more with the manner in which he conducts himself in working toward a given goal, then with the achievement of the goal itself, since he has made it apart of his thinking that no goal can be constant or absolute.

40

Coming down out of the abstract into the particular, he has learned by experience that unless he can adopt himself to changes in his personal life, he will be in perpetual turmoil and torment until he does so adopt.

This is not to say that he must approve of all changes which take place in his personal life, by any means. Many will seem most objectionable. Those over which he may have some control, he will attempt to influence at best he may toward the good of all concerned in his judgment. Those over which has no control, he must to at least some degree adapt himself, extracting whatever lessons in patience, understanding and tolerance may be gained from them. In either case he knows that black resentment or blind resistance will avail him naught.

IN HIS REACTION to public event, the same rules hold. All situations, all circumstance are constantly changing as the human personalities involved in them wax and wane in influence. Philosophies and ideologies are in a constant state of alteration as varying personalities and characters interpret and develop them, frequently not for the better!

The race question as it confronts us today is not the same as it was prior to 1863. Many new factors have entered into the picture.

Labor relations are not in the least the labor relations that existed even fifty years ago.

Religious concepts among reasoning people are vastly different from what they were a few years ago. The mere fact that reason itself is being applied more while superstition and authoritarianism are lessening their hold, is creating the largest change in this field.

41

Technology has turned upside down our whole philosophy of economics—or at least, is in the process of doing so.

Nature, by definition covering the entire, vast physical universe in which we find ourselves operating, ebbs and flows in great rhythmic tides in which general patterns may be traced, but which are never quite the same.

It is not the same water which flows about your feet when you step into the river the second time. The leaves on the maple just flooding into green outside your window today are not last summer's leaves. Each iris blossom follows a pattern, but each blossom is different.

So MAN, whatever the origin or destiny of his spirit, for now at least a part of the natural universe, moves in sociological and psychological waves, which ebb and flow in great general patterns, but each individual is not only different from all others, but each is constantly changing and developing as he extracts knowledge from experience.

It is not for us to know at the moment what the Why of the Universe is, or why it should thus constantly change within patterns set by a Power beyond our ken.

We are able, however, to recognize the force that creates the changes within Patterns set by a Power beyond our ken.

We are able, however, to recognize the force that creates the changes within Man himself, and consequently within Man's relations with his fellows and his earth. That force is simply knowledge. The more Man learns, the more he partakes of the knowledge that he seeks, the wider grow his horizons; the more he grows and changes, the higher grow his aims and the farther extend his goals.

There is no end in knowledge. Only the educated man knows how small is his education. Only the uneducated can delude themselves into believing they have reached the absolute!

Each must set his own goals as milestones on his life-path, firm in his faith that real attainment is measured not by the distances he may travel, but how he travels toward the limitless horizons!

Vol. 1, No. 6, June 1963

Therein is a great mystery; I say the day arriveth

When understanding of the mystery cometh

to you; then shall ye rejoice.

(*Golden Scripts,* Chapter 3)

Collision Courses!

FOR THE SAKE of presentation, let us assume that a single railroad track lies between two cities. Further, let us assume that simultaneously from each terminal is dispatched a full-length passenger train with all seats occupied.

Can you imagine the concern, the terrified, soul-chilling terror felt by the American people if nationwide radio and television interrupted all programs to announce that the engineer of neither train knew of the impending collision!

Wouldn't the whole nation be aroused to do everything within its power to avert and prevent such innocent tragedy?

Wouldn't the whole nation be aroused to do everything within its power to avert and prevent such inevitable loss of life. Some years ago a whole nation was emotionally moved by the plight of little Kathy Fiscus who had become entrapped at the bottom of a deep well. For several days she commanded the attention of an America whose prayers and concern were focused on her life and death struggle.

And even after her lifeless body was retrieved there was at least the consolation that every effort, including the endangering of other lives, had been put forth that her precious life might be spared. Will we be able to say the same if destruction should be our lot?

AMERICA has the heart, the mind, and the capability within to display both compassion and concern for human beings. It is not immune to hardships and misfortune in the individual or limited group sense. Why then is it insensible in open and outward reactions when a whole nation, a whole continent, a whole world are engulfed in overwhelming suffering and are following courses that can only lead to mass destruction?

Why is this so? Why would not the plight of Katy Fiscus be felt a million-fold in the plight of millions of little children in our own land that are fighting their own life and death struggle because of insufficient food to nourish their hungry bodies? Is not their plight even more moving and tragic because it is prolonged, and so needless?

Why is it that a whole nation can be emotionally aroused over thirty men trapped in a mine explosion while such heartfelt concern is not multiplied a billion times over at the prospect of a whole world of human beings entrapped in horrifying nuclear explosions, where a blackened planet gives mute testimony to a people who really don't care?

46

The answers are not difficult to understand. We have become a nation of people so propagandized, demoralized and brainwashed that we can't really comprehend the magnitude of human suffering and imminent disasters. Blindly, we have accepted other persons' half-truth and sanctified slogans instead of doing our own thinking.

The forces responsible for the plight of America, and the plight of the world, have weakened us in both body and spirit. We have reached the point of fearing to be ourselves.

Here lies the turning point that must be made. It is a decision that must be made by enough individuals so that the course of the whole world can be reversed towards construction instead of disaster. And why is there hope and faith in such prospect?

Because in the heart and soul of each individual there resides inherent rebellion against wrong and a susceptibility to that which builds and enhances life!

First, however, there must come intelligent awareness of those wrongs and intelligent grasp of those solutions that would cure them. The time for awakening and acting becomes shorter with each passing moment. . .

AMERICA is bent on collision courses. They not only embody needless suffering but must inevitably lead to needless sacrifice of many lives. Sanity and a collective will for good alone can stay them.

Economically the giant industrial cartels and financial barons are waxing stronger and stronger in their camp. In the other camp are the vast working and consuming public, among them some 30 to 40 millions who live in poverty, some 5 to 6 millions who walk streets futilely seeking employment. Children cry for food amidst plenty, work is denied when there is much to be done. These are intolerable conditions, which can only lead to open clash in wholesale collision.

It is not unrealistic imagination to foresee masses of hungry and furious citizens openly colliding with those who hold the keys to overloaded warehouses and who have thrived on the suffering of the millions.

Much space in this issue has been devoted to the problems, racially. Here again, we are a nation pursuing a collision course. Twenty million Negroes in the one camp and one hundred sixty million whites in the other. Already collision in the form of rioting and open threats and counter-threats give but surface evidence of smoldering combustibles that could envelop the whole nation in flaming controversy over racial injustices unsolved.

When we come to international relationships, the collision course pursued by both the leadership of Capitalism and Communism is completly devoid of sanity and rationality.

Right now we as a nation possess nuclear weaponry equivalent to 22 billion tons of TNT. Allowing for 30% error we have an "overkill" striking force that could level every major city in the world 125 times, that could level every city in Russia and China combined, 500 times, and that could literally wipe out Russia 1250 times! It must be assumed that Russia also possesses such "overkill" nuclear power.

Our whole economy has become so geared to the manufacture of weapons of war that hare-brained economists, bureaucrats and politicians are afraid to advocate peace. They have become the prisoners of an "industrial-military complex" that has come to dictate American policy.

According to the Melman Report, recently released, at least 22 billion dollars could be diverted from our current 56.7 billion-dollar military budget for schools, hospitals and direct assistance to the needy and jobless. And our striking force could b e kept at its current incredible level.

America, Russia, the whole world is on a collision course that can only lead to disaster for all. There can be no victors in nuclear holocaust. Strong hearts, and strong minds must prevail if we are even to have a planet on which to work out our differences and the destinies of all mankind.

WE at **Aquila** wish to play no role as alarmists. At the same time we know that we must fact up to reality, however distasteful and insurmountable the problems may appear. We have emphasized, and will continue to emphasize, that all problems are man-made and are thereby all solvable.

More than that, we are propounding such economic and political reforms, all within the framework of our Constitution, as would permit all people to profit through cooperative relationships and still maintain and expand the identity and worth of each individual. Only the vested interests and those who chisel on the human effort of others are opposed to those innovations.

Of course, there is reason to be disheartened and sad over the tragic times we live in. Of course, there is

49

reason to entertain a sense of hopelessness in overcoming the forces and obstacles that block the revitalization of America tomorrow.

But, if the problems are bigger and the obstacles are greater, doesn't this make every ounce of truth also that more important?

We have faith that the collision courses pursued can be averted. We know that the feet of American citizens can be placed on a constructive road that will lead to a higher and finer plateau of functioning where the spirit of "one for all, and all for one" underscores all relationships. But each must bestir himself and act!

Every person we can put on that road is an added voice representing increased strength for ultimate victory!

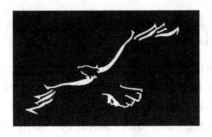

Vol. I, No. 7, June 1963

So must we labor that a return of spirituality cometh to

men in an age of great roarings, and the Glory of

the spirit manifest itself, even as in Galilee

when we walked by blue waters.

(*Golden Scripts*, Chapter 5)

Look Behind All Labels

EVERY now and then we receive a letter from someone who berates the No More Hunger Plan as some form of "socialism" or as "communism" in disguise. Unfortunately, these people have tragically misunderstood the fundamental provisions, mechanics and goals of a Cooperative Commonwealth. These people are the most pathetic, and tragic, victims of the subtle brainwashing that anything that questions the workability of capitalism must be foreign-inspired.

The technique of hanging odious labels on reform programs for the express purpose of discrediting them falls in the same false area as creating favorable connotations for labels of existing programs in order to cover up blanketly their injustices and failures. Thus, we are treated to the shallow conclusions that everything that is good falls within the operation of

51

capitalism or "free enterprise," everything that is bad is outside its jurisdiction.

This is cunning propaganda. This is premeditated subterfuge. It is hoped by the propagators that you will have neither acumen nor the courage to take note of anything wrong in our society and especially to advocate steps to correct those wrongs.

We say tommyrot to all labels, slogans, catchwords, and symbols! We are not interested in ambiguous words or sentimental phraseology bandied around without realistic application. We are interested and concerned only with whether or not the programs and structures identified are workable, whether they are honest, and whether they further the well being of all people.

Since when did it make sense to determine the character, intent and ability of an individual by the name on his birth certificate? Isn't it just as devoid of elementary logic to evaluate systems lived under, or proposed, in the same superficial manner?

THERE is only one basic yardstick by which we can honestly evaluate the structures and methods within and by which we live our daily lives. To what extent is the material, intellectual and spiritual well being of man advanced in light of our maximum potential? Make this searching inquiry into everything you pass judgment on and you will achieve real perspective in drawing conclusions and making decisions for action.

No longer will you be a victim of insidious propaganda designed to focus your attention on the label on the package and not on its contents.

Now to specifics. Why do we indict capitalism, as a system, for the wrongs and problems that confront us? The answers couldn't be simpler. It just does not work. It has built-in flaws that violate every basic tenet of sound economics. As a system of determining production, distribution and compensation, it has brought about wholesale poverty and bondage on the richest country in the world..

One of the most important distinctions we must make in our economic thinking is that capitalism, by our definition, is not our network of technology and productive industry. In short, is has nothing to do with our know-how or potential to produce. It has all to do with the ownership and direction of what shall be produced, how much shall be produced, and who shall have the ability to enjoy such production!

Most accurately, and pointedly, it should be stated that by our definition, capitalism is the whole intricate system of "paper" values---shares, mortgages, basic credit and reserve lending, interest, notes securities, bonds---that has placed the nation's entire productive capacity into the greedy grasp of a mere handful whose only god is Profits, and more Profits. Unsuspectingly, the American people have accepted that such "paper" representations are the same as real wealth and have been blind to behind-the-scenes manipulations that have beggared them in consequence.

How does a Corporate Commonwealth differ in approach? It sets down that the cardinal purpose of any economy is to produce for use, not to see who can garner the most and biggest profits. It adheres to the principle that only human effort, both mental and physical, can exert any rightful claim against that

53

which is produced, not by those who have contributed nothing intrinsic to production but are the manipulators and unentitled holders of fictitious paper values.

Under a Corporate Commonwealth there would be full employment with full utilization of our technology to meet the needs of all the people. Instead of power-blocks dictating scarcity, with resultant millions unemployed and hungry, we as a nation would enjoy abundance with the people owning full equity in the nation's productive capacity.

We now come to the charge, "But that is some form of communism or socialism!" Again, we say, tommyrot! Ask yourself this question: "Why is it communistic or socialistic for all the people to own and benefit from a corporate structure which meets their needs, but it is not communistic or socialistic for a handful to own and benefit from the same corporate structure"? Strange, isn't it?

No thinking person objects to the bigness of operation of our giant, monopolistic corporations. The technology of the Twentieth Century makes this necessary. This is simply coordinated efficiency and scientific progress through know-how.

What we do strenuously object to is the system, capitalism, that has permitted "paper" ownership to be lodged in the hands of the few to the detriment and widespread suffering of the many.

Above all, get it straight in our thinking that technology, know-how, industry itself, is not capitalism. Capitalism is a system, or mechanics, by which a nation's entire economy is owned and directed!

When you understand this distinction clearly, you will appreciate the need and practicality of the recommendations of **No More Hunger.**

IT MIGHT further help to dispel these charges of our advocating any form of foreign "isms" by pointing out that these so-called "socialistic" economies in question are under the arbitrary and absolute political dictation of the State, with the incumbent political regime having sole direction of the nation's economy. This is regimentation and mass control of the citizens by the political elite and the dictatorial powers of the State.

Under a truly Corporate Commonwealth, we are talking about people's ownership, not State ownership. We are advocating that the people themselves would arrive at both the economic planning and the determining of individual worth through negotiation. This is a far cry from government or the State determining production, prices and wages by fiat.

What consistency is there in the reasoning that it is quite proper and right to run a nation by the democratic process politically, but that it is "socialistic" to apply that same democratic process to the running of the economy? In the final sense there can be no partial exercise of sovereignty!

It would be well to heed the words of Thomas Jefferson who stated, "I know of no safe depository of the ultimate powers of society but the people themselves."

Not all nations are by any means advanced enough historically, intellectually or technologically to be able to utilize this highest form of self-government. We believe the United States is ready, and specially gifted among the other nations by Nature and by temperament to act as bell-weather toward a veritable Golden Age among all nations.

Labels, slogans, sentimental phrases are for the mentally lazy, the philosophically immature, or for those who don't object to being bamboozled and denied their rightful places in society. Commence to look behind all labels. Study the content of the package before you cast it aside.

Our destiny, our very lives are dependent on our ability now to be forthright and clear of mind!

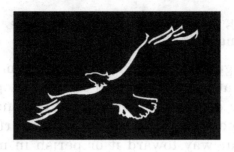

Vol. 1, No. 8, August 1963

There is no greater love than this, that a man

should bear the burdens of his brother.

(*Golden Scripts,* Chapter 5)

Road to Utopia . . .

THERE IS a story about the tourist who braked to a stop besides a wandering stonewall in Vermont and inquired of the farmer sitting thereon the way to Newfane. The Vermonter is reputed to have eyed the outlander sharply, shifted tobacco to the other cheek and ruminated long before responding, "Well, if I was goin' to Newfane, I wouldn't start from here!"

Just so with the Road to Utopia. So far have we seemed to wander out of our way in our progress up through history that it seems unlikely, not to say impossible, to find the right track onward.

Let us quickly note that Utopia, the perfect society, will never be reached, for at the precise moment that we enter into that hallowed condition, there will be no further need for the great mud-ball we call the planet Earth. Our lessons in human relationships will all have been learned, and so-called humankind will be

57

passed along to the next grade of a more complicated but rewarding education.

Since such graduation and elevation seems to be the mortal aim, at least in Western culture, Utopia must be the ultimate goal. Whether we like it or not, whether we think it possible or not, we've got to start from here, and work our way toward it or perish in meaningless oblivion. We may be closer than we think to either denouement

Why? Because we have only just now turned a momentous corner into a New Age. This is not yet realized by 99% of struggling humanity, but it is nonetheless true.

THE CORNER we have turned for the first time in our recorded history is from an Age of Scarcity behind us to an Age of Abundance before us. This is not to say we have full command of the Abundant Life at this moment. Quite to the contrary!

Hunger, disease, deprivation still stalks three-quarters of the globe as terrifyingly as ever. Even in America, long labeled the richest nation on earth, malnutrition and poverty are on the increase in large areas, millions unemployed and 8,000,000 of its citizens over 65 unable to defray medical bills on yearly incomes of less than $1,000.

No, the cornerstone appeared when we achieved the technological potential. In other words, when we found ourselves potentially capable of supplying the necessities of the world for the first time. The actual doing is another question!

58

With the advent of this momentous potential, what do we find? A world on its knees giving thanks that most of its troubles are over? That it may now be sure of food when it is hungry, of shelter when it is cold, of rest when it is weary, of medicine and treatment when it is ill? That may at last free its nose from the harsh grindstone of constant labor to purchase the things it wants to do in self-improvements, in education, in the creative arts, in research, exploration and invention?

Unhappily, no! We have instead a world of mounting confusion, of jangled nerves, of heart-damaging anxiety and tension. A world in which the horrors of war are not only not lessened, but indeed are increased to our possible extinction. A world of hostile factions whose only law is Might and whose only god is Mammon.

No, if we were going to Utopia, we wouldn't start from here!

Except that we have to!

Very well. Let us take a moment here to study the terrain we must travel. Let's note the obstacles, and decide to face up to them instead of going in endless circles to avoid them. Let's decide where we can make it and where we will take time for scenic beauties instead of wandering aimlessly in desolates wastes.

FIRST, are we agreed upon the goal? Are we aiming toward a society in which all men have learned to live together in reasonable harmony, respecting each other's differences in habit and culture, and viewing each other without fear and prejudice, in which the development of the fullest creative ability of each individual is paramount, in which the only restrictions to be placed on anyone are those that prevent his interfering with the equal rights of any other? The statement of such an aim is a long way from its actuality, but we will certainly have to agree on where we are headed.

Now as to mode of travel! The advent of the Age of Abundance now enables us to change here and now from horse-and-buggy progress to streamlined, swift and effortless locomotion. Technological developments of automation, communication, mechanical power, production and know-how, all these make up the chassis of our new transportation. We are still at this point as far from our goal as ever. We are simply in a position to go more comfortably and more quickly.

How about fuel? What is our go-power? What will make us progress? The answer: Advancing knowledge, not only individual intellectual achievement but also the increasing ability across the globe to read and write, to learn how others live, to make comparisons and evaluations. The increasing awareness, in short, that the earth is no longer made up of a vast number of provincial, far-flung and isolate communities, but is willy-nilly and headlong becoming one small spaceship hurtling through Cosmos. Either we accept this concept and agree to work out our differences somehow or the whole shebang will blow up in our faces and the joy-ride is over! This must be the motive-power urging us toward our envisioned Utopia.

Two questions of paramount importance must now be decided upon:

1) Who is to sit in the driver's seat? Are we, the people, who make up nine tenths of society, going to make the decisions of our own destinies, or shall we leave it to a small handful of self-appointed, power-hungry manipu-

lators who have finagled the reins in their own hands and have been for some time plotting the journey to suit themselves?

2) What about a road map? Is there a plan of action already laid out that will help to guide us toward our desired goals?

But of course the Christian Cooperative Commonwealth presents the fairest, the straightest, the most widely acceptable chart that has been offered.

And what of obstacles? The first is a mountain of apathy. The confused, the despairing, the weary must be awakened to the possibilities. When they understand the new factors, hope will rise again.

Another obstacle is the wild beast of greed. That time when ambition for personal wealth or power meant simply competition is now past and gone. It must be sublimated into the desire for good for all men. Otherwise greed will lead the mighty in wealth and power to their own undoing, in nuclear holocaust, which respects no man, or in complete economic collapse in which their paper riches become useful only to wrap the garbage.

The third obstacle is a great bog of Fear. Fear is rooted always in ignorance. We are not required to accept what we fully understand, but neither shall we fly into blind panic at its mention. A fully informed people will be at least more rational in decision than a poorly informed one. Be not afraid to investigate for yourself!

Does this seem to you a fanciful and unrealistic portrayal of a journey in Time and Space? It is of the grimmest reality. Think on it well!

61

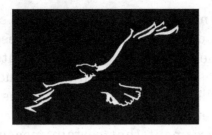

Vol. 1, No. 9, September 1963

I say, how can ye fail to go forward, sure and calm

and free? Use all that hath been given you,

Mind, and Soul, and Spirit

(*Golden Scripts*, Chapter 7)

The Three B's . .

"HAVE Bigness, the Bomb and the Buck destroyed our old Morality?" asks Look magazine in an article appearing in its September 24, 1963 issue. The question should be profoundly disturbing to all Americans who yet possess the old-fashioned virtue of Conscience.

If there were no concepts available in the world for a supposedly civilized nation to choose from except Capitalism which has created the worship of the Almighty Dollar and Communism which has created the worship of the Almighty State, western civilization would have small hope of recovering from its present dangerous illness.

Great concentrations of power and great concentrations of money before which average human beings must bow down and do homage must eventually be broken up by sheer force of necessity if civilization is to survive at all. Whether it is done by brute force, the resentment and outrage of the Have-nots boiling up into revolt and violence against the Haves, with consequent suffering, misery and disaster for the innocent as well as the guilty, or whether it is to be done by concerted and thoughtful agreement that certain measures must be undertaken, first to alleviate and eventually to cure the spreading disease is up to the conscience of thinking Americans.

The concepts of the Christian Commonwealth would do just that.

"Power corrupts," said Lord Acton, "and absolute power corrupt absolutely." A good dictator may be more efficient than a lumbering democracy, but what is our purpose in this world, the creation of the most efficient state, or the development of the individual human spirit?

Only by breaking up and redistributing the power of decision to the people themselves can the nearest approach to a non-corruptible government be reached.

We are corrupt and morally decadent as a society today because we have lost faith. We have lost faith in God and in each other.

Our faith in each other has gradually diminished as we have lost personal responsibility for our actions. A man with a sense of responsibility can be depended on, can be trusted, is worthy of our faith. A man without responsibility (especially if he has once had it and it has been taken from him) couldn't care less what happens to the rest of the world.

For a great share of our citizens, responsibility in personal matters is still a functioning quality as in taking care of family or doing one's duty in the PTA or the Boy Scouts, but responsibility in the larger matters, in matters of government, of business, in national organization has been taken from us, or we have let it go, and now we no longer seem to care. "Everybody's doing it," we say, or "You gota look after your own interests in this world, because nobody else will!"

We laugh uproariously at the story of little Abie and his papa, in which Abie's papa tells him to jump from the mantelpiece, that it'll be perfectly safe because Abie's papa will catch him. Abie jumps, Papa lets him crash to the floor without lifting a finger, and Papa completes the lesson: "Now, that'll teach you! Don't trust anybody, not even your own papa!" Any society that finds humor in that anecdote, however ironic, has got to be little sick.

Our faith in God has slipped collectively because Science has in the apparently heartless fashion destroyed so many of our dearest sentimentalities and favorite superstitions. Unless we have opened our eyes to the Greater Divinity manifest in a rational Universe, we are lost and scared.

God is no longer a kindly old gentleman whom we ask for favors, much as we ask Santa for new bicycles. Neither is He a thundering God of Vengeance who will take us personally by the heels and hurl us into everlasting fiery pools if we do not follow the dictates of His church, whichever one it may be.

God is always the Outside Limit of our personal concepts, and as our concepts have grown, have become less provincial and superstitious, our concept of God

65

should have grown with them. As we come to know more and more about the magnitude and complexity, both of ourselves and the Universe, so should our appreciation of the Thought behind it increase, till there be no end in majesty. . . .

Coming back to these horrendous three B's, where shall we find the cure?

The Bigness is not to be feared in itself, nor is it to be deprecated. It is only our mission to it that must be adjusted. Because America is a physically big, and physically complex country, even cutting away the hundreds of unnecessary bureaus and thousand of weavers of red tape, its government must necessarily employ many persons in order to operate. American industry is physically big and complex and by its size and complexity has created the phenomenon of mass production and the potential for the Economy of Abundance. It is not the size of either government or industry which has created our problem, but the control, or lack of it, of these enormous bodies. We lack personal identification with either.

A GOVERNMENT in which each citizen had a basic share, represented by his own vote on all matters pertaining to his general welfare, would have much more personal identification for each individual than a government run entirely by representatives who at best are subject both to their own personal preferences, and the inevitable pressures of all-powerful financial and economic groups.

An industry in which each employee, both labor and management, had shares proportionate to their physical or mental contribution to that industry would

66

foster in that employee a personal identification with it that he cannot possibly have now when the policies of his employer can be no concern of his whatsoever.

Our only defense against the Bomb is peace. Peace through understanding will be a long time coming, but it is not impossible. Peace by watchful truce, until the leaders of all peoples have truly absorbed the realization that war is unthinkable, is quite possible. War under present conditions would mean the end of civilization, and those who speak otherwise are either dangerously shortsighted or utterly callous. Man's political philosophies over the years of recorded history are too changeable, too ephemeral to be worth the price of destroying everything else he has built in beauty and heroism and wisdom.

Two materialistic political philosophies stand face to face at this moment, each endeavoring to browbeat the other into submission. This seeming intransigence cannot last. Bigness again has terrified us, and distorted perspective. We forget that it is again a matter of control. Whatever differences exist between us in politics, in economics, in religion, in anything, neither the Russian people nor the American people, individually want war. Neither, we would be sure, do Kennedy and Khrushchev. Looking ahead, it is altogether possible that the American people and the Russian people, gaining control of their own governments, will make their feelings known.

In that day, it is possible that wise and altruistic men representing both governments, whose first allegiance is to the human race and second to their own nations may work out solutions to the problems that perplex us so much today. In that day both Communism and

Capitalism may safely be relegated to the history books as two more experiments of mankind in the way of conducting human business, unsuccessful, like slave-states and feudalism.

This leaves us the Buck to worry about in the here and now. Aquila's main purpose in life is to point out the truth of the old Biblical maxim: "The love of money is the root of all evil." If money ceased to have value, no one would love it, and evil would consequently disappear. This is not quite so facetious a statement as it appears at first glance, although it is over-simplified. The cold fact is there will be no solution to this basic problem until Money ceases to have a value in and of itself.

Only when human effort is rewarded by direct purchasing power, represented by non-transferable credits earned for constructive effort expended, will money cease to exert its seductive and ruinous attraction. When purchasing power cannot be hoarded, inherited, charged rent upon in the form of interest, or expanded fictitiously without basis in fact, then will it become sound and inviolate, then will merit alone become of worth, then will incentive have constructive and wholesome purpose, then will real morality begin to thrive again.

If all of *Look's* readers might also read and understand **No More Hunger** the problems raised in the article would be more than halfway to solution!

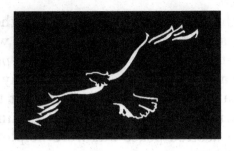

Vol. 1, No. 10, October 1963

He who readeth the human soul aright is the

prophet and seer, to whom spreadeth as a

scroll the secrets of creation.

(*Golden Scripts,* Chapter 8)

Hypocrisy and Sham

As WE go to press, President Kennedy has just officially announced the Administration's okay for the sale of wheat to Russia. Estimates vary as to the amount that will be sold but general calculations are that nearly 200 million bushels will be shipped. This will make a total purchase of over 250 million dollars.

The two basic reasons justifying this transaction are that it will tend to improve Soviet-American relations and will stave off hunger for millions who otherwise would lack bread, all the while reducing surplus we don't need.

On the surface both reasons sound plausible. Underneath the surface lies sheer hypocrisy of a magnitude that violates every standard of honesty and integrity.

Outside of the few, insanely blinded by their lust for both profits and control, every American wants every conceivable step taken that will lessen the possibility of hellish nuclear war. The vast majority pray for the day when they can retire at night certain that the morrow will not be witness to the blackened remains of untold millions who desired peace but were helpless to attain it.

But it is one thing to desire peace with all one's heart and mind and another thing to have the survival and well-being of this nation subjected to cheap, nebulous, ambiguous acts that only befog clear thinking and misdirect the people's attention from existing reality. A few harsh, but pertinent question are in order.

SINCE when did the hungry people of Russia, or any other country, communist or non-communist, deserve to have priority over the destitute and hungry of America? Doesn't the Administration or our elected representatives know that over 40,000,000 Americans are inadequately nourished? Or don't they care?

If the plea that reduction of our surpluses has a financial advantage to the American taxpayers, why not now make available to America's hungry the remaining four-fifths of the surplus wheat, plus the 3 billion dollars of other food stuff, and save in direct taxes the literal billions of dollars represented in storage costs year after year? Or is this too sane and humanitarian a gesture? Or, haven't we learned by now that native Americans have no seniority when billions upon billions of their tax-dollars are doled out with gay abandon to the remotest parts of the globe?

There is, however, a much more serious consideration that should arise in the minds of the American people: Are the leaders of both Capitalism and Communism carrying on an ideological sham battle while the tens of millions of taxpayers on both sides are simply the fall-guys?

This year alone the American taxpayers are carrying a 50 billion dollar tax burden to underwrite Capitalism's fight against Communism. The Melman Report recently released cites the Defense Department's own figures to prove that 20 billion dollars of our defense budget is needlessly spent. Without this latter sum we can still support a nuclear striking force that could destroy all Russians 1,250 times!

Is this 20 billion dollar excessive tax just extorted to underwrite our military-industrial complex that has made a mockery of free competition and man's right to work? Is the cold war deliberately prolonged lest our war economy collapse? Will Vietnam be another Korea where another 33,000 American boys give their lives in treacherous landscape far removed from our own shores? And what of the 100 billions of dollars in foreign aid that has been spent since World War II?

WE do not hold one solitary brief for Communism, or any other foreign ideology, or its leaders. Nor in clear conscience do we hold any brief for Capitalism, which has failed to recognize the dignity and worth of the individual.

We are, on the other hand, moved deeply by the suffering of people as human beings whether they be Russians or Americans. We know that there would be no wars if the people themselves were truly sovereign

71

in their respective countries. Murder is no less murder just because it involves millions and is done in uniform.

Could it be that when all the pieces of the cold-war jigsaw puzzle are put together the composite picture will simply reveal two "ideological" economic power-blocks whose only interest in cutting each other's throats was that more spoils would accrue to one than the other? The people, the hundreds of millions, may appear as just a hazy backdrop.

It merits some serious thinking!

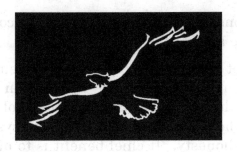

Vol. I, No. 11, November 1963

These are my beseechments, that you love one another,

That ye labor as the ox, that ye ripen as the corn,

That ye sing as the linnet, that ye play a

Great melody even as the bowstring.

(Golden Scripts, Chapter 22)

Whence Come They?

A READER in California has put into words a question that may bother many who see the Christian Commonwealth as the only answer to our national dilemmas, but who are likewise aware of the obstacles to its installation. He has put it this way:

"Upon each re-reading of **No More Hunger**, I am confronted with the perplexing question: Where could enough honest and conscientious people be found to inaugurate and perpetuate the blue-printed plan for the Christian Commonwealth? The question comes from the fact that there are, and have been, plenty dedicated people who have entered Government service and after having had a fair sample of the manipulations, have become thoroughly corrupt. Do you have the answer?"

At the outset we may dispose of the problem of finding honest men after the installation of the Commonwealth, to perpetuate it. The whole point and purpose of the Commonwealth is to be a system which prevents dishonesty. It chief benefit is to provide such safeguards as will make dishonesty impossible.

If all men were honest, or altruistically motivated, it would not matter a whit what kind of system we operated under, or whether indeed we had any at all.

If all men were honestly motivated, that is, not wishing to profit at the expense of others, the profit system would never have come into being in the first place. All would be taking only their fair share for the effort they put forth.

By removing the profit motive without removing the competitive spirit, by equating purchasing power with the effort put forth, by making it impossible to acquire power by inheritance, by patronage, or by haggling, the chances for corruption, as well as the reasons for it, would vanish.

The net result would be that a man could be nothing else than honest. The motive for dishonesty could no longer exist.

It is reasonable to suppose that human nature being as contrary and as cussed as it frequently is, there would be attempts made from time to time by the greedy to acquire illegal power over their fellows. Human nature, after centuries of dog-eat-dog morality, will not change over night.

74

However, the over-all safeguards of the Christian Commonwealth are such that the possibility of such attempts would be reduced almost to zero, and when they were made, could, by the very openness of the society, be readily detected and prevented.

WE DO not envision a perfect society set up on this planet. We are striving only to work out human relationships in social structure so that the best ability and brotherhood can be brought out of each individual. There will always be the recalcitrant, the lustful and the greedy.

Eternal vigilance being the price of liberty, it will always be necessary to keep watch against rats chewing away in dark corners, or termites endeavoring to undermine behind the scenes, but the important thing to grasp is that under a Christian Commonwealth, the tools of the profiteer, the usurer, the exploiter would be eliminated. Illegal gain would be impossible.

Imperfect human nature would at last have real incentive to improve itself!

At the moment, only those who are possessed of a growing awareness that something is sadly amiss in our national life, and are actively seeking solutions, are attracted to the abundant goal of the better social structure.

NOT ENOUGH people as yet even realize the magnitude and the nature of the problems we are facing.

Not enough people are able to see yet the underlying and interlocking single basis for those problems.

Not enough people yet see that behind and under the increase in crime, the racial unrest, the political shilly-dallying, the labor-management difficulties, the constant struggle of the plain man to make ends meet, the steady rise in costs and in taxes, lies a single, gnarled root: the antiquated and unworkable capitalist system which we stubbornly cling to and mistakenly glorify as the American Way of Life.

Not enough people yet are aware that the economic system under which we continue to sweat and strain is an import from foreign shores, fastening itself upon us after the Founding Fathers had outlined our political form of government, and only waxing of consequence after the middle of the Nineteenth Century with the introduction of the factory system.

Not enough people are aware of how they are being victimized by a financial system which gives them one penny for each bucket of water they bring to the watertank, and charges them two for every bucket they carry away.

Not enough people can see yet that they themselves, and only they have the power to correct these evils, and that there is no power greater than they on the face of the earth.

WITH EVERY DAY that dawns a few more people are beginning to see. A few more people are putting two and two together. A few more people are beginning first to realize that certain problems exist for which the present ruling authorities have no answer.

A few more people are beginning to realize that there is no need for unemployment, for slums, for higher and higher taxes. A few more people are beginning to

76

realize that they are being euchred out of their hard-earned dollars by some of the slickest skin-games going: high pressure advertising, price-fixing, hidden taxation, installment come-ons, and always and forever compound interest making it seem impossible even to make headway on always increasing debt.

A few more people are asking questions of themselves rather than "authority." And they are beginning to get more honest answers from themselves that ever they got from "authority."

A few more people are beginning to realize that it is time that the American people work together for their own protection and improvement than to let remote bureaucrats and millionaires with a taste for politics do it for them.

PLENTY of people around the nation are scared, frightened stiff of problems for which they have no answer as yet. Presently they will be forced by circumstance to seek more and more fundamental types of answers. This is equally true for those who to date have profited from the current system.

All must come to see that a structure as the Christian Corporate Commonwealth will provide the only sound solution, both to the problems our own system has wrought, and to the threat of Communist domination.

Time will provide the honest men to inaugurate a New Order in the affairs of people. That time can be shortened by the efforts of those who already see the answer to get it into the hands of those who are searching.

It may be sooner than you think!

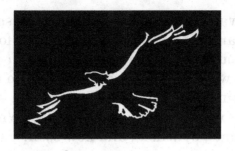

Vol. 1, No. 12, December 1963

Times of import open vastly, weapons of utterings

rust to be wielded, men have a clamor

to seize things of Spirit.

(Golden Scripts, Chapter 24)

Harbingers of Change

WE KNOW that most people on first hearing of our efforts to promote a "Cooperative Commonwealth" immediately place themselves on the defensive. Such initial reaction should not be surprising. People by nature, and even more largely by "conditioning," are prone to oppose change of any kind.

This is doubly true when the person singled out is asked to exert himself in some way to bring about the proposed alternation in the affairs of the nation.

Now it would be very easy for those spearheading needed renovations in the nation to conclude quickly that the people aren't worth helping and to proceed to less exacting roles in life themselves. But this doesn't solve injustice and inequities in any society. More seriously, it would be an unfair indictment of one's fellow citizens.

All people want a better and more wholesome life for themselves and their children. They pray for an end to violence in our nation, an opportunity to enjoy all the good things which industry can produce to abundance, and an elimination of all the stresses and strains that make daily existence a wearing ordeal. What changes should be made, by whom, and how soon?

We at Aquila of course wish that we had access to all the media of communication: radio, TV and press, with which to answer the foregoing questions adequately. We are confident that we could do so to surfeit. It is our considered feeling that under such conditions a whole nation could be re-educated, and educated, in a matter of weeks to the soundness and practicality of the recommendations we advocate for rebuilding a Dynamic America.

BUT WE DON'T have access to the same avenues of communication employed by those monopolistic forces in our society who have every reason to protect and preserve the status quo in order that their merry game of exploiting the majority can continue unhampered. Should we therefore conclude our whole cause is hopeless and succumb to the manipulated strength of the opposition?

We give forth with a lusty and unequivocal retort, "We have no intention of quitting because what we stand for cannot lose. No arbitrary power built on human suffering can have permanence. Already there are irreparable cracks in its armor!

Our strength has nothing to do with the number of TV stations at our disposal, with the size or circulation of our magazine; in fact, in its intrinsic sense, it has

80

nothing to do with the number of people who share our objectives. Our strength lies in the dynamism of the idea itself, which we propound for mankind's betterment!

This is the thought to imbed in your consciousness and in your approach to other people. It is with this conviction and unshakeable belief that real strides can be made in gaining converts to our way of thinking and taking those very realistic steps that lead to achievement. . . .

THE FIRST cardinal point to bear in mind is trying to apprise new people of the Cooperative Commonwealth Idea is to realize that people by nature fear that which they don't understand. Couple this with the fact that they have been subjected to a life-time of propaganda to reject and fight any attempt to reform our capitalistic system, and you can realize why the average person is unreceptive to a new way of conducting our national business when first approached. By necessity it takes time and determined patience.

However, the unchallengeable factor on our side is the obvious breakdown of the so-called "free economy" itself. Each day it is becoming more stymied and patently unworkable in meeting the requirements of the people. All the propaganda in the world cannot perpetuate an "ideology" by name alone, however bolstered with high sounding slogans, if the system it identifies just doesn't work.

We go further than merely stating that it doesn't work. Our charge is stronger than pointing out that it contained built-in evils from the beginning. It even exceeds identifying the monopolistic forces in finance and industry that have siphoned off the greater part of the wealth of the nation.

Unreservedly, we indict a system that denies men work, who are able and willing to work, and denies medical attention to the sick who need it, as being uncivilized.

YES, people fear change even when it is presented to them as a solution to their problems. Ironically enough, it is also fear of loss of job, fear of losing their homes, of inability to meet mounting bills and taxes, and educating their children for jobs that don't exist, that will force them to seek out those who have answers to their increasing dilemmas.

In direct ratio to a worsening of the times, our numbers will increase progressively.

In the meantime there are tens of thousands who see the handwriting clearly on the wall and who always make up that special vanguard of souls that light the way for stumbling humanity. These are the Men and Women Unafraid who have entered life to lift mankind onto higher plateaus of performing. Their simple recompense is the opportunity to serve their fellow man.

Let us seek these out that we may forge camaraderie in purpose that must be reckoned with!

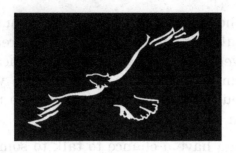

Vol. II, No. 1, January 1964

Beloved, lead my cohorts! Their banners

Droop without you, their trumpets

Weep with silence. . . .

(*Golden Scripts,* Chapter 24)

Yes, They'll Listen!

MANY people who first hear of our efforts, or have a copy of *The Eagle's Eye* thrust into their hands, immediately show disinterest. Why? Because they quickly note that we deal with the subject "economics" and average Mr. Citizen has prematurely concluded that this subject deals with nothing but a lot of statistical reports, chart and graphs, and such deadly dull phrases as "marginal profit" and "economic stabilizers."

So, pardon me, sir, but I'm not really interested," is his only comment. Before we can correct his mistaken grasp of what "economics" really means, and should mean to him with impact, he has taken leave of our presence.

You can see how wrong it would be for us to take the person at his initial reaction and dismiss him as someone who just isn't concerned about his own welfare, let alone that of the nation. The real fault lies with ourselves. We just have not communicated to him what economics encompasses and what we seek to achieve by our efforts. When we do, make no mistake, he will listen.

Next time you have a chance to talk to someone about our efforts, leave out completely any reference to "economics" as a subject. Instead tell him certain things we believe and ask him questions.

For one thing tell him that we believe that the only reason people should produce goods and services is for use and not to see who can make the most profits by manipulated scarcity. Emphasize that we believe that no man can be denied work who wants to work, and we believe in absolute security of home which cannot be foreclosed on because all forms of mortgages and liens against man's future can be dispensed with under a sound ownership arrangement.

Ask your friend if he believes a man should be denied medical aid for himself or his family just because he lacks the necessary pence. It is interesting to witness his reaction. He will be caught between two influences. His heart tells him "of course not," but his mental conditioning has been to reject all forms of permanent public assistance. Holy horrors! that's socialism . . . or communism!

MAKE further inquiry of your prospect as too how he feels about giving every child a free education from elementary grades, through high school and then through college. Immediately he will parrot what he has been conditioned to believe. "But that would be

84

contrary to our principle of a free society where every one works out his own advanced education," he protests.

Quickly you counter by asking if it makes sense to deny a child the right to go to college, or high school for that matter, simply because it is his misfortune, through no fault of his own, to have parents financially unable to underwrite his higher education. How "free" is a society in which one child has to assume his role in society in competition with all others yet without the same opportunity of education?

When you emphasize the highly technological era we have entered the importance of every child being insured equal opportunity of the highest learning will register more convincingly with your listener.

WHEN we talk about economics we aren't talking about just statistics, or something in the abstract. We are talking about the kind of food all citizens have on their tables; we are talking about the kind of homes they live in and whether or not they own them; we are talking about the kind of clothes, the kind of recreations, the kind of education and the kind of medical needs every citizen can provide for himself and his family.

In its simplest terms, we are talking about the size of the paycheck of every citizen, how regularly he gets it, and the standard of living it will provide.

So when anyone reacts to our efforts as simply something dealing with "economics" and having no bearing on his life or well being, we have failed to communicate.

Economics is the study of human relationships. It covers all our dealings with each other. And you can't have dealings with each other, in the sense of basic human relationships, without at all times invoking spiritual essences and values,

As for our efforts we seek those economic and social adjustments so that every individual can have the fullest opportunity of displaying his best ability and receiving acclaim and compensation in direct ratio to his contribution. Such goal is possible under a Cooperative Commonwealth.

All men in their hearts and souls desire to live in peace and in a society where life for all is decent and prosperous and honest. We have a real message for these people.

Let's do the best job we can in reaching them!

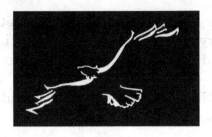

Vol. II, No. 2, February 1964

I say unto you, The Universe is Light

Manifesting through Thought, by

Love, unto Eternal Time.

Golden Scripts, Chapter 25)

Debacle Ahead! . .

THERE HAVE always been the Gloomy Gusses to predict imminent disaster. From times before Homer, men have wept over, jeered at, or pointed with alarm to, the rapid downward progress of mankind. The Good Old Days were always to the rear, never before us, and the swansong of civilization had been sung.

On the other hand, there have also always been the Pollyannas, the bright and cheerful voices that hold that in spite of his aberrations, in spite of his contrariness, his meanness and his smallness, Man has progressed. That has to be so, they contend with a good deal of reason, or he would have destroyed himself already and vanished from the earth's face like the brontosaurus and the dinosaur.

At this particular point in the world's history, however, the contentions of both the profound pessimists and the exuberant optimists appear to carry a disturbing new weight. The world could suddenly get very much worse, or very much better. The question is which? And how? And when? It is no longer a matter of slow deterioration of an empire with an out for the oppressed or the despairing always provided by having new wilderness to settle.

Nor can life be viewed any more as a long, slow climb upward with a bright heaven-on-earth shining far up the years ahead if we just keep working at it long enough.

THESE are the Instant Days, instant coffee, instant soup, instant annihilation, instant Utopia. Things move fast. Atoms, population, knowledge, all are exploding faster than we can comprehend. Peoria and Peking, Moscow and Miami are only half a day away from each other. For peoples, for missiles, it is something considerably less.

Information that would have taken a man years to compile has within his lifetime become available to him through computers in a moment. Man has hurled objects a quarter of a million miles through space and made them land where he wanted them. (Incidental thought: You might know the one place on the Moon in which man had to stir up the dust was the Sea of Tranquility!)

Things happen in science, in finance, in foreign relations, in almost every field of human activity faster than we have time fully to digest them. Now we are beginning to hear the roar of breakers ahead. We are building up to Something, something very good or very bad, but certainly, not indifferent.

The nature of the crisis that lies before us is interpreted variously by the people who contemplate it, each according to his own interest. A tremendous scientific breakthrough may lie just around the corner, overturning our whole concept of matter and energy. The little pool of inflammation and conflict over the face of the earth may suddenly escalate into the fever of total annihilating war.

Economic crisis in a world where all economies are now dependent on each other to greater or lesser degrees might suddenly precipitate financial disaster and chaos. The swelling push of underdeveloped or under-privileged peoples, or the demands of the have-nots upon the haves, could burst into bloody conflict, setting the brotherhood of man back a thousand years or more.

Aside from the ultimate destruction of nuclear war, all the foregoing crises might be either weathered with some profit in individual and national experience, or avoided by the taking of thought ahead of time. Man has powered his various Ships of State with the incalculable strength of atomic energy, reaching into every field of his activity. It now behooves him to discover whether he can control that energy or whether it will drive him willy-nilly onto the reefs of total destruction.

It behooves him, in short, to re-evaluate his aims, individually and nationally, to make clear toward what harbors he is steering, to decide what is vital to save in that voyage and what must be jettisoned in order to pilot his ship through the dangers ahead. . . .

IF and how Man survives are directly dependent on his attitude and behavior respecting life itself. The yardsticks that sufficed in the past no longer can be employed to measure either our conduct or decisions.

War as a means of settling international differences must be unequivocally outlawed. All instruments of war must be gradually limited and destroyed. It is now sheer insanity even to consider the use of nuclear missiles for it could mean the end of all civilization.

Belatedly man must bring about social change so that all people, on the simple premise of being human beings, can have the benefit of our tremendous capacity to produce abundantly of all goods and services. Riots, bloodshed, and even revolution, are the only alternatives to our failure to act immediately.

The foregoing must be done if man is to survive physically. But this is only half the battle. Man is not a materialistic being. He is a thinking and spiritual entity.

No society can endure meaningfully that is geared to material profits at the expense of human dignity and intellect.

In our hands rests the decision!

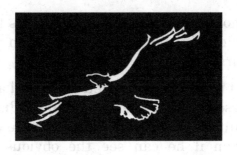

Vol. II, No. 5, May 1964

Out of such suffering they achieve their en-

noblement; they arrive at a tenderness;

They behold the Father's essence.

(Golden Scripts, Chapter 26)

There Is An Alternative

$\mathbf{A}$ GOOD deal of the confusion and perplexity in our thinking today can be materially lessened when we come to realize that almost all the problems confronting us individually and as a nation are more closely interrelated than they seem at first glance. The fact is that they have a common origin.

All of them arise from malfunctioning economic machinery.

This is the underlying cause that the majority of Americans either cannot see or refuse to admit. Such blindness is understandable. The average American has been led to believe first, that his own economic system is perfect as it stands, the only thing wrong being a bunch of conniving bureaucrats that want to take it over, and second, that there could be only one alternative to it anyway, that being communism. With these two thoughts firmly imbedded in his thinking, it is extremely difficult to focus his attention on the true state of affairs.

The fact that problems do indeed exist, and are growing steadily worse by the moment, should indicate to him that something is lacking in the system he contends is perfect. Even if he can see the obviousness of his observation, he cannot, however, permit himself to consider any alternative, owing to the second factor ingrained in his consciousness, that any change at all means communism.

The saddest and grandest irony of all is that these same average Americans who refuse to see or refuse to admit that they see these problems as interrelated and fundamentally economic in nature, who shout the loudest about our only danger being the Communist menace, who parrot meaningless slogans in praise of "free enterprise" and "rugged individualism" are unwittingly permitting themselves to be led into the exact spot where the regimenters of freedom want them to go.

The Communist can afford to wait. Internal dissention, increasing debt, enlarging pockets of poverty, a younger generation increasingly disinterested to education for a questionable future, weakening moral integrity, preoccupation with money and sex, every encouragement for individual power-grabbing, lead us straight to complete political, economic, and social chaos.

If America wakens in time to her peril, if sufficient of her citizens can make themselves heard, if growing numbers of her people express a genuine desire to restore and preserve the freedoms she is supposed to, but does not in fact have, she may again resume her leadership of the free world. If she discards her philosophy of ruthless competition in favor of nation cooperation, if she remembers that Main Street is more important than Wall Street or Madison Avenue, if she at last begins to value Man instead of Money, she will begin to recover from her present grave affliction.

When this nation disengages itself from the money system that is throttling it, when all science and productive potential are employed for the benefit of all citizens, when government is once more the servant and not the master, when real Christian ethics replace the worship of Mammon, when the individual American citizen actually becomes the master of his own fate as was envisioned in years long gone, then America will rise again and fulfill the great American dream.

Man has just begun to tap the tremendous resources of a limitless Universe. He has just begun to scratch the surface of understanding himself and what he individually and in the accumulate is trying to do. The adjustment period ahead of us can be of short duration, and we shall then be on to the greater challenge of mind and spirit that await us up the years.

In the solving of our present problems, therefore, let us begin to think, not as squabbling, self-important, provincial yokels, but as rational, responsible citizens of an Expanding Universe.

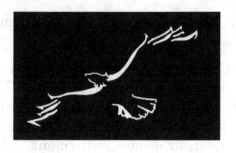

Vol. II, No. 6, June 1964

My speech is your shibboleth to bear you on to valors.

Let your responses be lovely as roses; let them scent

a sweet landscape and perform a fair flowering.

(Golden Scripts, Chapter 28)

"Social Planners"

OF RECENT months we have received several handsomely printed 2-page folders put out by the Dollar Federal and Loan Association of Cleveland, Ohio, entitled "Dollar Hollar." In the folder we have seen, Herbert A. Philbrick has given over the "I Led Three Lives" man to articles whose entire space is associated with so-called "Rightist" groups.

In an article entitled "Let's Talk About Economics," Mr. Philbrick, wittingly or unwittingly, permits himself to become a voice for regimentation as exacting and as stultifying as that which he abhors in Communism. Whereas he quite correctly identifies the symptoms of a sick society such as a devalued dollar, increased Federal dictation, a swelling bureaucracy that has choked and stifled us with forms and red tape, he displays no diagnostic acumen in citing the real diseases.

In fact, Mr. Philbrick seems content to say simply that our only national ailment is the "Social Planners" in Washington. And across the width and length of this land ring forth three lusty cheers from the Right Wing cohorts for his courageous indictment. To which is added, naturally, the compliments of his sponsor.

The tragedy lies, of course, in the fact that the larger number of so-called Rightist organizations and their leaders can't see the forest because of the trees. They can't penetrate through and behind existing wrongs, and government abuse, and identify the real "social planners." When they do, they will make the irrefutable discovery that all our problems, almost 100 percent, are economic in origin, that the social inequities and political over-lording making life a perpetual nightmare stem from the basic flaws inherent in our economic structure itself.

It is the very nature of our economic framework to encourage and allow ruthless power-blocks to exploit and plan the lives of all the people!

STRANGE, it seems, Mr. Philbrick, that your adeptness at undercover work shouldn't have led to an uncovering of the machinations of the privately owned Federal Reserve System. If it had, you would have gotten the full impact of the statement attributed to old Amschel Mayer Rothchild: "Let me control the purse-strings of a nation, and I care not who makes its laws!"

No greater crime has been perpetrated against humanity than the "legalized" power of private banking institutions to put into circulation, with the stroke of a pen, unearned "credit" dollars, to compete with earned dollars based on human effort. If this weren't irrational enough, consider the additional fact that it is the credit of the people and the wealth of the United States that serves as the collateral upon which all bank loans are secured.

How could a nation enjoy either solvency or economic well being when it permits its economic bloodstream to be diluted and dissipated by financial vampires bent on sucking the last ounce of vitality from the National Body?

Strange, too, Mr. Philbrick, when you speak of "social planners," you avoid almost painfully, like a barefoot boy sidestepping sharp pebbles, any mention of the 150 monopolistic corporations that have accumulated over two-thirds of all productive assets. Are you not aware that these giant industrial cartels, "plan" all production for the one purpose of making as exorbitant profits as possible for the few?

Certainly, in view of court convictions, and current indictments, you cannot plead ignorance of the actual conspiracy engaged in by the cartels to defraud both the government and the people of billions of dollars through price-fixing and planned scarcity!

Such "social planning" is only for the few at the expense of the many. It should not be compared with constructive planning which combines intelligence and cooperation in achieving the maximum economic security for all citizens.

THE RIGHT of the people to make their own decisions, and their inherent right to perform in conducting their own affairs, are fundamental principles we share wholeheartedly with Mr. Philbrick.

However, these ideals of the Founding Fathers have been made a hollow mockery because without economic liberty there can be no personal or political liberty.

The framers of the Constitution made no specific provisions for economic security. They could not encompass the untold wealth that was to be dug out of the generous New World, grown on the fertile western prairies, slashed out of the towering forest primeval. They could not know at that time about billion-dollar international communication systems, about automation, cybernation and split-second computers, about world-destroying thermo-nuclear bombs.

They could not seriously consider an economy of abundance because for them, even the necessities of life were hard come by. Economic security did not enter into their thinking because there was no such thing, and there was no way to envision the future.

In 1776, the Founding Fathers laid down a revolutionary new political principle, dedicated to the proposition that the people are sovereign. The time is here and now to lay down a revolutionary new economic principle, dedicated to the proposition that the people must also be supreme.

We must do this, soberly and in all conscience, or all that America is supposed to stand for will come tumbling about our ears, and we will be prey for Russian ideologies, Chinese ideologies, or internal strife ending in brother pitted against brother.

Mr. Philbrick's error lies not so much in misstating general principle, but in not digging deep enough into the causes which have produced the dilemmas we face as a nation. We must have both the intelligence and courage to face up to reality.

Let us all, for the preservation of our own sovereignty, of our own ideals, be honest with ourselves. Circumstances demand no less.

Our destiny can rest only with our own minds and hands!

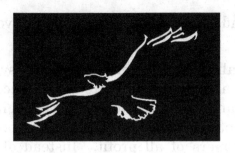

Vol. II, No. 7 and 8, July-August 1964

I say unto you, beloved, the times are ripe on earth

for heavenly manifesting: a cycle hath

performed; a new cycle openeth.

(*Golden Scripts,* Chapter 29)

Importance of Man

IF THERE is one basis, underlying fundamental, poignantly contrasting a Cooperative Commonwealth to both Capitalism and Communism, it is the importance of every individual. Grasp this fundamental in all its cardinal ramifications and you will readily accept the beauty, worthiness and workability of what we are espousing.

The importance of every individual! This should be the crux of all human relationships and social structures. Everything else has to be made subordinate to man as a human being. Whether it be government, whether it be science, whether it be the tools of production, all these "things," outside of man, are meant to serve man.

When they do, man is free and has the opportunity of expanding his inherent talents to the utmost. Conversely, when man is made a servant of that which he builds and sets up, he has become a slave of his own making.

Both Capitalism and Communism are systems that relegate human beings to mere cogs in economic and political arrangement. Instead of people being the chief beneficiary of the systems, it is the systems that are the chief reapers of all profit. Instead of all human effort being geared to perfect each and every individual as a thinking creative entity, all work is geared to perfect artificial entities, corporate institutions, with greater rights than human beings.

WE HAVE permitted our whole order of life to be shaped diametrically opposite to what it should be. Unsuspectingly, we as a people have allowed our lives to be so directed that we work, slave and exhaust ourselves in building a national productive plant whose progressive efficiency is in direct ratio with our progressive inefficiency to acquire what is produces.

As a consequence we have as a nation become insolvent on paper in the form of mass indebtedness. We have permitted the unearned profits of the few to be more important than the earned well-being of all.

No nation can, in the final analysis, go bankrupt as long as it has resources, manpower, and the science and machines to refine raw stock into usable products. It can, on the other hand, so unwisely employ its tools, including government, that its people are bankrupt both materially and intellectually.

Belatedly, people are awakening to the fact that both the people of the Soviet Union and the people of America are the victims of minorities in positions of extreme power. Whereas in Russia the main

102

domination is exerted by the political State itself, in America the main domination is exerted by financial and industrial monopolies, privately owned, that in turn make all levels of government bow to their wishes.

Again, let it be reiterated that both systems are predicated on the slave-principle of subordinating the individual, and making the State and monied forces supreme.

THE real tragedy of our dilemma is found in the misconceptions that we hold respecting the economy and the individual. Ironically, the very economic concepts that we accept by which to support our idealistic beliefs, are the very concepts that the abnormal forces in our society use to justify their exorbitant profits and their corralling of the nation's wealth and assets.

We fail to see that there is nothing sacred about property as property. It is whether or not property is utilized for the benefit of people or for affecting their bondage. It comes as a real shock to many of us to realize that in most of our "idealistic" thinking we have given no real thought to the paramount importance of man himself.

Those people who conclude that a Cooperative Commonwealth would conflict with their idealistic concepts of "private property," a "free economy" and "rugged individualism" have not thoughtfully read **No More Hunger.** They have failed to grasp that these concepts would be given real substance and meaning.

The first consideration under a Cooperative Commonwealth is that every family shall have inviolate ownership of its home. It can neither be taxed nor subjected

103

to liens of any kind. Contrast such secure possession to the current wholesale foreclosures, resulting from confiscatory taxation and fictitious loans of banking institutions, which compel you to pay twice the price although they don't add as much as one shingle to your home.

Inviolate ownership of one's home will be the first step to making the concept of "private property" an absolute right.

This is only a very small part of the picture respecting private ownership. Each and every citizen will be a shareholder in the whole incorporated economy. Under the current "water-tank" system, stock ownership of the nation's productive assets have been lodged almost completely in the hands of roughly 5 percent of the nation's families.

Under a Cooperative Commonwealth, recognizing every citizen's rightful claim, stock ownership would be extended to include the entire citizenry. For the first time the "right to private property" would exclude no one. For the first time physical properties would serve man instead of being his stultifying overlord.

OF COURSE, the monopolistic interests, that own and direct that nation's major productive assets, have constantly emphasized the fact that all the American people are the stockholders of the corporate cartels. They cunningly left unsaid that the vast majority of people, all told, own only a pittance of the stock. A Cooperative Commonwealth would turn their myth into a reality.

It is high time that the concepts of "free economy" and "rugged individualism" be likewise placed under

104

analytical observation. In so doing we will see that these are idealistic terms for exploiters and corruptionists to hide behind.

By what gymnastic of reasoning can we conclude that we now live under a "free" economy when millions are denied work who are willing to work and there is so much work to be done in building hospitals, schools, decent homes, and erecting modern factories and cultural institutions befitting the science and technology we possess.

What claims can we make that we live in a "free" society when tens of millions live in poverty, with no opportunity to better their lot, and all citizens are at the mercy of monopolistic price-fixing and money manipulators whose malpractices have landed the people and their government hopelessly in debt?

Since when did bondage, exploitation and denial of work describe a people who are free? Since when did mental anguish and inability to pay bills and to educate one's children, and the fear of attack and murder on one's own premises characterize liberty and freedom?

Is it not a true fact that we as a people have been so enslaved that we are afraid to challenge the real oppressors?

What hypocrisy to speak of "rugged individualism" when we kowtow and acquiesce to every whim and dictate of those who hold economic and political advantage in our society! What audacity to charge that a Cooperative Commonwealth would destroy independence and individuality when no area of our current

105

daily lives tolerates any meaningful non-conformity. We must now either conform or suffer in consequence.

A people who wish to be free must first make the decision to set aside preconceived notions, remove the shackles from their thinking, and show a disposition to consider new ideas and fresh outlooks. Coupled with this decision must come the realization that people are not statistics, or cogs, but human beings.

When one recognizes that every person is important, half the battle has been won in formulating human relationships that makes life inspiring and worthwhile for every solitary individual!

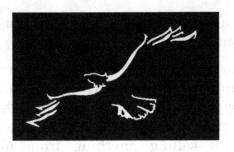

Vol. II, No. 9, September 1964

I tell you when the call cometh for higher things to be

revealed, the Bright Word shall manifest: men

shall behold the beauties that were hidden.

(Golden Scripts, Chapter 29)

The Roots Lie Deep

A PROMINENT anthropologist has suggested this week that our present era should be called the Age of Confusion, rather than the Space Age or the Atomic Age.

We can be sure there must have been, in the long span of history many such periods of confusion as revolutionary advances were made in man's knowledge of himself and his environment, before mankind as a whole got used to each new idea and accepted it.

There is this difference between previous ages of Confusion and our own: In times past with high illiteracy and slow communication, the confusion was confined to small areas, either intellectually or geographically. Communication over the face of the globe has now become so far-flung that everyone can now be aware of everyone else's confusion, which makes the outlook the more terrifying.

Even more to the point is the necessity to recognize the full power and sweep of modern propaganda, carefully controlled by those in a position to foot the enormous costs of advertising, whether it be in creating public images, or in selling anything from ideologies to deodorants.

To say that the developments of the technology of communication is both a blessing and a curse is trite, but it might be safer to view it, as we also must atomic power, as a great beast that has crept up on us unawares. It remains to be seen whether man is wise enough to tame them both to reasonable burden-baring and honest blessings, or whether he spinelessly permits them to drive him into panic and annihilation.

Unquestionably man's increased ability to commun-icate is largely responsible for our present state of confusion. Voices pour into our homes and our cars constantly. The written word flashes before our eyes in a continuous stream. Beseechments, warnings, boasts, threats, promises, denunciations, information, misinformation, siren songs of a thousand tunes pull at our conscious and subconscious moment by moment, day in and day out. If we don't get it directly, the neighbors are sure to come over and tell us about it.

NO LONGER can we concern ourselves simply with the daily village gossip and a national scandal once or twice a year. The weal and woe of millions, individually and collectively, assaults our sympathies every day. No longer are we permitted to worry over our own private troubles alone---we must worry for the world.

All this not to say that nothing has changed very much, and the world will rock along as usual, only we know more about it. To the contrary. Not only are there vast changes in all facets of living, but the fact that more and more is creating change in itself. Add to this, calculated misinformation and distortion of fact and confusion is inevitable. Confusion in Viet Nam, in the Congo, on Cypress, in Malaysia, behind the Iron Curtain. Confusion in Harlem, in Mississippi, in Congress, in City Hall---in any city hall. Confusion next door. But that is only half the story.

Confusion worse confounded---a hundred thousand signposts labeled "This Way Out!" have been posted, some pointing backward, some skyward, most of them nowhere at all. Trying to follow them, we run in circles. Running backwards, trying to escape to the simplicities of the past, we crash into hordes trying to get out of the hardships of the past. Looking skyward, we wait in vain for some kind of divine interference, some miracle, to deliver us from responsibility and plain hard work.

If we follow our own accustomed habits of thinking, our own prejudices, we seek a single scapegoat on which to blame all of our troubles in the vain hope that if such could be driven into the wilderness, the world would come to rights once more. Blame the Communists. Or the Jews. Or the Catholics. Or the Democrats. Or the Republicans, the NAACP, the ADA, the bankers, the labor leaders, the Supreme Court, anything you don't happen to approve of, and having absolved yourself of blame, concentrate henceforth on destroying your chosen enemy with a clear conscience.

THERE ARE individuals and groups about the nation and the world who have taken trouble to look deeper. Without singling out any group or person for indictment, they have recognized the tremendous impersonal forces unleashed in our lifetimes that must design the shape of things to come.

These forces lie in the hearts of all men, who have begun to taste the heady wine of freedom. Men who want freedom from the iron chains of war, of conscription, of regimentation. Men who want freedom to work, to play, to enjoy the good life without the constant threat of war, of poverty, of indebtedness, of violence and criminal insanity.

Men who want freedom to study, to travel, to make their own individual contribution to a society that treats them with the respect and courtesy they will have earned. Men who want freedom just to be themselves, independent, self-respecting, healthy, enthusiastic members of the human race.

Much of today's confusion will fall into orderly pattern when people understand the main forces that are compelling man to alter his thinking if he is to survive.

First, the power of the atom, now stockpiled for destruction. Man must make war impossible or he will not even be alive to work out his problems.

Second, man's inherent desire for individual recognition. Growing resentment and frustration will break out in increasing discontent, disturbance and violence everywhere until dignity and security are recognized as the natural right of each and every individual.

The third great force is technology, which has brought us at last to the threshold of the Age of Plenty. We are held back from plunging into it by man-made systems of monopolistic control, of inadequate distribution and privately created debt-money. Until these restraints are understood the people will remain confused as to the real causes of their discomfort and deprivation.

Aquila is convinced that the time is not far distant when these adjustments will be made, when political, economic and military regimentation, whether Capitalistic or Communistic, must in sheer self-preservation become things of the past, when each human individual will be recognized as the most important unit in society and it is his well-being and spiritual growth that supersedes all considerations.

Aquila's chosen role is to remove the confusions that currently confound us, to make the coming changes understandable and desirable, to preserve what is good of the present system, and to guide in the installation of those innovations which are necessary to make life meaningful and joyful for oncoming generations.

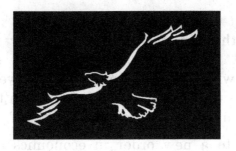

Vol. II, No. 10, October 1964

Perceive that we are brethren: the work we do is

Beauteous: we dwell in a fellowship:

We make the earth beautiful.

(Golden Scripts, Chapter 30)

How About Specifics?

A SUBSCRIBER to the Eagle's Eye recently expressed disappointment that we did not devote the magazine exclusively to blueprinting the exact details of how a Cooperative Commonwealth would operate. He lamented that there were a number of economic plans being promoted but none spelled out specifics as to the literal functioning of an incorporated economy.

His criticism merits some explanation. Yet, it is obvious that he is unaware of the fact that the majority of Americans are ill-prepared fundamentally to accept the "specifics" he wishes to see in print.

There is little question but that the person who wrote us has for some time recognized the built-in evils of private capitalism and he is awaiting someone to set down the literal mechanics of a new economic system whose fundamental premises he has already accepted.

Slowly, but surely, our readers are coming to appreciate that an incorporated economy is the only sound and equitable alternative to debt-money capitalism, with its corralling of all the wealth in the hands of the few, but what's our approach to people to whom our magazine goes for the first time?

Conversion to a new order in economics and politics requires persons to discard old concepts and embrace new ones. Reluctantly and stubbornly, people fight major adjustments in their conceptual thinking. Therefore the emphasis has to be on basic fundamentals before specifics become acceptable.

To those who feel there should be more specifics, and make no mistake, there will be increasing detail as we go along, it should be pointed out that the circumstances existing one year from now might demand entirely different mechanics from those called for today. However, the fundamental premises underlying the rights of every individual and all social structure should not alter.

Currently, we have to deal with people exactly as they are and not as we would wish they would think and conduct themselves.

ALL people want a better life for themselves and their families. Within every breast is an inner urge to improve his lot. Give a man an opportunity to procure a job with higher wages and he will exert himself to secure such employment. Give a mother an opportunity to buy extra things for her children, or perhaps help pay off the mortgage, by also becoming a breadwinner, and she will gladly add outside work to her already pressing family chores.

And the same holds true for children whether it be paper routes or the obtaining of a higher education. They are born with the irrepressible urge to have identity and be the arbiter of all material things.

Just because a people succumb into apathy, or explode in rebellion and crime, does not alter their innate desire to be free, to express themselves constructively, to participate in all decisions that affect their lives, and to enjoy the full fruits of their labor. They have been alienated from their true selves and been estranged from a good and rational Universe. Confused and restrained, people must seek escape or supinely accept their predicament.

Everyone of us has seen the reactions of the animal that has been taken out of his natural environment and placed in a cage. Immediately he paces his man-made prison seeking some avenue of release. He gnaws at the steel bars that confine him. In desperation, and blindly seeking freedom, he vainly bangs his bloodied head against the walls of his imprisonment. It is all to no avail.

Beaten and stymied at every turn, the animal finally succumbs to his environment of restraint as a "natural" condition of existence. In fact, he would reject freedom if he were given his sudden release from persistent confinement. It would require new conditioning, or education, for him to embrace an environment true to his inherent nature.

So it is with humanity. The people in this nation, and the same holds true for the people of other lands, have been so "caged" by economic and financial stresses and restraints over a prolonged period of time that they have accepted their prison-environment as something that could not be otherwise. Not realizing that their servitude is enforced and man-made, the majority has lost all incentive to fight back. More to the point, they know neither why to fight back nor how to fight back.

When imprisonment of both body and mind is falsely wrapped in idealistic terms of "free enterprise' and "rugged individualism" the people are simply glorifying their own enslavement!

How can a people be freed to enjoy the abundant life possible, if they don't know they are slaves? What good does it do to present a list of specifics as to the minute workings of a Cooperative Commonwealth when as yet they haven't accepted the soundness and practicableness of the structural framework itself that must be erected in which to work out all human relationships?

Right now the most important hurdle to be surmounted is to get people to grasp what their inherent rights are so that they can realize to what extent they have been flagrantly violated under predatory capitalism, and how they can be fully exercised under an incorporated economy within which every human being has a stake in the nation. Simultaneously, the people will grasp that all the power rests in their own hands to make every change deemed necessary.

An enlightened people will understand that neither capitalism nor communism is predicated on the dignity or inviolate rights of the individual. Both have political systems that exclude any meaningful voice of the citizenry.

Under communism, the political power of the State controls all productive assets. Under capitalism, the owners of the productive assets control the political parties.

For the moment we are not overly concerned as to the final details, or "specifics," that must be worked out. First, we must chart the right road to be taken, a road that every human being can travel, free from the highwayman and the robber in ambush.

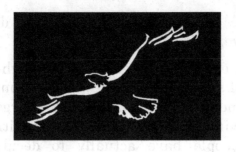

Vol. II, No. 11, November 1964

Light hath power to achieve: it goeth up and down

the Universe, verily impelling creation before it.

(*Golden Scripts,* Chapter 30)

The Great Election

MUCH STEAM has been generated over the recent Presidential election. Much of that steam has condensed into tears. Aquila has been questioned, several times sharply, for its refusal to endorse one of the candidates.

The simple fact is that Aquila could not, in all conscience, support either. Neither got at the root of our problems. One spent all his time soothing; the other spent all of his time scaring. (Naturally the soother was the winner, with the immeasurable help of the power he wields as an "in") What the American voter needs is neither soothing nor scaring. What he needs is a realistic briefing on the facts and a coming to grips with the fundamental issues that face him.

Whether neither candidate understands these issues, or understands them but refuses to face up to them, is beside the point. Neither did, and the American voter is confused, disappointed, frustrated, doubtful or apprehensive.

The whole elective campaign, with high-flown and empty idealism sullied over with personal recrimination, scandal, and innuendo, was largely surface twaddle having little or nothing to do with what the American people have actually to decide in these explosive years of the mid-Twentieth Century.

The best thinking of the Conservative mind fears the growth of an all-powerful State, which will take from its individual citizens all decision, all initiative and all independent will. The best thinking of the Liberal mind fears the growth of a rigid and exclusive code, which like that of Jahweh of old, would wreak personal vengeance on all who dared to disagree. Both are legitimate but superficial fears.

A workable resolution of these two viewpoints has not yet been adequately discussed in public, certainly not in the recent campaign. Instead, the American people were offered a choice between one candidate who was "all things to all people," and another who set the tone of his beliefs early by saying in Los Angeles in April, "Our job as Republicans is to get rid of people who will even listen to those who say we should pay people whether they work or not." Both positions are irrational, untenable and impossible.

THE TRAGEDY is that American voters do not have time or substance to waste on such shallow histrionics, such emotional rampages, such personal trivia as was evident through the late summer and fall of 1964.

American voters, together with every other human being, are now face to face with an election path, which

120

may well affect the lives of all who come after for the next thousand years or more.

The necessity to make this election could not have occurred before in human history because man had to reach a certain point in his social development. The capability to make this election will progressively lessen if we continue our present irresponsible and thoughtless course.

The choice is simply stated, immensely complex in exposition: Who is to be master in the years ahead, Man or the Technological Giant he has created?

By the Technological Giant is meant the whole of the present organization of civilization.

Unfortunately, most persons are inclined to think Technology in terms of the machines of mass production, of computers, of Telstars and missiles. This is only a part of the Technology of our age.

For clearer understanding of the meaning of Technology, let's break down the word. It comes from "techne," the Greek word for "art, skill or craft," and "logy" the Greek ending denoting "doctrine, theory or science." Very quickly we can see that the word "technology" basically means the "science of skill," or "the art of doing things better."

This is the end toward which Man has been working since first he began to function on Planet Earth back in the shadowy, misty eons before Recorded Time. Always goaded on by the desire to "do things better and better," he has taken thought, invented and organized.

He has succeeded in dominating the earth. He has reared cities, pushed back mountains, set up complicated networks of communication and transport that

121

have, in practice, cut the size of the earth to what one man may circumnavigate in less than a day.

He has succeeded in causing the abundant earth to b e even more fruitful, he has utilized the vast storehouses of Nature to his own ends, he has even unlocked some of the secrets of Nature's limitless energy, to use to his own profit or peril.

More than this, he has recorded his accomplishments. He has established schools, libraries, theatres, churches, centers of communication of countless kinds, for the purpose of exchanging, enlarging and, to an ever increasing extent, controlling his own most highly developed tool, ideas.

Technology then, in this wider definition, means much more than being able to produce shinier and faster motor cars in a constantly decreasing time, or being able to toss a man up in a basket and direct his further progress around the perimeter of the globe. It also means more than the use of automatic mechanisms and computers, which can do a great deal of man's thinking much more quickly and accurately than he can do it himself.

Technology used in this sense, also includes finding more efficient ways to run a great corporation, to elect a man to public office, to disseminate propaganda, good or bad, across enormous distances, over vast territories, in the twinkling of an eye. When we talk of living in a Technological Age, we must bear this broad interpretation clearly in mind.

To THIS GREAT technological organization, and to its control, are tied most of the problems that beset us nationally and internationally, and because neither of

122

the candidates addressed himself to this fundamental issue, neither succeeded in leading an inspiring, moving and honest campaign.

Until Man recognizes that his No. 1 problem is figuring out how he is going to harness these monster organizations to his own benefit, instead of being absorbed into them, or crushed, he will get no where that he wishes to go. He will instead be traveling further down the road to Huxley's Brave New World, fast becoming a terrifying reality. Even the Communist world of today would seem a riotous splurge of "rugged individualism" beside it. This is the danger of Technology, left unchecked, unrecognized for the hidden power it is, and controlled at present, worldwide, by the few at the expense of the many.

The steps, which must be encompassed by all, are as follows:

1. Men in general must be made aware of the realities of the world surrounding them, of new forces that are secretly shaping the future. This means a broad educational campaign.

2. Men in general will then come to see that the power to control these great new forces must lie with all men as an inherent right, and not with the fortunate few who by inheritance or manipulation have undue control. The dawning of such awareness will split the Right and the Left of today's political alignment straight down the middle, into those on both sides who believe that control of the many by the few is right and desirable, and those on both sides who believe that the ordinary citizen is inherently entitled to a share in the control which he does not now exert. This is the crux of

the question, and on its resolution will depend the human course for years to come.

3. Those adjustments must be embraced by legislative means, which will more effectively ensure the individual his inherent rights in the social order of the future. Such adjustments must eventually and inevitably be made or civilization as we know it will go down in chaos and the whole Human Experiment must be written off by the Powers That Be as a dismal failure.

It may, of course, come to that. But as long as there are those who see a bright vision of man's future and who are willing to work toward it, and as long as there are those who believe in man's limitless capacity of the spirit for justice, for mercy, for love, for honor, for forgiveness, for repentance, there is a great and growing hope that a genuine New Age can be achieved, where the crushing oppressions of Communism and Capitalism are both retired to the attic of man's social progress along with slavery and the feudal system, and where man's fascinating and incredibly exciting capacity for technological accomplishment will be, not his soulless and overpowering master, but his willing and tireless servant!

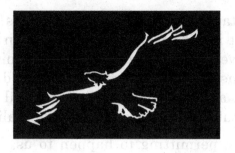

Vol. II, No. 12, December 1964

Man receiveth the Light and cometh to the Godhead:

He is swept in the path of it unto the eternal

Principle of Love

(Golden Scripts, Chapter, Chapter 30)

Christmas Renewed

THAT time of year has suddenly burst upon us again, Christmas when the hard edges of Reality are blurred, softened and overlaid with a resurgence of hope and a mellower attitude among men, to be followed shortly by New Year's Day, when the clean and shining pathway of unspent days stretch before our feet, unsullied and bright with promise.

What are we to make of this New Year? As the scroll of earthly time unfolds, it will certainly be one of the Years of Great Decision. We are called at this moment, individually and together, to decide which road Mankind is to follow, upward into the great challenge and equally great rewards of a New Age, or downward into mass regimentation, death of personality, and eventual annihilation.

Put this starkly, the proposition seems ridiculous, fantastic. It is not so. Men and women in every walk of life, in every social and business organization, and altogether as a nation, even as a world of human beings, are having to face up to great moral and ethical questions that suddenly have terrifying reality.

What are we permitting to happen to us, individually and as a nation? What are we doing wrong? What is truly important and worth fighting for? What are our purposes in life? As a self-professed largely Christian nation, our moral and philosophical ideas are undergoing an agonizing period of testing.

SCIENCE, with its sharp scalpels of Reason and its powerful microscope of Research, is cutting away and exposing sentimentality and superstition. Should this lessen our respect for a Supreme Power because the heavens are now measured in billions of light-years and man has penetrated into the very heart of the atom? Man's technological progress has carried the nation over the threshold into an era of abundance. Should we permit the material affluence among the vocal and the influential to gradually destroy the spiritual importance of every human being to the good life?

Coming down to cases, what about increasing poverty in a country, which boasts of its increasing affluence? What about a crime rate that grows faster than the population rate? What about the Negroes as human beings, yet caged as animals in our citie's ghettoes?

What about Communism and our own subservience to bureaucracy and government fiat? What about an economy and national policy devoted more to the

126

making of instruments of death and their allied products than to the education of the nation's children.

How far have we turned our faces from the Man whose birthday we honor this month? As we write our Christmas cards, how many times will our eyes fall on the phrase, "Peace on earth, good will toward men"? What does it mean to us?

There will be many who say, "Oh, come on! Let's relax and enjoy this one period of the year when men are a little kindlier, a little more thoughtful, a little more charitable. Life's rough enough all year. Let's be thankful for some respite in Christmas week. Go peddle y our preachments elsewhere for a while. . . . "

CHRISTMAS week is the one time of year when the average Christian gives more thought to the origins of his religion than at any other time. In the harmony of an old familiar carol floating up a darkened street, in the solemn hush of a candlelit church, in the wonder on a child's face before the tree on Christmas morning, somewhere each of us is called to a higher remembrance of the Man the Holy Babe was to become. Each captures a deeper glimpse, however fleeting, of His teaching as it ran in the ancient Scriptures: "A new commandment I give unto you, That ye love one another," or as it runs in the new, "Behold, every life, no matter how humble, no matter how tragic, no matter how broken and thwarted, hath a meaning and an inner glory and is precious in my sight."

A young lady said to us recently, "I am beginning to get what you are driving at with the Christian Common-wealth idea. It is not so much a formal plan to be superimposed on the American economy, as it is a

127

whole new way of looking at life. Once you get that outlook, the concrete suggestions it makes fall naturally into line as the only sensible way of doing things." She has indeed begun to "get" it.

The Christian Cooperative Commonwealth, based soundly on the ethical precepts of Christ, provides the only positive solution to Peace and the second greatest problem of our time: How may the individual preserve his own identity and express his true self in the face of the all-but-overwhelming forces which threaten his extinction?

ADOPTION of the Christian Cooperative principle is the only course which can prevent a head-on collision between those extreme forces on the Right which are devoted narrowly to the individual, an those forces on the extreme Left which are devoted exclusively to the State. Such course is not a mere compromise between these two forces. It is not a makeshift adjustment, permitting an unsatisfactory status quo to stagger on a while longer.

It is not a new idea, but a very ancient one, deep in the hearts of thoughtful men since Jesus taught us to pray, " . . . Thy will be done in earth as it is in Heaven." It has been unable to come to flower until man should have reached a certain critical point in his social, cultural and technical evolution.

We have reached that point in this generation. We now face a New Age. A New Order amongst men must be ushered in!

To the hardheaded realist, provided only that has faith in the basic worth of human beings, the Christian Cooperative Commonwealth presents its own answers.

As Lewis Mumford has said, there are two kinds of Utopias, the ones built for escape from the world, and the ones designed for its reconstruction.

If the Christian Commonwealth is called Utopian, it is of the later type. By whatever name it may be called its fundamental principles of human cooperation, human service and the development of the individual human spirit, which are of the very essence of the Christian message, must come to be our way of life if we are to endure as a nation, indeed, as inhabitants of the planet Earth.

So during Christmas Week, we enter our beseechments with all the vigor we can command. We send herewith to all who may read it, our warm greetings for the Christmas season, not in a conventional parroting of merriment and joy, but in a soberly expressed prayer that the hearts of men will open as the Stable Door and welcome in the spirit of the Son of Man, not only for one night, or one week, but for a whole New Age. . . .

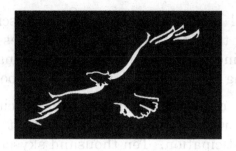

Vol. III, No. 1, January 1965

I tell you that little fears are as rodents gnawing

at the ropes by which men climb to heaven.

(Golden Scripts, Chapter 31)

Participants

IF WE were to underscore the one most important tenet underlying all human relationships it would be: **the inviolate right of every solitary individual to be a meaningful participant in organized society.** We will constantly plead this cardinal tenet in all our effort for social change. Without its recognition and acceptance it is impossible to chart a course leading to positive solutions.

We are fully aware that there are few people who will not accept this tenet. We also know that only those who will not see or will not hear are unaware of the five to six million jobless, the tens of millions enduring poverty and the large segments mentally ill or forced into crime. However, few are able to tie the two together and get the impact of the injustice that permeates our whole society.

Despite all the advancements of science and technology, the majority has become less and less secure and increasing numbers are breaking under the compounding pressures on both mind and body.

Belatedly it must be recognized that no citizen has a meaningful role in society if he doesn't even have survival participation. Ten thousand skyscrapers don't necessarily raise the stature of one man. Our vast network of highways, and our accelerated modes of transportation and communication don't by themselves increase a man's freedom of expression. Nor does the staggering potential to produce everything to abundance automatically improve the material lot of all citizens.

It is against this backdrop that we at Aquila come forward and demand to be heard. We propound a new order among men in which each individual may develop his innate abilities to the maximum, and in which he may not only participate to the fullest, but within which he will want to participate with enthusiasm.

The point we wish to stress in this editorial is the importance of being participants in social change itself. There is no need to await some idealistic future. However, whether we decide to be "standby's" or "prodders" in evolutionary social change is entirely up to each of us.

It should be clear to all of us that participation does not have to wait until after a new order has been established. Participation commences in the instant that the individual determines to help establish such an order. We can start participating in the next five minutes by unearthing a sheet of paper, an envelop and a five-cent stamp, and writing a letter expressing our

132

views to some other person. Have you written your Congressman as we suggested?

This is good for us. We are functioning. We are participating. We are becoming "cause," and we are creating "effect."

The effect achieved by our effort cannot be estimated. When we communicate an idea, whether by letter, by word of mouth, by a book lent, by a piece of literature passed by hand, we can never know how far the effort may go.

Just as ripples spread farther and farther from a stone dropped in a pool, so the effects of any positive action you may take spread in ever widening rings, long after you have forgotten the original splash. We never know where the results may lead from a chance remark to a fellow worker, from a book lent to a disinterested friend picked up by a visiting student, or a letter to a Governor, a Senator, or a newspaper editor.

The point to be emphasized is that nothing is achieved by apathy, or by pushing what is your own responsibility off on another. You cannot expect to enjoy the benefits of a democratic society if you are not willing to take some sort of part in the shaping of that society.

You cannot complain of the hopelessness of taking action if you catch the vision of what must ultimately come to pass. True love for mankind is born by one's willingness to sacrifice in its behalf.

So you meet with rebuff, with derision, with controversy? Remember that immediate agreement is not the goal. What is urgently needed in this confused and bewildered world is the free expression of all kinds of ideas, with a full examination of them in open discussion in order that the worthiest may be discovered and applied.

Only with minds open to the constant accumulation of new knowledge, new understanding and new insight can we cope effectively with the rising winds of Change that blow about us.

Be not dismayed by the infinitesimal size of your effort in the face of enormous problems, because finite scales cannot measure the value of such effort. You have done your share as a responsible individual, on the one plate of the cosmic scales. On the other plate of the cosmic scales, you have ceased to be a dead weight in the whole scheme of life, and have added that much to dynamic forward progress.

We may wait in vain for older and wiser heads to speak, or for younger and fresher voices than our own to be raised. Let us speak out, then listen and learn from the answers that come back to us. When we do, we have made the first step toward that desired better order. We are one who participates already. Others will follow.

Let us approach this crucial year, 1965, as functioning, participating American citizens!

The real increment from life is in meeting challenges boldly!

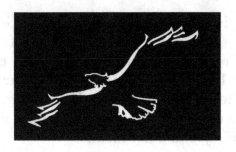

Vol. III, No. 2, February 1965

Beloved, I go before you opening many gates:

Trust me that I open the Last Gate of All.

(*Golden Scripts,* Chapter 32)

"Charity Is Criminal"

WE HOPE that statement shocks you. We hope you are sufficiently startled to ask about its source, and the reasoning behind it. It was uttered on a recent Sunday morning by a minister in Springfield, Mass. It is taken from context, of course, but a reading of the whole statement is not calculated, nor it intended to soothe ruffled sensibilities. It is an alarm bell sounding.

The whole sentence from which the above phrase was taken reads as follows: "When there are alternatives to tragedy, charity is criminal, an escape from our responsibility for one another. Charity makes it possible for the inequities in our economy to continue, for social stress and personal suffering to persist. Charity nurtures an inhuman process that brings hurt to persons, when what is needed is not charity, but corrective measures."

"No person is religious," continued Dr. George J. W. Pennington, minister of the Church of the Unity, Unitarian-Universalist, "if he or she gives charity, and fails to lend his or her whole weight so far as possible to correct the wrong of personal suffering, the loss of personal freedom, the death of individual dignity such as the loss of a job usually means."

Dr. Pennington is obviously one of the all-to-care individuals who are aware of the problems posed by the automated-cybernated society in which we suddenly are to be found. Note that we do not say, "one in which we suddenly find ourselves," because as a nation, as a people, we have not begun to awaken to the danger signals that are springing up around us.

The solid hard core of five million unemployed persons (the official figure, which is a gross underestimate of the actual total), racial tensions, the crime wave now epidemic, one-third of all high school students, and over half of all college students, dropping out before graduation, the steaming controversies in every State legislature over the increased costs of government, particularly schooling, and how taxes may accordingly be increased short of outright revolt by already over-burdened rank and file taxpayers, the paradoxical policies of a Federal government that makes a great show of economy in closing down veteran's hospitals, navy yards and military installations deemed obsolete while at the same time exacerbating an explosive situation in Viet Nam to keep us properly aware of the need for a defense economy costing $50 billion dollars a year.

These are among the danger signals of one single, monolithic impelling fact: The present economy of this nation is so woefully maladjusted, so unequally based, so antique, that without fundamental improvement in policy and administration, it is headed straight for disaster.

WHEN DOES Charity cease to be the greatest of virtues, and become criminal?

Charity becomes criminal when it is used to palliate suffering while its donors refuse to lift a finger toward removing the original cause of that suffering. When it is used as a sop to the conscience of the givers. When it is used as noble-appearing coverup to perpetuate subtle but powerful evils.

We are known as a democratic nation, supported by a great middle class. This is true, but when the biggest part of that support, in a steadily increasing amount, in fact, can be labeled pure charity of the criminal type, the system becomes something less than idealistic or realistic.

The great middle class today is supporting, through taxes both overt and hidden, the other two groups that make up the reality of the American people. They are supporting a small group of the very rich, to whom the "charity" comes in the form of unearned increment, and they are supporting a much larger group, constituting at least a fifth of the entire population, of the poverty-ridden, whose "charity" is received, not only directly from professional charities, foundations and churches, but also from tax-supported government welfare agencies at all levels.

If this were a static condition, it might be bearable. Foolish and unjust, but bearable. But it is not a static condition. It is rapidly worsening. Even the shameful

137

price of 27 billion dollars which we paid last year as the cost of crime falls into the category of "criminal charity" until we begin to get at its roots lying in poverty, ignorance and disease.

AT THE TOP, the industrial-military-financial complex gradually is absorbing or squeezing out the small businessman, the small farmer, the small independent entrepreneur, forcing his economic dependence on the great corporations or on government subsidy for existence. The consumer, besides losing his independence, pays the freight in hidden taxes, in controlled prices, pension plans, and insurance plans, in the highest profits to the great corporations ever recorded.

At the bottom, poverty is eating steadily upward, dragging along its concomitants of moral decay, crime, corruption, disease and violence. No firm line exists between the middle classes and the bottom, as there is between middle classes and the very top. Automation-cybernation is moving as inexorably upon the white-collar workers as upon the blue.

As jobs decrease, and therefore purchasing power in consequence, there comes a lessening of incentive, a frustration, a hopelessness, that leads a further step to school drop-outs, to apathy, to resentment, to riots, delinquency and crime. "Criminal charity" then takes over in the lengthening arm of government welfare programs, all the way from home and student loans, unemployment insurance, free school lunch programs, down to "commodities" and direct welfare to the needy.

In none of the "charity" is there recognition of the right of the individual citizen to life, liberty and the pursuit of happiness. The great middle class, saddled with personal debt and an increasing burden of taxes, is being ground between these two millstones, the very rich and the very poor, and in the nature of things as they are, slipping down rather than climbing up.

Nor will the situation improve until it is generally recognized that every citizen of this nation, by the very fact of his citizenship birthright, has inherited a stake in all that has been contributed by previous generations, that he has a personal unalienable interest in it which is his by right, not by charity; that the enjoyment of this right carries equal responsibility for it and that as he improves himself in physical, mental and spiritual wealth, his whole nation will to that extent improve also. Only then will prosperity, self-respect and dignity return to this land, individually and as a nation.

Charity is not wanted. What is wanted and sorely needed are economic adjustments that will provide work for everyone desiring it and in need of it, and a livable income for those who cannot by reason of age, or physical incapacity provide for themselves, not as charity, but as a right.

As the need for work-for-hire progressively lessens, as it inevitably will in this cybernetic age, we must be prepared to take further steps to provide income on a guaranteed bases. Not as charity, but as a right, as the only sensible policy in the new era of abundance. The potential for that abundance is here. Let us use it!

If this is not done, if charity of the present kind continues, the wages of it will sooner or later be economic collapse, moral abandonment, riots and chaos. And takeover by a collective, dictatorial ideology that will mark the end of American idealism.

Right now our best defense against this grim possibility is faith in the American citizen, making him a shareholder in an Incorporated Commonwealth, not a case of charity!

Think it over!

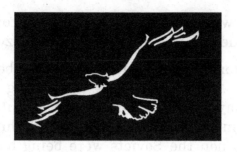

Vol. III, No. 3, March 1965

Lo, the brave in heart wrap their mantles

about them: they pick up their lanterns:

their loved ones give them godspeed.

(*Golden Scripts,* Chapter 33)

Search for Bedrock

AN ASSUMPTION is being expressed here and there about the nation that is not only incorrect, but dangerous. This is the thought that all who are against escalation of the war in Viet Nam must be either "appeasers" or sympathetic to the Communist cause. *Reductio ad absurdum,* it has even been seriously offered "only the Communists want peace, so anybody who's working for that is left-wing at the very least". However, an uneasy feeling lingers in the minds of many persons that if they came out forthrightly and flatfooted against further escalation of the war, they would be eyed with suspicion.

"We don't want war," these troubled people are thinking, "but we don't want Communism, and we are fighting the Communists in Viet Nam, so we'd better support the war, or keep still." This is, of course, where the danger lies, in fear and apathy and fuzzy thinking.

We, the editors of **The Eagle's Eye,** have been battling Communism for thirty years, from long before the benighted day when the New Deal was building up the bloody Stalin regime with Lend-Lease, through those later days when the Soviets were being hailed as our democratic Allies, helping us to stamp out dictatorship and imperialism all over the world.

In the 20 years since the end of the Second World War, we have continued to fight regimentation wherever it showed itself. We have always stood foursquare behind the banner of liberation for men's minds and bodies from any form of enslavement, mental or physical. We shall continue to do so.

Nevertheless, we are not for further escalation of the Vietnamese War. Our reasoning is based on two solid foundations stones.

First, the war against Communism is not going to be won militarily. War is the ultimate barbarism, the ancient and primitive way to settle differences. While the theory that Might makes Right has long been cynically accepted as the final determinant, it has been from the beginning of things morally indefensible, and now, in the face of nuclear holocaust, it is insane. There will be no winners in the event of nuclear war. Even if the planet were not totally destroyed, the psychological shock to those who were left would set civilization back to the Dark Ages.

THE ONLY other military alternative is a drawn-out, dug-in, ground war, in which case the Asian Communists would have us exactly where they want us, because they are in a position to carry on that kind of warfare indefinitely, and we are not.

Southeast Asia would turn into a bottomless pit into which we would uselessly pour the best of our manhood, additional billions of our disappearing money, quantities of our own natural resources, and our precious fleeting time. Attention which needs now desperately to be focused on the solving of our mounting problems here at home would be scattered, diffused and weakened.

And for what purpose? Either destruction of the planet, or, eventually, negotiation. Shall we wait till we are bled white, or shall we begin to think about it now?

Our second reason for opposing further escalation of the Vietnamese War is that with every passing day, like a magnet, we draw solidifying opposition from all segments of the Communist world. Instead of taking advantage of, and widening, the large cracks that have been appearing in the Communist monolith, we have by our belligerent attitude drawn them closer together, causing them to lay aside differences exactly as a quarreling family will suddenly unite to defend one member who is attacked from the outside.

Instead of protecting the peace of the world from a position of wise and mighty neutrality, we have by our unilateral action in Viet Nam descended to the level of brawling contestant. We have, by so doing, lost dignity and respect among other nations of the world.

Fantastic notions were advanced on a recent TV program entitled, "The Hawks and the Doves," such as maintaining an army of a million men in Southeast

143

Asia indefinitely, or occupying the land for as long as fifty years. This goes beyond all reason.

A standing army of a million men in Southeast Asia might indeed mitigate our unemployment problem temporarily, but it assuredly would contribute nothing toward international peace or abolishing poverty and disease as the real enemies of mankind.

As for the fifty-year proposition, we have news for its proponents. The world in a year's time will be quite a different place from what it is today, hopefully, a better one. In fifty years it will be unrecognizable. Such blind faith in a static condition of society as is expressed in this kind of thinking shows absolutely no awareness of the winds of change that sweep across the world today..

Stalin's Russia was not today's Russia; just as FDR's United States was not the United States of today. There is not and never has been any such thing as *status quo*. All things are different today from what they were yesterday, and tomorrow will be even more different from today. It is simply the accelerated rate of today's changes that upsets us and leaves us sometimes a little breathless and more than a little scared.

THE ONLY really basic enemies of mankind are poverty, ignorance and man's inhumanity to man. Both Communism and Capitalism as ideologies, while professing to be at war with these enemies, have nevertheless by their very nature and aims capitalized on and contributed to their continuance.

Circumstances change constantly. Principles do not.

144

The need for every human soul to find self-expression, the right of every human soul to life, liberty and the pursuit of happiness, and the eternal search for the just means of assuring this need and this right, these are principles, which do not change.

Violence, whether it shows its ugly face in war, in riot, in an individual attack and beating, sets back any constructive good and actually strengthens all opposition. Violence is waste of time, of substance, and of our most precious commodity, human life.

Education is the only sound and constructive weapon. "I know of no safe depository of the ultimate powers of society but the people themselves," said Thomas Jefferson, "and if we think them not enlightened enough to exercise their control with a wholesome discretion, the remedy is not to take it from them but to inform their discretion by education." This philosophy is not only as sound today as ever, but technology has at last made it possible and feasible.

It is education that is changing the face of Communism. As education becomes more widespread, so does the idea of freedom. Given sufficient time, it will so resolve itself in China, in Africa, in South America, in every one of today's underdeveloped nations of the world.

It must be borne in mind also that we Americans have permitted poverty and ignorance to make a humiliating assault on our own nation. Flaws inherent in a totally capitalistic economy stand revealed in the necessity for a so-called "war on poverty," in a terrifying crime rate, in the emergence of Establishments and an industrial-military complex that are rapidly destroying our illusion of democratic government.

145

Military force will not defeat these enemies of mankind. Let us negotiate ourselves out of a false position with as much dignity and respect as we can muster, as speedily as possible. Let us then begin to put our energies to work on the real and necessary and constructive work at hand, within our own nation.

Let us stop trying to remake the world after our own image by brute force. Let us instead endeavor to set up at home a model of national integrity, of national justice, of responsible individual liberty that is exercised by every American citizen which shall be an inspiration to every freedom-loving people around the globe.

Only when our national honor is once more shining bright, may we hope to command the respect and admiration we expect among the family of nations.

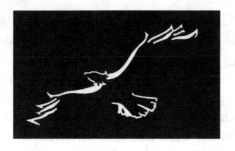

Vol. III, No. 4, April 1965

Our progressions are infinite: we do go from

star to star discerning Spirits vigilance.

(*Golden Scripts,* Chapter 19)

Ladder of Time

NOBODY EVER said the birth of the New Age would be easy. Seers and prophets ever since the hoary days of antiquity have foretold the coming of great cataclysms, of catastrophic clashes between tremendous forces, of upheaval and destruction. Not unnaturally, they have been periodically right.

During this short span of time, this flickering moment in Eternity, which we call the recorded history of Man, there have been long periods of gradual rise and fall in man's social and political growth, interrupted by short periods of agonizing stress and rapid explosion, lifting man suddenly to a higher plane of operation.

Child psychologists know that children take jumps in development putting them almost overnight into an older group. In a similar way, civilization has taken unexpected leaps upward in a century or less.

The Fifth Century was such a time, when Alaric stormed the gates of Rome and sacked the city, marking the end of the world's identifiable eras; it marked also the beginning of the so-called Christendom. The Fifteenth Century was another such time, with the awakening of a new intellectualism in the Renaissance, with the monumental invention of the printing press, with the discovery of a New World waiting for development across the western ocean.

Since then, revolutions have come more rapidly, and their upheavals have lasted for a briefer time, but they have been no less noteworthy. The American Revolution with its tremendous declaration of the equality of man, the French Revolution sounding the death knell of the divine right of kings, the Industrial Revolution of the mid-Nineteenth Century, all of these have had radical influence on the collective thinking of man, on his attitude toward his fellows, and on the way of conducting his affairs.

These have been genuine revolutions, genuine changes in man's approach to life, genuine steps up toward an increasingly meaningful and better life for more inhabitants of this small and troubled earth.

We are now in the throes of another one of the sudden steps upward. If we recognize this as an historical fact, we will be in a better position to understand the problems that such an upward step has caused, and to think through sensible enduring solutions.

Oddly enough, the bare recognition of this fact (that we are actually taking one of these giant steps up) not only would help in providing solutions to the problems but would even immediately eradicate a great many.

Only by viewing man's long journey, as a whole, up from savagery (still being aware of his occasional backslidings) can we retain hope for this generation in its present state of turmoil and conflict. Mankind, as a whole entity, must be considered, to some fraction of a degree at least, to be more "good" than "bad" or civilization not only would not have progressed, but would never even have gotten started in the first place. And make no mistake, for all the wailings of some of our very vocal philosophers, mankind *has* progressed.

It is not so much that certain evil practices such as slavery, or feudalism or dictatorship have been banished from the earth, for they have not, but that in the western world at least a phenomenon known as public opinion has labeled these practices bad for humanity's progress. Private power has committed strange atrocities on public opinion, but even so, it has survived and continued to grow as the moral conscience, outwardly expressed, of the collective human mind.

Getting back to those jump-ups in human progress spoken above, certain moral principles seem to have forced themselves on the attention of humanity at the same moment as certain technological developments, resulting in confusion and seeming hardship. Out of the Renaissance was born modern Science, the development of the printing press, the revolutionary concept that literacy and education were not the exclusive privilege of the wealthy.

Out of the American Revolution came the concept that all men are entitled to the same opportunities and the same treatment under law. Out of the Industrial Revolution came the concept that machines can gradually remove from man the necessity of performing hard physical labor in order to stay alive.

These concepts, which seem not only sound but commonplace to most of us in America today, were not accepted easily, and indeed have not yet been accepted by many. Against the acceptance of these concepts a war has always been waged by those who insist on trying to maintain a certain status quo which is to them desirable. It follows of course that those wishing to maintain the status quo are those in favorable positions of prestige, power and influence. The fact that this is only a perfectly natural reaction on the part of those who are comfortable makes it understandable but does not make it right.

Those who are uncomfortable, who are pinched by poverty, who are deprived of what they consider to be their right, who find it impossible to grow and expand as their spirit demands, will protest. The natural protest meeting the natural opposition of the status-quoers creates conflict, all too often bloody and painful on both sides. But eventually and inevitably the status quo is upset. Later generations will look back and realize that civilization at that point took a jump upward and then entered into a longer, quieter period of assimilation.

So today we have three concepts assailing us, demanding attention and creating conflict between the status quoers and the advance guard of the New Age.

The first concept is that war now becomes suicidal for the whole human race and thus, if humanity is to endure, is impossible. The old-fashioned who still look on war as a necessary evil have not yet developed their "sociological imagination" to the point of envisioning what war means today. They cannot accept that it is now necessary to work out a different method other than brute forced to sell ideas and ideologies.

The second concept is that of human rights. A growing spirit of the democratic idea begins to pervade the earth. While it is true that many countries, like infants deprived of parental supervision, do not seem ready for the obligations and responsibilities that accompany the benefits of democracy, it is also true that many nations which have had too tight supervision are demanding a greater measure of freedom, in movement and in thought. Many are the crimes hypocritically or ignorantly committed in the name of democracy, but the spirit is hardy and remains to spread across earth's face.

The third concept is that of technological potential. We have become a world that needs not hunger or lack no longer as far as our physical capabilities and resources are concerned. Additionally, we have also arrived at a point where men no longer have to labor by muscle and blood in order to satisfy all these wants and needs. This is the hardest, the most unthinkable concept of all for most people to grasp. So ingrained in our thinking is the ancient rule of man earning his bread in the sweat of his brow that any other outlook appears to be impossible, if not downright criminal.

Most of the answers to the problems raised by the two previous concepts lie in the frank acceptance and sensible utilization of the third concept, that of our present potential for abundance. When the common man ceases to be hungry and cold, communism will hold no more enticements. When the capacity of all men to better themselves through education and equal opportunity is realized, conflicts between all groups presently antagonistic will weaken and fade.

When the status-quoers either realize themselves or are at last persuaded of the need to take these three concepts into account, when they realize or are persuaded that they cannot preserve a society whose time is past but must, for the good of all including their own, accept a society which is in some ways altered, when they realize or are persuaded that they are not being coerced by any single group of their fellowmen but by circumstances that the natural evolution of human society itself has brought about, then and in that day the New Age will be in and on its way.

Our problems will not be over, but they will be different. They will be on a higher level, not physical but mental, and far more worthy to be challenged by the indomitable spirit of Man.

We shall then, indeed, have taken a giant step upward on the Ladder of Time!

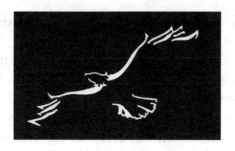

Vol. III, No. 5, May 1965

Great things are designed, great things are executed,

great things are made potent, but the greatest

things are made beauteous by the hands

of him who runneth like river toward

the sea, unmindful of its course

except that it be forward.

(Golden Scripts, Chapter 121)

What Price Security?

THE ONE GOAL toward which Americans work
harder than for anything else in this world is security.
But security is the one thing they *talk* hardest against.
The refusal to recognize this contradiction in actual
goals and stated goals causes most of the confusion in
our economic thinking.

Every normal, conscientious American father wants to
provide a comfortable life for his family. He wants
them to have sufficient food, respectable clothing, and
adequate shelter. He wants to be sure his children are
financially able to acquire as much education as each is
capable of absorbing, so that each in turn will be
competent to provide security for *his* family as it comes

along.   He wants to be sure these necessary requirements will continue to be met if anything unfortunate should happen to himself prematurely. He strives constantly to shore up the foundations of his home against all threats, both man-made or acts of God. He desires, in short to provide his family and himself with as much security as he can command in an insecure and uncertain world.

Side by side with this desire there exists in the minds of most normal, conscientious American fathers the contradictory fear that if sudden security in these essential matters of food, clothing and shelter were to descend on the American people as a whole, nothing but disaster could result. It seems as if the goal for which they so earnestly and devotedly strive individually is dangerous, indecent and anti-Christian when considered collectively. Why this very uncomfortable and seemingly insoluble paradox?

Both the desire and the fear are honorable, commendable emotions. Both lead far back into the shadowy, undefined origins of Man himself in which anthropologists, psychologists, theologians and philosophers have yet failed to find common ground. No matter what it is labeled, the desire to protect the family group exists. The fear of total security is there also, manifesting as the fear of losing identity in the overwhelming blanket of the group. Each man strives to make his mark, to perpetuate himself somehow in the pages of history. This fear of losing identity is very likely father to the desire to protect the family, since it is in the family group that the individual most easily exerts his personal influence and in a sense perpetuates himself through his children. It is this same

154

basic fear that is all bound up in the current conflicts and problems of Twentieth Century living.

ONLY comparatively recently did we become consciously aware of this business of individual identity, and consequently of the danger of losing it. Christ's message to the western world of the individual's importance got lost somewhere in the dark years of theological wrangling, at last emerging only with emphasis on the soul's importance in other realms, the safeguarding of which had to be left to those versed in such matters, to be guaranteed, of course, by donation of appropriate pence.

Only with the ringing words of the Declaration of Independence did this subconscious recognition of individual worth take clear and understandable form. Every man had always been aware of his own importance but here for the first time, the world at large went on public record that it too considered him important.

Unfortunately, the expression of an idea does not signify triumph. Thomas Jefferson's monumental announcement did not win the battle; it only provided a standard around which fair-minded men might gather to begin the real war.

In the two centuries since, different segments of the human race have become aware of self-identity to different degrees and stand now in different stages, both nationally and individually. Leaders of the "emerging" nations are having to cope with peoples whose recognition of national and personal self-identity is still in a nebulous stage. Leaders of collectivized nations are sacrificing or suppressing the individuality of their people in order to create collective strength. Leaders of the so-called "free" nations are endeavoring to manage people to whom "freedom" has become a many-splendored but fuzzy defined thing.

Across the face of the earth the real battle is becoming joined, for the preservation and establishment of individual freedom in a world that not only is not improving freedom's opportunities, but indeed threatens them increasingly with every passing day.

Man fears losing his identity today with good reason, as threats to his individuality beset him on all sides. As the organizations he belongs grow bigger, his voice grows smaller. Big government pays him scant heed as it rolls on its ponderous way. Huge corporations are constantly gobbling his own small businesses and farms, forcing him to join the toiling millions in the swollen cities. Complex machines are not only taking over his work, but much of his thinking as well. Marvels in communication and transportation have shrunk the size of the globe to backyard proportions, but instead of its making him feel like a larger human being, he feels more and more like a frustrated ant in a particularly angry and seething anthill. He becomes doubtful of his own soul, even that he has one, as science demolishes once-beloved illusions and comfortably rationalized superstitions.

Fear is hate's foundation, and man finds it easier to hate as he finds more to fear. White and Negro fear each other and therefore hate each other. Labor and management, conservative and liberal, the wealthy and the under-privileged, Communist and Capitalist fear and hate each other across the globe. Above all, man fears the unknown future, and therefore hates the

156

thought of Change. Fears are lost pathways . . . downward to destruction and ruin.

It is a matter of lost perspective. We are a society in which all elements are at loggerheads and cross-purposes. Out of the confusion, the envy, the fear and hate must come the realization that only within the framework of cooperative endeavor, *of all for one and one for all*, can each individual rise to higher plateaus of performance. Group well-being, or group security is only desirable in a social structure when it makes possible maximum individual security and freedom. Under a Cooperative Commonwealth, wherein the people themselves are both economically and politically sovereign, this can be a reality.

TODAY man fights his senseless battle, for and against security, both at the same time. His error lies in what he considers to be security. Security in home, in a full larder, in adequate clothing, in some of the extra graces that make life comfortable and enjoyable are, for the first time, possible to him now, without a lifetime of struggle and sacrifice. He now, that is, in possession of the potential, needing only to adjust the matters of equity and distribution.

But man has not yet realized that security on one level, that of basic necessities, does not remove the challenges from the levels above. Such challenges as he never dreamed of in his search for knowledge, for invention, for research, for creative enterprise of all kinds, for sports, for constructive entertainment, for a richer, more enjoyable life for *all* men, not just a favored few.

Security in basic material necessities will never mark the end of human achievement. It would instead unlock and free talents and abilities that are now stifled, starved and beaten down.

Think only of how you, yourself, would feel if you knew for sure that your most basic necessities were guaranteed to you for life. Suppose you knew that you would not be evicted from your home, that you could be sure of having enough to eat, that serious illness or accident would not drain away your life savings, and you could count on your children's having the best education they could absorb without having to take care of you as well in your sunset years.

Does the thought fill you with horror? Remember we are talking just about basic needs. Do you really think you would be ruined? Do you really think you would become a vegetable-like parasite, without further ambition or initiative? We do not think so! With the constant worry for physical survival removed for sure, would you not be encouraged to turn your interest and energies to the broader enticements of the mind and spirit? We think so. We truly think so!

Had we not then better get our thinking straightened out about this security business? Should we not begin to realize that it is not basic security itself, which would blight our lives but the lack of ownership-participation, our lack of identification with our own efforts that blights and kills initiative and ambition?

Security, in its intrinsic sense, has little to do with eking an existence. It should mark man's birthright to perform with distinction!

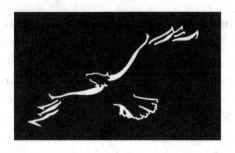

Vol. III, No. 6, June 1965

I bid that ye go into the world and say, the

Prince of Peace awaiteth in his person,

Ambassador to every heart.

(*Golden Scripts,* Chapter 35)

"Eye Troubles"

IT BECOMES apparent as time goes on that a great many Americans are afflicted with eye troubles. Psychological eye troubles these are, not the kind to be overcome with a pair of contact lenses or horn rims.

Every human being is afflicted to some degree at least with the first trouble, "blind spots." Lack of experience, lack of sensitivity, lack of information are among the causes of a complete lack of awareness of certain surrounding conditions. The inescapable awareness of the danger of our time ought to stir some curiosity to find out the facts. Less forgivable cases are those of persons simply refusing to accept what lies before them. Ostrich-like, they work on the principle that if they can't see it, it won't see them, and thus they will not be affected by it.

For them, poverty is either non-existent or grossly exaggerated. Everyone knows we're the richest country in the world. For them, the war in Viet Nam is a faint and faraway disturbance, which a handful of faceless and (of course) invincible Marines will soon have well in hand. For them, civil rights disturbances and stormy campus outbursts are only deliberate agitation by a few trouble-makers which the authorities should handle more quickly than they do.. Talk about the dangers of automation is nonsense. Everybody said the assembly line would ruin the economy and look what happened. For these people, nuclear war will never happen, the economy was never better, and what's all the shouting for, anyway?

Whether these poor souls actually believe such rosy propaganda, or whether their minds put up an impenetrable shock barrier because acceptance would be more than they could cope with, they wander nonetheless in a fool's paradise. The day of rude awakening will come.

The second trouble is something we might call "surface vision." This affects the victim by preventing his seeing beneath the surface of any given problem. For him, there is a war going on in Viet Nam which he does not like, but the only solution is to get in there and fight, winning it as quickly and decisively as possible, no matter what the cost. For him, there are race disturbances and riots on campuses, which are serious, but they must be put down and order restored. Such upsets cannot be permitted in civilized society.

FOR THESE people, automation and cybernation are merely extensions of our already remarkable mechanical technology, which will probably result in more jobs after all. As for all these so-called poor people that the sob sisters and fuzzy liberals are weeping over, it's about time they got back to work. The affluent society has just made people too soft!

These people affected with surface vision have never bothered to look underneath to the lower layers of cause, to the deeper questions that are plaguing the thoughtful, such as: To what extent do we have a right to interfere with the self-determination of people in Viet Nam, and elsewhere? What economic and political axes are being ground in the name of world freedom? Are race disturbances something newly devised by recalcitrant left-wingers, or are they the result of a social maladjustment that has been building for decades? What are these college students really trying to express in their excited shouts and broken phrases? Are they plain "chicken," or are they just disillusioned with a messed up world they are about to inherit?

Where is automation-cybernation leading us? If machines displace men by the millions where will people get the buying power with which to buy what the machines produce? How come all the assets go to the few when it was the contributions of all which made the productive assets possible? In a nation that has progressively increased its capability to produce everything, what is amiss in our system of doing business that our troubles have increased instead of decreased? How really soundly affluent is our society, after all?

A third group consists of those afflicted with "peripheral vision." Instead of looking squarely at the problems and evaluating them honestly, these people look only to the Far Right or the Far Left as the cause

161

of the trouble. To them, all our difficulties are brought on by agitation from the Rightists or the Communists, and each side is firmly convinced if their opponents could be suddenly wafted away to Mars, all would be peaceful and prosperous in the world.

These people on both sides are generally well motivated, but good and sincere intentions are not enough in these complicated times. There are equally well-intentioned and unquestionably more thoughtful people to whom the preservation and the enhancement of the whole human race are of greater moment than political ideologies and party allegiance. Extremists on both sides are exacerbating the problems, confusing the goals, and blurring the images, making it harder than ever to grapple with the stubborn roots.

The Communists did not cause the very real and widening abyss, which exists in this nation between the affluent and the poverty-stricken. The tear gas and police dogs of white southern authorities did not cause the very real and explosive argument, which exists between black and white. The escalation of the Vietnamese War and the increasing unpopularity of the United States across the world may be blamed equally on Left and Right.

The central problem which these peripheral viewers cannot see is that these problems are not political in nature, but economic. No political questions facing mankind around the globe today can be fairly and equitably settled. We need honest and straightforward appraisals, not scapegoats.

We come now to consider the "concentrated I." This is the widespread affliction that causes so many of us to expend effort only on our own problems, without

162

relating them to everyone else's. Each of us is having his own troubles trying to make ends meet, trying to keep up a standard of living he considers proper, trying to cope with the emotional crises of private teenage rebellion, old age dependency, business deterioration, and the distractions and pressures of our atomic-age living. Most of us feel the necessity to keep posted on national and world affairs, but keeping posted is as far as we are able to commit ourselves. We don't in simple fact seem to have the time. We feel the urgent need to participate in varying degrees, usually, not very much.

THIS is not enough. Bearing witness to the country's decline is not enough. Withholding oneself from participation because of "not enough time" is not sufficient excuse. If enough American citizens do not get under their hides that their own good, their own future well-being and that of their children also, depend on more than their own individual interests, we might as well give up right now.

If we continue to refuse to see the handwriting on the wall, if we refuse to accept responsibility for the welfare of others besides ourselves, if we continue to refuse to take active as well as passive interest in our nation's welfare, then this nation is bound for catastrophe.

Regimentation will take over, regimentation of minds as well as bodies. The spirit of individual liberty for which this nation has acclaimed itself for so many years will have perished utterly. Whether it be collectivism of the Communists, or the collectivism of the monopolists, or the collectivism of the money manipulators, or the collectivism of "thinking machines," it will all be one to the poor dupes living there under.

We must get rid of the blind spots. We must see the problems for what they are. We must stop judging on surface values. We must dig down to the actual causes of our problems, even if it does mean soul-searching and agonizing mental work. We must stop trying to escape responsibility ourselves by looking only to the right and the left. And we must stop concentrating exclusively on our own problems. Our problems are caused 90% right now because too many have sought security for themselves without realizing their own security was dependent on the security of all.

Now if ever is the time for clear vision!

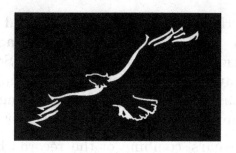

Vol. II, No. 7 & 8, July-August 1965

Tell it with trumpets, emblazon it with radiance! verily,

beloved, it seemeth a mystery. I say it shall be

unfoldeth in every life that testeth it.

(Golden Scripts, Chapter 34)

What Makes Sense?

THESE are days when decisions must be made by mature and rational minds, days when we must be concerned with ideas and principles. Let us examine the trap that many are prone to fall into, so that it may be avoided in the future.

There are those who remember a similar time before Pearl Harbor when the war clouds loomed large on the horizon and emotions were being played upon and stirred even as today. They will remember that all who opposed Red Russia, who opposed Lend-Lease, who opposed escalated embroilment in hostilities and who felt we should remain strong and aloof from foreign wars were dubbed Red-baiters and pro-Nazis. The Roosevelt Administration took the attitude that all who were not "for us" were "agin' us" and should be so excoriated.

After Pearl Harbor had become a provoked reality, the stage was set for legal action against the Administration's most forceful critics. Some thirty-three individuals were indicted in the infamous "mass sedition trial" on charges of interfering with the Russian-American war effort against Hitler.

After three years' combing of the records here and in Germany, after a million dollars of taxpayer's money had been wasted, the Roosevelt Administration openly admitted it lacked sufficient evidence. Chief Justice Laws of the Washington Federal Court threw the whole case out with the ruling that "it would be a travesty on justice to permit it to continue."

Strange, isn't it, that the professional smear artists didn't take note of the fact that Mr. Pelley was one of the defendants exonerated in the Washington trial when they were so busy hurling epithets at his dead body! Not that the same evidence used against him in Washington was the same insufficient evidence upon which he was railroaded to prison four years earlier at the peak of war hysteria!

The supreme irony of the Mass Sedition Trial is the fact that the only single concept binding the defendants together in any way was that they were all anti-Communists!

Almost a quarter century later, the nation finds itself with the dogs of war growling ominously near. Once again those who dare to question or criticize the powers-that-be find themselves dumped unceremoniously into the enemy camp. All those who aren't with us are agin' us, only this time they are Red-sympathizers or downright Communists.

166

It is, once again, hard not to fall in the trap. Unthinking public opinion, following sheep-like after the policies of the powers-that-be, are glad to hang opprobrious labels on all opposition. It makes things so much simpler to have it all divided into black hats and white hats, the good guys and the bad guys.

Observe the confusing muddle into which devotion to slogans and personalities have led the American people. "Rugged individualism," and "free enterprise" have led us into an economic stalemate where monolithic monopolies control the whole economic system in a Twentieth Century feudalism far more stringent than endured in the Thirteenth. Being a "patriotic" American has focused our eyes on Communism as our sole enemy, blinding us completely to weaknesses at home. It has led us into the blandly complacent and perilous attitude that "self-determination of nations" is what we want, just so long as each nation determines that what it wants and needs is the American way.

"Defense of freedom" leads us into supporting the most outrageous dictatorships just so long as the dictatorship professes itself as anti-Communist. Even if such dictatorships mercilessly trample on the liberties of their people it is of little concern to us provided of course we are permitted to dictate the military policy, and the political policy, of the nation we are supporting with tax dollars, and the blood of our fighting men.

The Eagle's Eye will subscribe to no double standard. It is earnestly trying to promote the dignity of every human being and his right to live under systems that enhance and secure that dignity. It believes that no

167

government has a right to send a boy to die for rights in a foreign land that he and his loved ones were denied at home. Killing is no less murder because it is done in a uniform, and no government is acting in the basic interests of the people if it does not take every step possible to preserve human life.

This magazine has contended from its first publication that a nation's foreign policy can never exceed one iota in integrity and honestly what its national policy represents. It is on this premise that we have pleaded for the putting of our own house in order before essaying to reform the world according to our own domestic failings and denials of liberties.

Indeed, we should pluck the mote from our own eye before we stand qualified to do it for all others!

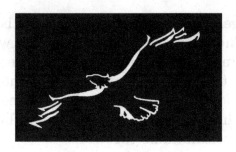

Vol. III, No. 9, September 1965

I say ye shall rise up and give his plotting contest: ye

shall spear him with a courage: ye shall rise up

and cry, and who are thou, that the

righteous bend before thee?

(*Golden Scripts,* Chapter 36)

Our Own Day of Infamy!

EVERY year newspaper, TV and radio devote some coverage to the anniversary of America's dropping of the atomic bomb. During the past month considerable space has been allotted to it due to the fact that 1965 marks the 20th anniversary.

On the evening of September 19, a special program was presented by NBC entitled "The Surrender of Japan." In contrast to all previous presentations, this was to be different. For the first time, the direct testimony and positions of both the American and Japanese government leaders in the closing days of the war were to be revealed.

The first part of the coverage dealt largely with the progressive weakening of Japan militarily. There was much footage of the actual devastation of both life and property. The horror and brutality of war were not left to the imagination. American Marines were shown as defenseless targets as they stormed the shores of Okinawa and later one saw the Japanese soldiers turned into human torches as they were flushed out of caves by American flame-throwers.

Then came the bomber onslaught on the Japanese mainland with the pulverizing of major cities by incendiary bombs and bombardment from naval vessels having increasing access to the costal cities. Pictures taken by American airmen, and many apparently taken by the Japanese, ran the gamut of the soul-searing effects of indiscriminate bombing. Cities were shown in the process of being blown up. You knew that thousands of old people, women and children were being blown to bits and scattered throughout the rubble. Also, there were the scenes of thousands of homeless, frantically seeking escape from the fiery destruction that kept pouring down from above.

Japan was in a state of chaos and her industrial capacity devastated. Testimony, as substantially presented in the TV coverage, bore out that the official leaders both of Japan and the United States recognized that militarily Japan had been defeated. She must inevitably surrender or face the alternative of complete destruction and annihilation.

It was against this background in July of 1945 that President Truman demanded that the Japanese "unconditionally" surrender. We blanketly refused to make any concession respecting any modification of our position despite the fact that any assurance of protecting the status of the Japanese Emperor would

170

have meant immediate peace. This was the circumstance that obtained when President Truman met with Churchill and Stalin at Potsdam.

To this point in the TV presentation nothing had been offered that had not been made public before. But then, a most pertinent and significant revelation was made. Two messages were delivered to President Truman. One announced the United States had successfully detonated an atomic bomb. The second was that representatives of Japan were *enroute via Moscow with an acceptance of the United States terms of surrender.*

According to the memoirs of secretary of War Stimson, as read by McGeorge Bundy, now advisor to President Johnson, Mr. Truman immediately took counsel with Premier Stalin. Out of that get-together came the decision to send a "blurred" message in response to the Japanese representatives. There would be no immediate acceptance of peace with Japan.

Upon President Truman's return to the United States a decision was made to drop the first atomic bomb on a Japanese civilian city. There is no need for details. On August 6, 1945 in a blinding flash, lasting but a matter of seconds, the city of Hiroshima laid waste with some 100,000 of its inhabitants burned to ashes. Two days later, on August 8, 1945, a second bomb was dropped, this time on Nagasaki. Again, a blinding flash and a similar number of human beings annihilated, with those on the outskirts writhing in agony and dying from death-dealing radiation.

Now to some serious conclusions. Over the years most Americans have salved their consciences by the persuasion that the ending of the war with Japan was

171

only possible by a massive invasion of the mainland, with the probability that upwards of a million American soldiers could be sacrificed in the undertaking. Therefore, there was justification in dropping the bombs because it would bring the war to an immediate end without the loss of so many American lives.

The documentary of Sunday evening on "The Surrender of Japan" completely destroys the foregoing justification. Not only was there official testimony to the fact that Japan was already pulverized and disposed to surrender, but the most deadly evidence was that we deliberately turned aside a specific overture to end the war which would have precluded both the loss of further American life and any necessity to "test" the bomb on massive civilian aggregations.

To those who still contend that there was a military necessity for use of the bomb to display our exclusive power, what justification could there have been in demonstrating such horrendous taking of innocent life the second time? Couldn't either or both of the bombs, as some military men pleaded, have been dropped away from human targets to underscore our invincible strength? What of the fact that, according to testimony by Japanese officials, the second bomb was dropped before the leaders of the Japanese government could apprise themselves of what had happened?

This editorial, does not mean to interject here the causes of World War II in which 406,000 American fighting men gave their lives. The ramifications are much too long and detailed. A well-documented coverage can be read by obtaining a copy of "President Roosevelt and the Coming of the War" by the historian,

Charles A. Beard. But even if we granted that the Japanese attack on Pearl Harbor was an unprovoked "day of infamy," what then of the two bombs we dropped on the defenseless cities of Hiroshima and Nagasaki?

As the record stands, our own leadership created our own "day of infamy" when it wantonly and needlessly snuffed out the lives of 200,000 other human beings! But this was the lesser of the crime that was committed. What of the additional thousands condemned to lingering death by the radiation burns and the children yet unborn condemned to live their lives in malformed bodies?

On September 2, 1945, Japan signed the surrender papers. By 1952 she was restored as an independent nation bound by a mutual defense agreement with the United States. In this year of 1965 we no longer refer to the Japanese as those "dirty little Japs." We try hard to forget the cities of Hiroshima and Nagasaki, and the inglorious chapter of World War II when thousands of Japanese-Americans were imprisoned without trial while their blood relations were fighting and dying for the United States on Italian beaches.

Isn't it time the American people called a halt to this "devil-theory" of warfare and the slaughtering of millions at the behest of economic and political oligarchies? Isn't it time we recognize that all human beings are the product of the same Creator and have the same inherent right to life?

Isn't it time we recognize that our own leadership is subject to the same corruption of morals and justice when it is given too much power? Isn't it time that we recognize that a nation's treatment of people abroad is never any more honest than its treatment of its own people at home?

A candid appraisal of our own "self-righteousness" should be the first step toward peace in the world!

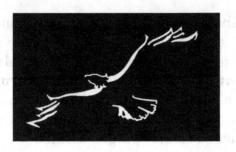

Vol. III, No. 10, October 1965

Tranquility giveth a man the essence of himself: It maketh him to see his soul as in a mirror: It showeth him his diadem: it lifteth him up and beareth him along: he seeth the world as one who hath wings.

(Golden Scripts, Chapter 38)

The Most Precious Gift

THE GREAT PARADOX of our time is our preoccupation with the saving and prolonging of human life, and our callous indifference to it on the other.

Science, the recorded, orderly accumulation of man's knowledge to date, burgeons and expands before our startled eyes, without regard to moral principle. It is the responsibility of man himself to apply moral principle in the use of that knowledge. As the human race steps over the threshold into a new age, scientific knowledge is increasing so rapidly that there is imminent peril in it's getting out of hand completely.

Like Dr. Frankenstein, all the science of the world's history (90 percent of whom are now alive!) have

175

created of their subject an enormous monster, whose strength far exceeds their own, and whose capacity for good or evil is limitless. The monster in Mrs. Shelley's novel had unwittingly been fitted with a criminal brain, allowing for the development of a classic tale of suspense and horror. The future for our monster, Science, is not so clearly prognosticated.

Its future will be directed by the human leaders of mankind, and whether its good outweighs its evil, or vice versa, is the responsibility of human beings themselves, who will either be, or will choose, those leaders.

The whole difficulty, of course, lies in knowing what is good and what is evil. Who is to say? Every man has his own idea of what constitutes good and what is evil. Sincerity, altruism, high purpose, these are not enough to guarantee wisdom in the choice. Many absolutely sincere and high-minded men can be proved sadly mistaken in their goals with the passage of sufficient time.

Further, time itself, the existence of which may only be identified by change, alters standards of good and evil from one age to another. Custom, space, increased knowledge, all these are factors bearing strongly on man's understanding and acceptance of what is good and what is evil.

A verse in the *Golden Scripts* reads as follow: "The world groaneth, mankind wracketh, the races shout lustily, many run to and fro declaring their perception that a new order cometh . . . . But ever do they perceive it after the order of their desirings, that their enemies be felled and a bitter fate await them. . . ."

Man's faith in the absolute rightness of his own standards, of his own decisions, of his own judgments, is as old as he is, and without it he would long since have perished with the dinosaur and the dodo. It has been responsible for man's self-assurance, his self-confidence, his faith in himself, and these are the qualities that have kept man operating, functioning and improving his lot in life from cave to what, the Cow Palace?

Through the ages man has stuck to his beliefs, arguing quarreling, battling with his fellowmen to try to prove the correctness of his own judgment. He has swayed into acceptance of the other fellow's ideas, into compromise or at least into co-existence with them, through reason, through "faith in authority," more often by brute force, and the whole process has made up the warp and woof of man's material, and sometimes spiritual, progress.

There is another verse in the *Golden Scripts* which says: "Man hath risen until he knoweth his divinity evinced in manufacture, in science, in art: lo, he hath kept tryst with talents supernal and not been disappointed; lo, hath made himself lord over matter and shaped it to his ends: lo, *he hath not made himself god of his own spirit!*"

Now, up here in the middle of the Twentieth Century after the birth of the Prince of Peace, man has come to a great, new Moment of Decision. Up the centuries, the increase in technology, meaning broadly man's total "know-how," has led to tremendous concentrations of power unheard of before in human history. Never before has the power been available to one human

177

being to push a button and consign the earth to annihilation.

Never before has one man had the capability to speak, and be seen and heard by half the people of the earth simultaneously. Never before has the power of controlling the manufacture of all goods to fill all human needs been concentrated in the hands of so few human directorates. Never before has control over the financial bloodstream of the entire earth, its buying power, been concentrated in the hands of so few men operating in a global network.

Never before has the well-being, indeed the continuing existence of so many human beings been dependent on the moral judgment of so few. The greatest protection to the common run of ordinary mortals, those without power and without influence, lies in the fact that the powerful few do not agree among themselves, and so, as they align and realign, merge and split, agree and disagree, a precarious balance of power is maintained, permitting the world to continue in its peril-fraught, blundering and confused way.

The great question facing the world today is: Shall the human race continue, or shall we as human beings deliberately commit suicide and let this tiny planet pursue its little orbit in the vast celestial progression of the heavens, as dead and old and silent as the moon?

You cry quickly, "But there is no question about it! Everybody wants to survive for as long as he can. Survival is the first law!"

Survival may indeed be the first law, but unlike the great natural laws of Cosmos and the universe, it can be broken, and frequently is. The human race is

178

generally overpoweringly concerned with individual survival, but it has not yet learned the necessity for raising its concern to the all-inclusive, to the survival of the human race as a whole.

It is a fact that human beings are, so far in our experience, unique. We do not rule out the possibility of human life elsewhere in the broad, blue expanse of the universe, and we may indeed be standing on the brink of contact at this moment. But it has not happened yet.

Where we came from, and where we are going in the infinite reaches of unfathomable time, we cannot state with certainty. We find ourselves in animal bodies, subject to the natural laws governing those bodies. We are born, we eat, sleep and feel pain as animal bodies do, we reproduce and we die just as horses, monkeys and white rats. But we know we are more. What more we cannot estimate, for we have not learned exactly what we are. But the human race, from Hottentot savage to university president, differs from the beasts of the field, and is within its own broad spectrum, unique.

Shall we endure? Do we want it to endure? The earth is fruitful, varied and generous. It holds much that is beautiful, satisfying and inspiring to human beings. There is now, here in the Twentieth Century after Christ, largely due to man's own ingenuity, a potential at last to provide for the needs and wants of human beings, so that none of them need suffer cold, or hunger or want. Because the full development of this potential requires adjustments in our present attitudes, in our present modes of operation, should it be declared undesirable, illegal, immoral for *all* men to be free of

179

these age-old miseries? Is this not what we each most ardently desire for ourselves? Why not work toward it for all?

Perhaps the highest individual attribute, the one most clearly distinguishing man from the beasts of the field, is his unwillingness consciously to be pushed around, his innate desire to be himself to express himself in a way that is special to himself alone, in a word, man seeks *individuality.*

It is the subtle attack on this most basic of human desires by the great agglomerations of power that imperils man today, and so insidious is the attack that he is liable to fall a helpless victim through subversion where he would resist magnificently any open attack.

War is the most corrosive of all attacks on man's individuality. The propaganda attendant upon war is the most subtly subversive. In time of war, all citizens are called to sacrifice all personal ambitions for the national safety. One is expected to give up all personal desires to the authority of the military. When one's home is attacked or one's nation is invaded by alien humans intent on taking over by force, there is an instinctive and noble urge to rise up and defend one's own hearthstone, one's native soil, to drive the invaders back to their own bailiwick, and there let them work out their own destiny.

But when one is sent to fields afar, there to kill or be killed at the behest of other humans whose motives are not clear, whose methods are confusing, whose word is frequently suspect, for reasons that are not satisfactory as given, tragedy ensues. Where does one's allegiance lie? Individual argument or discussion has no place, and opposition is legally suppressed.

War does more. Not only does it destroy individuality, reducing groups of human beings to single, many-legged, mindless monsters, but it is at work constantly to blur, break down or utterly destroy respect and reverence for human life.

War is, at we have said in many places elsewhere, the ultimate barbarism. There is a barbarism less easily recognized, just as deadly. Man's headlong and reckless pursuit of material things, his ingrained desire for the "fast buck," is leading him to despoil the riches and the bounty freely offered by Nature.

Deforestation, air and water pollution, soil erosion, the promiscuous use of fertilizers and pesticides, thoughtless waste and destruction of reusable resources, all these are destroying the hospitality of the good green earth upon which we are privileged to reside. By this wanton waste and destruction, we are destroying our chance of continuing to live here. This is not necessary destruction. These things can, with a little thought and some sacrifice of excessive profit, be almost entirely prevented. Without such thought, we continue on our suicidal course.

Death on the highway is becoming a national American scandal. Somewhere in the neighborhood of 50,000 people will die in traffic this year, most of them sacrificed to an insane love of speed and physical power, together with criminal carelessness and disregard for courtesy and common sense.

There are other ways in which our present material standard of values is furthering and fostering the national disregard for human and spiritual values. Crime, mental breakdown, pornography, venereal disease, illiteracy, broken homes, delinquency, drop-

181

outs, all these destroyers of respect for human life are on the rise.

How may this tide be turned?

It is not enough to shift the blame for these growing perils onto our favorite enemies. The responsibility falls on each of us individually, simply as members of the human race, to do whatever each of us can, great or small, to lift our own perspective and that of all others we may contact, to include *all* men and their right to exist. Whether they be saints or sinners, publicans or dogcatchers, whether we love them or loathe them, we are going to have to learn to respect the right of others to live and to differ from ourselves in their desires and in their needs.

When an individual, or a group of individuals, attempt to stifle the right of other individuals to live, to stifle their right to think, to grow, to develop their own God-given individualities, that individual or that group must be restrained, if need be ostracized, but never destroyed.

It has been said that while there is life, there is hope, but he who destroys hope while there is yet life is the greater destroyer.

We cannot gain to a better life by dealing in death in whatever form. Let us view life for the precious gift it is, the lesson to be learned, and the experience to develop us, the opportunity to learn how glorious it could be.

The hope of the human race lies in respect for the precious gift of life!

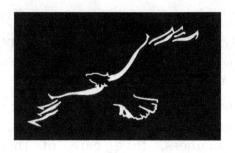

Vol. III, No. 11, November 1965

Perceive ye the universe and see that it is measured:

The wren's song is pure; the babe's tear is silver:

The summer wind is vagrant, art hath her resonance:

There is singing on the sea's shore that the ships

have found their havens.

(Golden Scripts, Chapter 38)

The Uncommitted

IF EVER, Heaven save the day, the United States should fade from the scene as a world power, if ever it becomes a single closed chapter in the history books of the future like the "glory that was Greece and the grandeur that was Rome," the fault will not lie with the spies and the subversives, with the right-wing extremists or the radical left, with the criminal or hoodlum element, the hate mongers, the rabble-rousers and would-be revolutionists. The fault will lie squarely upon the shoulders of the millions of decent, quiet, honest folk who make up the great bulk of the citizenry of the United States.

The fault will lie squarely on them because of, paradoxically, their very decency, quietness and honesty. The fault will lie on them because they failed to take a stand.

Descent, quiet, honest people do not seek our trouble. They avoid hurting other people's feelings. They mind their own business, take care of their personal responsibilities and ask favors of no man. They believe in the virtue of thrift and the healthfulness of industry. They deplore the seven deadly sins, and bring up their children likewise. Their name is legion, and they inhabit every nation on the planet. They are the Good Neighbors, the Model Citizens, the backbone of any nation, yet they may lose the world and not gain their own souls, even so.

Keeping out of trouble is not always a sign of probity. In the days in which we live, it may be fatal.

Socrates failed to keep out of trouble. Martin Luther failed to keep out of trouble. The early Christian martyrs failed to keep out of trouble. The Founding Fathers failed to keep out of trouble. A certain Carpenter of Nazareth failed to keep out of trouble. . .

Not one of the foregoing went out and actively stirred trouble up. They simply took their firm stands against Wrong and trouble engulfed them. But history has sung anthems to them up the centuries, nevertheless.

Here in the last half of the last century of the second millennium after Christ, we find the earth shaping itself to an Armageddon of sorts. It is immaterial whether it is *the* Armageddon foretold of old in Scripture. It is the most serious we shall be called to face in our present lifetimes and the most serious history has yet recorded because the future of the planet and the survival of the human race itself are at stake. The Battle between the Builders and the Destroyers is a-building fast. . . .

Who are the Builders? They are those who see in the individual human spirit the fulfillment of the purpose of mortality. They are the ones who subscribe meaningfully and in function to the Eleventh Commandment, who respect the rights of others to express themselves, to grow in mental and spiritual stature individually, who accord to all other humans the same rights they themselves need and own.

They are those who confront the Destroyers and draw a line, saying, "Thus far and no farther. You may have your just desserts but no more. The good earth belongs to all men by right of being born onto it. No man by force or guile may build a fence around any part and say, This is mine and thereby deprive another of the right to life itself. We build not for ourselves alone, but for eternity!"

Who are the Destroyers? The destroyers are the Self-Seekers, the Power Hungry, and the Materialists. They are those who hold themselves in high esteem as rulers and arbiters, and the rest of the human race as beneath consideration. They are the disrespecters of Nature's bounty, the greedy riflers of her spacious cupboards. They are the makers of the fast buck, the "Business-is-business" Boys.

"It's a rat race," they say, "a jungle-world. We'll get what we can while the getting's good. We'll see who's cleverest at this chess game of power-grabbing, and let the suckers beware. Why should we worry? We'll be a long time dead!"

185

The lines are drawing tight around us. The choice moves closer with each morning's sunrise.

The decent, quiet, honest people of the earth must take their stand and make themselves known. They belong not with the Destroyers. Have they the will to stand with the Builders, or shall they in their desire for peace, flee from the trouble that surrounds them, and hurl themselves, lemming-like, into the Sea of Eternal Oblivion?

Where shall they take their stand, these decent, quiet, honest people? Where shall they decide to place their unconquerable strength:

Shall they continue to permit war, brutal, inhuman, demoralizing war, to rage unchecked upon this, the good green earth, their own beloved home? Or shall they combine together and make it known that they desire peace, that they command the war makers to cease and desist in their destruction, in order that peace and construction may take place?

If the decent, quiet, honest folks of this nation, or any nation, should suddenly join together in raising the loud word "Peace!" it would echo down all the corridors of time, and war would plague the world no more. This the Destroyers know, and they'll make what they can while they can.

WHERE ELSE should the decent, quiet, honest people take a stand? Shall they continue to permit poverty, illiteracy, disease and crime not only to exist but also to proliferate on the face of the earth? Shall they avoid trouble by pretending these dark problems do not exist, or do not touch them, or someone else will clear them up? Or shall they, for the love of their lives, take time

186

to study these problems, to see what inequalities, injustices; stupidities, shortsightedness and ignorance cause these sores to fester? Then shall they take steps to cure these inequalities, eradicate the stupidities and the shortsightedness, as Divine Creation has given them the courage and intelligence to perform?

Shall the decent, quiet, honest folk of the world permit the greedy, the avaricious, the misanthropic to strip the earth, to upset the delicate balances of biologic life, to destroy in a day what Nature has been centuries in creating? Shall they permit themselves to be poisoned slowly by man-made pollution or the sunshine and sparkling water? Or shall they take counsel together and see what may be done to prevent further heartless and needless ruin to the earth, to begin to use wisely and gratefully the bounty and the beauty Nature offers?

Shall the decent, quiet, honest folk continue to avoid trouble by paying and paying and paying the dishonest tribute demanded by the Destroyers, in interest, in unearned profit, in extortionate taxes, in tribute money of a hundred sorts, or shall they join together and decide that they have had enough? Shall they draw tight the purse strings on the money they have earned in the sweat of their brows and demand an accounting for the squander bust? Shall they decide that henceforth they will pay an honest fee for honest work and not one penny more to support the lazy, the greedy, the dishonest or the tricky?

Decency, dignity and honesty know no national boundaries, just as greed, ignorance and hunger for power do not. When the good and constructive and altruistic citizens of one nation speak out, they will be answered by the good, the constructive, the altruistic across the earth, and their voices will blend into a psalm of peace and quiet happiness such as the world has never known.

Keep out of trouble? *No.* Because this time, he plays the game for keeps. As he stands firm against trouble, he stands firm against evil, against all who would overpower humanity, exploit it, imprison it or destroy it. As he battles trouble this time he battles those who endanger his own survival.

As he overcomes trouble, this time he gains the world and saves his own soul!

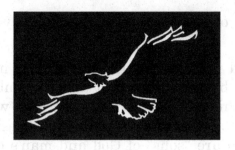

Vol. III, No. 12, December 1965

Harken to this well: Change is your friend. Go forth in Change, be strong in it to run a race, have confidence in it believing it good, for change is Consciousness performing in event.

(Golden Scripts, Chapter 41)

A Rational Religion

MORE and more people can be heard to exclaim, "Only divine intervention can save mankind!" Looking around they see only an increase in corruption an increase in crime, and escalation of war with mounting death, and conclude that the problems are all beyond mortal solution. Their only faith in the future lies in a belief that somehow, and some time, the Creator of all things will intercede and put everything in order.

It would be unfair to question the sincerity of these people. They are the victims of religious belief that has so emphasized the dogma of "pie in the sky" that man has been reduced to a mere puppet without either will or purpose. The irony lies in the fact that they have unwittingly placed human beings outside the jurisdiction of the very "God" whom they purport to identify.

Rare indeed is the "Christian" who does not accept a God that is both Omnipresent and the embodiment of Love. If this acceptance is true, and we have no disposition to militate against it, then doesn't it follow that all men are "sons" of God and man's own actions can be logically interpreted as a form of constant "divine intervention"?

What we are trying to get at here is no attempt to interfere with anyone's belief as to life before birth or any religious persuasion respecting the after-life. Such convictions belong solely with the individual. True freedom of religion should encompass the right of every person to believe whatever he wishes in all areas of the "unseen."

However, in this three-dimensional existence, both his survival and well-being are inter-dependent with others. The conduct of one person does have a bearing on each and every other person. Thus it does become incumbent upon every individual and every nation, to have common meeting grounds respecting man's treatment of man.

All the great religions, in fact, were originally predicated on ethical principles relating to human relationships. They all accepted a literal world inhabited with literal people and propounded rules of conduct recognizing the natural rights of every inhabitant. It was the priesthood of the great spiritual leaders who amplified the "unseen" into irrational dogma completely over-shadowing how each individual might be protected and assisted in extracting the maximum profit from the life experience.

What the times demand, more than anything else, is a world-wide ecumenical movement, that considers the broadest ethical principles acceptable to all mankind. The tenor of the approach would be that there was no need to interfere, change, or disturb present religious beliefs concerning the origin of life or any convictions concerning the Hereafter. On the other hand, there must be recognition that all problems which are man-made are susceptible to solutions based on universal ethical tenets.

Is it presumptuous to conclude *that* the first common agreement would be that every human being born onto this planet has *an equal right to life?* No man, no group, no government has the rightful power to play "God" and destroy a solitary human being. No civilization can lay claim to being rational that condones or tolerates the taking of one life as a method of settling differences.

Secondly, there must b e common agreement that this is an impartial Universe that we inhabit. Nowhere is there to be found any Celestial plaque depart-mentalizing the planet. All the resources are the heritage of all the people. Thus, all economic solutions must be premised on the equal opportunity for all mankind, both within nations and within the scope of the world, to have access to Nature's bountiful storehouse. All economic systems, or international policies, that build fences around natural resources for the exclusive benefit of the privileged must be corrected or eliminated.

Thirdly, there must be common agreement that just as there is no "divine" priority on resources, there is at the same time no "divine" priority on human opportunity.

Each and every individual, irrespective of skin-color or nationality has an equal right to develop his innate capabilities. No group, or government, has the rightful power to decree the inferiority of an individual by denying him the opportunity to prove his own worth through performance.

Perhaps the most paramount agreement would be the recognition that only through the principle of cooperative action can the foregoing agreements have meaning and realization. Belatedly it would be recognized that it is out of mutual endeavor, not survival of the fittest, that individual excellence is attained. This would be the cornerstone of a rational religion to which all mankind could subscribe.

Strange, isn't it that the underlying principle, and spirit, of all religions has emphasized, *"By losing yourself in service to others, you shall truly find yourself"*?

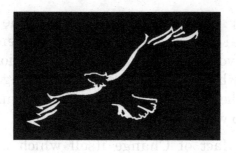

Vol. IV, No. 1, January 1966

The dawning hath its fever: the night-time hath its

Solace; behold every good and perfect thing

hath its place in God's order.

(Golden Scripts, Chapter 42)

Proliferation of Change

As A NEW YEAR opens, it seems appropriate to spend a few moments in speculation on the future. We are not concerning ourselves with push buttons, monorails, rockets or robots, intriguing or commonplace as these individual advancements may become. They constitute only physical manifestations of the future we are called to envision. They are simply the inevitable outward trappings of a burgeoning technology.

What we are facing in the latter half of the Twentieth Century is a New Age of concepts and structures dealing with human relationships. It will be an age as profoundly different from all previous ages as Alexander the Great differed from Neanderthal Man, and much more in fact than any of us differ from Alexander.

We are, in short, sitting smack in the middle of technological and scientific change that embodies not just one revolution, but a dozen revolutions, each of them earthshaking in itself. The average person is frightened because he has lost identity and practical relationship with all that surrounds him.

It isn't the fact of Change itself which terrifies and confuses most people, but the crowding in of so many changes, and so fast. They don't have time to digest, to discriminate, to decide what course to follow. It seems at times like a plot to befuddle them, to take advantage of them, to somehow get the upper hand over them, and they blindly resent all shake-ups or the status quo. They yearn to lay hands on the plotters and lock them up so that they can safely resume their accustomed, conventional pace.

It may, or may not, be comforting to learn that the underlying cause of the proliferation of Change cannot be laid at any human door, but is too be explained by the evolutionary cycle spurred by something called Geometric Progression. This is the mathematical principle of doubling a number, then doubling the result, and continuing this process as far as you with to go. Let us illustrate. . . .

HAS NO 14-year-old ever tried to snare you with this proposition? He will be happy to work for you for a month, he says, and all you have to pay him is a penny the first day, two pennies the second day, four pennies the third day and so on. When you figure rapidly ahead, and note that on the tenth day, with the month a third over, you will only be paying your prospective young worker $5.12, it seems a pretty silly business. There is a gleam in his eye, which goads you to

194

continue. It may surprise you to find out that on the twentieth day, with the month two-thirds over, you'd have to shell out $5,246.88 for that day's work. To your teen-ager's glee, it will really jolt you to find out that for the thirtieth day alone (not for the accumulate, you understand) you would owe him $5,373,805.12!

Or, if you have more time than we have, you might try counting how many grains of wheat you'd have on the 64th square of checkerboard, if you began by putting one grain on the first square, two on the second, four on the third and so on. If you double the amount each time, by the 64th square, you could feed the population of the world!

You get the picture? The amount of anything, whether pennies, or grains of wheat, or *population*, or even *ideas*, gets off to a slow start in the doubling process, but just as you get bored with the whole idea, something happens and the result overwhelms you.

Thus it has been with technological development up the centuries. For every new idea advanced, two more have branched out from it, slowly growing and doubling their number until suddenly we have turned the corner, and are about to reap the whirlwind. Unless, we construct a framework within which man is dominant and master!

Let us consider the last 100,000 years of the history of our era. It took man something like 90,000 years to discover how to harness fire, and invent the wheel and the lever. Only 10,000 years ago, he invented the plow and our present so-called civilization got under way. It was slowly evolving agricultural civilization until just about a hundred years ago when mechanization began

195

to turn Western development into an industrial civilization.

One hundred years out of 100,000! Now, with the shocking speed generated by geometric progression, has come, in the experience of most adults now alive, the harnessing of unlimited energy through atomic power, and the potential of unlimited production through automation and cybernation. We in the West have turned that corner from growth that is so slow as to be almost imperceptible to a proliferation that scares us. . . . .

ALL CHANGE is evolution. It is the slow process of adaptation to new circumstances, new requirements. Revolution, on the other hand, might be termed the need for sudden involvement or adjustment to change. In its most common stage, revolution is "quick and radical change." Examples would be the Industrial Revolution, the American Revolution, and now the Technological Revolution.

The two basic *evolutionary* movements which have now been speeded into *revolutionary* movements by geometric progression are A) the explosion of population, and B) the explosion of knowledge, and its application, which we call technology. Out of the growth of knowledge and technology have developed four major revolutions, among others: 1) Weaponry, 2) Communication, 3) Production and 4) Habitat.

1) The Weaponry Revolution, having reached the capability, not just of annihilating the enemy, but of destroying the planet, has made the hitherto accepted art of war an insane pursuit. There is no alternative to peace if mankind is to survive.

196

2) The Communication Revolution has suddenly shrunk the wide, wide, world to backyard proportions. Each can now know everyone else's business and there is no escape beyond the horizon. Existence for each can only be thought of in the context of all peoples.

3) The Production Revolution is forcing the whole economic world too focus its thinking on systems based on Abundance instead of systems based on Scarcity. Too long has man had to accept that only by the sweat of his brow could he expect the right to live. The power to accumulate wealth has always carried with it the ethical justification of exploitation.

4) The Habitat Revolution is the growing footlessness of man. Not only is there a general movement to the city from rural life, due to technological development, but people no longer choose to live in or near the place where they were born. Others are lured by the inducements of education or pleasure to frequent travel.

In their basic sense, the four revolutions just listed deal with material things such as bombs, television, jet transportation, cybernated factories, and homes. While one cannot separate people from them, the predominant emphasis is on the science of *things*. There is no emphasis there on the science of human beings. It is in this latter area that belatedly the most basic revolutions are erupting. They deal with human relationships in every aspect of people living together, and how the well being of each person is inter-dependent upon the well being of every other person.

INCREASING numbers of people are recognizing that their insecurity, their hardships, their anxieties, and their unhappiness are caused directly by the failure to emphasize the paramount importance of people as *human beings*. Man was not meant to move at the behest of things. All things are to serve man. It is in this context that the world now finds itself in the midst of revolutions dealing with the survival and destiny of human beings.

If we were to divide such revolutions geographically, we could say that they find expression in the form of Civil Rights demands within nations, and in the form of emerging nations on the worldly scene. Underlying both is man's exertion to find recognition as a human being and to have equal opportunity to create the good life for himself and his family.

While the Civil Rights Revolution is generally related to the Negro in the United States, we must consider it in the scope of sovereign people in all lands seeking such economic, political and social reform that the natural rights of every solitary individual are protected and given exercise.

Emerging nations frequently turn toward Communism, seeking to escape from Capitalism and Colonialism. Actually, neither Capitalism nor Communism provide a viable framework. It is a New Order in social structure that must be ushered in.

Natural Rights are inseparable from man's spiritual makeup and so there is a parallel resurgence in the form of Religious Revolution. All religious dogmas, all churches, all religious beliefs are being shaken up, tested and tried against the new faces of truth being everywhere unveiled.

In its most encompassing context, the whole world must undergo what we might label a Philosophical Revolution. Thinking men and women all over the world must find common denominators for God, Love, Morality, Altruism and Wisdom that will be acceptable to all men, not just to give life meaning and purpose, but to permit life to continue at all.

The next three decades are crucial in man's existence. We choose to believe that during those crucial decades a sufficient number of people of good will will involve and declare themselves. They will realize the need to turn from competition to cooperation. They will gradually learn how to relate their ideals to the new realities so that succeeding New Years must be a happier and safer one.

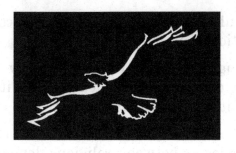

Vol. IV, No. 2, February 1966

Love hath radiance, love hath a softness, love

hath a witchery, it hath a magic happening.

(Golden Scripts, Chapter 8)

The Uncommon Man

THE FIRST HOPE of man is that he is capable of a certain amount of objectivity.

There is no record of the dinosaurs ever getting together, either in solemn conclave, or over the teacups, to discus the causes of decay in their society, and to offer constructive suggestions for its improvement.

Men, on the other hand, from the beginning of recorded time, have relished this activity. Never more so than at this moment. Endless hours of speeches and conversations, gallons of ink, acres of paper, miles of tape and film are being filled with viewing and questioning, with analyses, criticism, comment, suggestion, diatribe, polemic and exhortation. The failure of all this great burst of talk would seem to be in the fact that everyone is so busy expressing his own ideas that he fails to hear what anyone else is saying.

The real fault lies in a lack of communication where communication is most sorely needed.

Human thought in the Twentieth Century has curdled into widely divided schools, each with its own glib spokesmen, its own rigid platform.

No longer can lines of demarcation be drawn between political parties or between religious denominations or between racial groups. Nor can they be drawn between age groups or social castes. All these previously homogeneous groups are split drastically within themselves, each faction ready to war on another at the drop of an opinion.

With few notable exceptions, all of the analyses, all of the suggestions, all of the comments are reserved for consumption within the speaker's own group. One speaks thoughtfully, it seems, only where one will be understood, agreed with and appreciated. Catcalls and epithets are sufficient for the opposition.

A favorite topic whirling along the closed circuits is "the common man." He is constantly talked *about*. He is almost never talked *to,* except by the trouble-making Left Wing. He is thought of, generally, as a nonentity, a filler of space, a faceless blob in the vast sea of humanity.

Views of the common man vary, of course, among the groups. The military think of him only in terms of units of destructive strength. In political groups, he is a vote to be controlled. Industry considers him only collectively in terms of buying power, or of labor power, which last in these cybernetical days is becoming of less and less importance. Among intellectuals, he is a poor relation. In financial circles, he does not exist.

Everywhere, the common man is consciously or unconsciously, looked on either with pity or contempt, if he is looked on at all.

Jeanne Riha, on another page of this magazine, wonders whether the cynicism of some intellectuals regarding man's efforts to shape a better world stems from their profound knowledge of man, or from their being at too great a distance from him. It is an open question.

Industrial leaders are rapidly severing all connections with him on the one hand by refusing to countenance his plea for economic adjustment, while on the other, they are freeing themselves from the labor problems and costs he causes them by the installation of automated and cybernated machinery.

Historically and necessarily, the military quickly reduces the uncommon man to a number in a column, to a none-thinking robot, responsive only to orders from a superior officer.

Reductio ad absurdum, industrial and military hideaways are being constructed here and there about the nation, a notable one at Iron Mountain, up-country from New York City, where "selected personnel" will be "safe" from all dangers of atomic war except a direct hit, and where they will be able to carry on the business of their far-flung empires. As Cleveland Armory points out with savage irony in a recent *Saturday Review,* their far-flung empires may be flung a little farther than they expect. The picture of these busy little centers of safety trying to do "business as usual" in an incinerated and dying world suggests that common death might be preferable to uncommon life.

The leaders of these worlds of intellect, of military, industrial and financial power would be well advised to move closer to his forgotten and hapless creature, the common man, and thereby see themselves as in a mirror. For the sober truth is that *the common man is anyone outside one's own particular group.*

The common man is simply the prototype of all of us human beings. Our base structure is so standardized that any straying from the norm is instantly measurable. Our basic urges for survival, for shelter, for family, for recognition, for being loved and needed are so similar that deviations are likewise apparent and subject to cataloguing. In basic physical structure and in basic urges, all men are "common" and the obvious fact needs calling to mind every once in a while.

Beyond this, the common man can be considered "common" no further. Molded by genetic line, by racial, ethnic and tribal custom, by environment, by luck, by a thousand diversified experiences, by whatever spiritual background may lie behind him, the common man is variegated beyond belief. He is one separate, unique and individual part of the three billion other parts of the whole, a single complex particle of the Divine Infinity we call the Universe. This fact must also be called to our attention periodically.

On this continent, 190 years ago, the United States of America was founded on the principle that all men were created equal, meaning that all men were born with certain natural rights and that each was entitled to equal treatment before the law of the land. The official, government endorsement of this principle is this nation's magnificent contribution to the progress of mankind, the shining ideal toward which the world painfully struggles. It marks the first public acceptance of the "common man."

This radical and upsetting idea is beginning to permeate the entire globe in this day of advanced communication, and the common man moves restlessly, demanding recognition of his individual "commonness."

Long a sleeping giant, he shows signs of awakening. Even Americans are asking themselves how closely their present way of life resembles the glorious ideal of individual liberty they thought they had been assured.

Across the world, the beleaguered common man is striving. Communism whispers in one ear, trying to rouse him to intemperate action. Capitalism murmurs in the other, trying to persuade him back to sleep. Both are blind and dangerous courses.

The need of the hour is to awaken him, not to violent and destructive action, but to reasonable and rational cooperation. The artificial ivory towers must crumble. "Leaders" must return from their distant and elevated positions above the dusty scene of human drama. They must for their own survival rejoin the human race.

If human beings are not to follow the dinosaurs into eternities of silence, the race of common men must learn to talk together, to recognize their common desires and common destiny as inhabitants of one small planet in an endless ocean of Space, to grant to each other the same rights they claim for themselves, and to work out a set of rules for living together which would permit to every common man the possibility of becoming quite *uncommon*.

If we will, therefore, in our talking, permit equal stretches of quiet listening, we may hear the common heart of man beating steadily and sturdily under the tumult. May we be granted the wisdom to know that it is our own! . . .

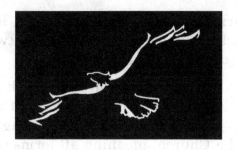

Vol. IV, No. 3, March 1966

Easter —1966

Ye are Spirits Incarnate, destined to make unto

humankind a benevolence; ye do come

thus together for fruition of service.

(Golden Scripts, Chapter 45)

TWICE A YEAR the attention of the Western World is directed toward the religion, which the majority of its inhabitants profess.

Once at the start of winter and again around the beginning of spring, Christians of all denominations and degrees of faith turn their collective thought toward the Man around whose image their religion has been built, in all its manifest ramifications and dissensions.

It would not be fair, perhaps, to speculate on how much significance would remain to the periods of Christmas and Easter if the trappings of Santa Clauses, Christmas trees, bunnies and eggs were removed, or if the commercial coercion to buy Christmas gifts and Easter outfits were to cease. No matter what the circumstance, how artificial or pagan they may be, even among the irreligious a spirit of kindness, brotherhood and constructive rejoicing is regenerated twice a year, which is unquestionably beneficial.

However, at this moment in history the Christian religion has entered into another period of great stress and strain, in which its viability is again put to question. The Church, meaning all forms of organized Christian worship, is under attack not only from the outside but also from within.

Another period of agonizing self-appraisal, similar to that which sparked the Reformation and just as fundamental, has been entered. The winds of revolution sweep as disturbingly down cloistered aisles as within all other areas of human thought.

While the ecumenical movement, on the one hand, has made more actual progress in the last decade than it has in the whole of the last millennium, on the other, religious denominations and groups within the whole are splitting themselves in twain over the matters of war, civil rights, birth control and the fundamental question of how much the church should enter into worldly affairs.

The Supreme Court has provoked rancor by its legalistic endeavor to keep church and state separate, while the State of Alabama sees fit to ask again whether the teaching of the theory of evolution should not be legally barred as being against the revealed Word of God.

One group of disillusioned youngsters chant, "God is dead" while older groups call for a return to "that ol' time religions."

208

THE SOLUTION to the problem cannot lie in declaring religion to be separate from the world. Like politics and economics, religion is an integral part of our thinking, whether we are aware of it or not. No rational person can get through life without reacting one way or another to the stimulus of religious thought. Even the anti-religionists make a religion of their anti-ness. Those who endeavor to separate religion from all other departments of life are doomed to defeat because it is there and will not be disposed. Consciously or unconsciously, men's actions in all walks of life are influenced by religious ideas, not infrequently by their very desire to divorce themselves from it, all too frequently by their ignorance of religious influences of the past.

Notable cases have been made, for example, for the development of modern capitalism by the Calvinist or Puritan philosophy together with the Jewish philosophy working to produce the so-called "free enterprise" system, the taking of profit, and the making of money into a commercial commodity. Modifications of various sorts have appeared in both the Jewish and Calvinist philosophies since the Seventeenth Century, but the system they encouraged and fostered as an outgrowth of the Age of Colonization and the beginning of the Industrial Revolution has grown apace and produced for us up here in the Twentieth Century a way of life that is materialistic, still feudal in concept, and possibly eventually suicidal.

Without getting too deep in this fascinating area of study, and at the risk or over-simplification of a very complicated subject, it can be asserted that neither the Puritans nor the Jews concerned themselves with

209

Jesus' message. Theirs were strictly Old Testament philosophies, based primarily on Mosaic law.

The original religious bases of capitalism have long since been overgrown by more practical, worldly considerations and now permeate every phase of western economic life. Thus a very real conflict has developed within the confines of Christian thought between the Old Testament's blessing of wealth and work as an end in itself, and the New Testament's disparagement of worldly riches and its emphasis on the importance of common humanity. That this conflict is submerged and generally unrecognized only enhances its difficulty and its painfulness.

GEORGE Bernard Shaw is credited with the comment that he did not know whether Christianity would work or not, it has never been tried. Other men, less witty but no less earnest, have for generations tried without success to popularize the teachings of Jesus. It appears that we are now coming to some kind of real test of faith. We are being forced by the realities of the world in which we find ourselves in this last half of the Twentieth Century to re-evaluate our religious beliefs, as to which of them have vital meaning and which are merely warmed-over superstition, which have application today and which had value or application only in years bygone, which are universal in appeal and which purely sectarian and exclusive.

At this Eastertide of 1966, it is hopeful to consider the possibility that Christianity may be at last coming into its own. Not, unfortunately, by the free choice of men, because the precepts of Jesus are not easy to live by yet, but because circumstance is forcing us to it for the sake of our survival.

Emphasis on the universal brotherhood of men, on the need of thoughtful regard even for those we don' t like, on the importance of each individual soul in the Great Scheme of Things and on the complete irrelevance of a man's worldly possessions as compared to what he *does* and *is,* is increasing.

When the Christian church as a whole wakes up to the fact that it has for centuries been trying to correlate two irreconcilable philosophies (that of the Old Testament and that of the New) many of the current theological arguments can begin to be resolved. More importantly, it will be much further along the way toward promoting a "rational" religion of universal appeal.

By developing the Man of Galilee's central theme of altruistic love and hope for all mankind, Christianity may yet become the Light of the World.

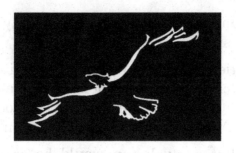

Vol. IV, No. 5, May 1966

Change is the benefactor, Time is the counselor: I say

that we do all things in Time, that we have patience,

in that patience giveth us a garland.

(*Golden Scripts,* Chapter 45)

The Priceless Ounce

IT WAS as an established custom in old China, so they tell us, to pay one's physician only as long as one was well. If you became ill, you immediately stopped payment, because your doctor had obviously fallen down on the job. Whether or not this exemplary custom is still practiced under Mao Tse Tung is beside the point.

The principle back of it makes the most profound sense, and bears translating into further areas of living. It is the principle of prevention rather than cure. Its practice demands emphasis on, and study of, the laws of cause rather than the laws of effect.

A well-known New York columnist was once quoted as answering a questioner: "Well, no. I can't really say from my own experience how good an osteopath may be when you are sick. The fact is, I have had an osteopath treatment once a month for over twenty years and never had a sick day in all that time."

Keeping patients well would seem an infinitely easier job than patching them up when they break down, but such is not our system. Neither for the doctor, nor for the average American, nor for our society in general.

Consider what a revolution would be created by the passage of a law saying that all doctors could receive their regular income as a matter of course, but only so long as their regular patients remained well, that they would be "docked" for all patients who became ill. Naturally, this would require some cooperation on the part of the patient, since it would hardly be fair to dock the physician for a diabetic who insisted on a diet of caramel creams!

What interests us, however, is what the effect would be on the physician's own philosophy, how he would react to such a completely new approach. Instead of sitting in his office, ministering with knowledge, skill and sympathy to the endless stream of damaged, diseased and distressed people parading through his waiting-room, he would be out beating the bushes for the underlying reasons accounting for that streaming parade in the first place.

H would be moving mountains in areas hitherto given only token attention except by a few dedicated and selfless altruists. He would begin to crack down on the causes of occupational disease, on accidents and disabilities caused by improper working conditions.

He would light vast fires under negligent congressmen regarding water and air pollution, insufficiently tested drugs, improperly used pesticides, and false labeling.

He would before long begin to get even deeper than this substratum of disease-causes. The study of psycho-somatic illness (the effect of the mind on the physical body) would become a primary concern, and with it would come not only awareness of the effect of mental problems on the physical body, but he would be led into the whole area of the causes of mental breakdown itself.

He would inevitable be led to the basic scourges of mankind, poverty, ignorance and war.

The point that we are trying to make is that if the size of the pocketbook of the average physician were suddenly dependent on the health of his clientele instead of their illnesses, what wonders might be performed.

This is not meant as an indictment of American doctors, most of whom are dedicated, hardworking individuals. It is an indictment of a system, a way of life, which concerns itself much more with results rather than causes, with treating the victims rather than the causes, which made them victims.

Our prisons and jails, our hospitals and mental institutions overflow. Our welfare rolls are long, and juvenile delinquency grows apace. Narcotics addiction, alcoholism, abortions and venereal disease increase. Sickness permeates the whole society.

What an expensive and futile process, treating the patients after the damage has been done, and doing nothing to basically change the environment in order to prevent others from falling prey to the same difficulties!

When we take a real good look at our society, it is obvious that our whole approach to dealing with the health and well-being of our citizens is cart-before-the-horse thinking. This is the real shortcoming of most of the movements engaged in seeking social justice. They are more alleviators of suffering than social reformers.

Instead of concentrating all effort on trying to feed the poor and improve their lot by patchwork welfare, we should be at the serious business of determining why and how they have become so destitute in the first place. What is wrong about our system itself that 30 to 40 million people can be denied a decent living when the nation has the ability to produce more than enough for all the people?

Instead of spending billions of dollars to operate our prisons and mental hospitals, we should be asking what is wrong with our society that so many hundreds of thousands of our young boys and girls turn to crime. We should ask what are the pressures and strains in our society that causes 18 percent of our entire population to mentally crack in confronting life?

Instead of trying to assume further indebtedness in building needed hospitals, schools and homes, we should be looking to causes why a whole nation has to become hopelessly insolvent when it possesses all needed materials, manpower and know-how to build all the nation requires. Who or what group controls the money supply so that hopeless indebtedness and consequent bondage are the lot of a self-sufficient people?

The biggest realization, and the most important conclusion, that will come to the American people will be that it is our economic-financial-political system itself that turns out criminals, that causes the mentally insane, and forces tens of millions of our citizens to live like caged animals in the slums and Appalachia's of this nation.

A slave society is not one, necessarily, where there is deprivation, grueling work and mental breakdown. A slave society is one in which all these are present while at the same time there exists the means and capacity to erase them from the society.

Tragically, this is the serious indictment that must be leveled at our own society. Half the battle is won when we have the courage and wisdom to face up to this reality.

While there is merit in alleviating suffering at all timers, the real merit lies in getting at the causes of that suffering so there are no victims.

It is interesting to speculate on how many of the current officeholders in Washington would stay on the job if it were stipulated by the people that henceforth the amount of their salaries would be directly related to the degree to which the nation was kept healthy, on the elimination of the *causes* of a nation's ills and not their mere *treatment*.

Not only in medicine but also in government is an ounce of prevention worth a pound of cure!

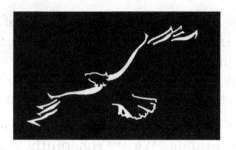

Vol. IV, No. 6, June 1966

Verily, my beloved, we are spreading light gloriously

Over all the earth: to rich and poor we cry,

Come and see the radiance!

(Golden Scripts, Chapter 12)

White Hats vs Black

SENATOR RUSSELL LONG, in one of his rare appearances in the televised Senate Foreign Relations Committee hearings, voiced a question, which typifies much of modern American thought, or lack of it.

"Are we," he bellowed at the witness, General Maxwell Taylor, "the Good Guys or the Bad Guys?"

A trace of wry amusement flitted over the General's classic features as he murmured, "I hope we are the Good Guys."

This is the way most Americans want their thinking served up these days, neatly divided into packages wrapped either in white or black and let's not bother with any in-between value shadings. We haven't got time.

Here lies our dilemma. The complexities of modern life demand an increasing number of judgments for which adequate consideration-time is lacking, and yet the results of many of those judgments are so serious and far-reaching that survival itself depends upon them.

Adding to the problem is the current American idolatry of "standard" brands. We are constantly being told that "standard" brands of goods provide us with the trust of worthiest products. "Bloop is a name you can trust!" If Bloop is in a position to say this often enough and widely enough, it becomes gospel. Since Bloop does maintain an even standard nation-wide, there is a certain truth in what Bloop says. It becomes of small moment whether the Bloop Corporation could raise its standard for the public benefit (at some small sacrifice of the stockholders' profits, of course). The great thing is that by its size and influence, Bloop sets the standard and maintains it, and for Americans it becomes one of the household gods.

Unfortunately, because we have become *thing*-oriented society, this blind worship of standardization carries over from the industrial into all other areas of our culture, religious, political, economic, even aesthetic. How greatly life is simplified by hanging standard labels on our leaders, on our social groupings, on our national organizations!

The danger should be obvious. As in the industrial area, so in all other areas of thought: The average American accepts the standard label as "safe" and "trustworthy."

Individual thought becomes a real effort. Individual action is suspect.

THE ONLY drawback to this comfortable practice of standardization, and incidentally the only hope of the human spirit, lies in the fact that it is an even more basic tendency of the human species to assert individuality, to make a distinguishing mark, to be different, each one from his neighbor. Against the power of materialism and its label-making rises up the human spirit with its desire to be free. Hence the revolt of the young, who view the sheep-like complacency of their elders with a jaundiced eye. Hence the revolt of the intellectuals, who deeply value their right to think as they please. Hence the revolt of the underprivileged, who refuse to be squeezed any longer into a shapeless and voiceless mass at the bottom of the heap.

With the winds of revolt blowing in all directions, the label-makers are having trouble making labels stick.

Who then are the Good Guys and who the Bad?" Who wear the White Hats and who the Black? The fact is that every human being from his own experience knows no one who is *all* good, or *all* bad from *all* points of view, *all* the time. All of us wear hats that are piebald. It follows that if no single human being can be classified as all good or all bad, still less may any group of men, and least of all, nations be so classified.

In today's concentrated, complex, confused world, there is only one meaningful simple question: Are you interested in the whole human race, or only a part of it?

Because the sobering truth is that whosoever is interested in only part of the human race may find one fine day that the parts he has been ignorant or despising or endeavoring to eradicate may with equal justice be ignoring or despising or endeavoring to eradicate *him*. The world is now too small, too crowded, and too complex either for arrogance or for provincialism.

Let's forget the Guys in the White Hats and the Guys in the Black, and remember instead that the Greatest Altruist of all walked bareheaded among men!

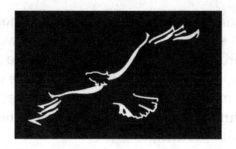

Vol. IV, No. 7 & 8, July-August 1966

Love is the medium by which contact obtaineth; Without it is emptiness and a great lamentation.

(*Golden* Scripts, Chapter 46)

Chasm

THE GREATEST stumbling block to the orderly growth of civilization is widespread ignorance of the chasm, which divides this generation from the last. The very width of the chasm makes it unbelievable; its depth makes it unthinkable. It has been growing slowly for centuries but only between this generation and the last has it assumed perilous proportions.

It appeared at first as a tiny crack when men first began to have self-conscious relationships with one another. It was a thin line drawn in the sand by a timeless and ageless hand marking divisions between humans who thought of themselves only as individual units and humans who thought of themselves in relation to all other individual units.

For millennia the line was all but indistinguishable, to be hopped across as was expedient at the moment, a matter of small import in general commerce between human beings. Except for those who read into that fine line an eternal significance. Except for those who had the vision to see that man's relationships would forever become more and more involved, more and more dependent upon each other, more and more snarled and knotted as man in his infinite cleverness assaulted, conquered and controlled the earthball on which he found himself operating.

More than all else responsible for the drastic widening of that crack in human progress has been technology, the result of man's peculiar trait of seeking out, storing up and disseminating accumulated knowledge, permitting each succeeding generation to accomplish more and more in the conquering and controlling of its environment. Technology, as it bound men ever closer together in physical dependency, has created this ever-widening division in spiritual growth, this invisible chasm which we must somehow cross if civilization is to continue.

The salient point is that technology has arrived at the state in earthly time (between this generation and the last) where we are individually forced to make the choice as to which side we are going to be on, either entering gratefully and enthusiastically into the New Age of Cooperation, or clinging frantically and blindly to the Old Age of Greed.

The chasm cuts deeply through the three fundamental areas of civilized life, politics, economics and religion, fragmenting them and creating the disruption, which we are today calling, either happily or unhappily, revolution. Political revolution is the most superficial. The economic revolution is deeper. But even more profound is the spiritual revolution, demanding that we begin to make clear what we think about man's

224

purpose, about life's value, and what our real responsibilities are to ourselves, to our fellows, and to the universe of which we are part

Technology has created the vast modern network of transportation and communication, which puts everyone in everyone else's hip pocket. This condition, new in the last generation, is irrevocable. Whether we like it or not, we are stuck with it. We cannot go back to our isolationism and provincialism ever again. We are become in fact and from here on out the Family of Man living in the small house called Earth, and if the roof is not to fly off or the walls to cave in, we had best learn how to get along with one another.

Technology has created automation-cybernation, a monster whose strength is as yet untamed, but which, broken to saddle and bridle, can be ridden to undreamed of heights. It can lift the burden of physical toil and drudgery from man's aching back, and is now pointing the way to a material abundance unimaginable a generation ago. As yet uncontrolled and running free, it is increasing unemployment and poverty and widening despair and resentment. Few men as yet realize its power and its potential, and many of those few are using it selfishly only to line their own already well-filled pockets.

Technology has also in the last generation created the power to destroy itself, the earth and the human experiment altogether. Men of wide worldly power, but without imagination, without vision, without spiritual wisdom, are toying with this enormity as if it were a popgun or a water pistol. Technology thus has widened the chasm to alarming proportions, has lengthened the gap between those who think in Old Age terms and those who think in terms of a New Age.

The United States leads in the development of this great technology that has suddenly broadened the chasm. The rest of the world watches uneasily, waiting for the assurance that American leadership knows just where it is going, that it will lead to a better world, not a worse one, or perhaps none at all. They have not yet received that assurance. Current American leadership in most fields still goes on the Old Age standard that might makes right, that worldly success implies the blessing of heaven, that God is on the side of the strongest battalions and the biggest money-bags.

It is more fact than fancy that the Golden Calf of Baal has been hauled to the very brink of the chasm, its high priest continuing to demand sacrifices in blood and treasure, totally insensible to the pressures building up behind it that will push it over to annihilation. The tragedy is that millions of mortals, ignorant of its deceits and unaware of alternatives, will follow it down to destruction.

The bridge across the chasm is already there, carefully and soundly constructed by centuries of human experience and spiritual growth. The Ten Commandments, the Sermon on the Mount, the Declaration of Independence, Pacem in Terris, all these exhortations to justice and human dignity, to mutual respect and cooperation, are planks of the bridge to the New Age.

We are forced at last to take them seriously. Men of vision, of imagination, of reality, are already on the side of the New Age. They call to their fellowmen, advising them, exhorting them in every way they know how, to lift their eyes to the bright horizons in the

226

distance. No mortal eyes can discern the pathway clearly that leads to that distant upland, but those who have placed Man above material things, have attained the other side of this chasm, and are pleading with their fellows to follow over the bridge. The question is, will enough people hear them in time?

It is too late now to hop back and forth as expedient directs. The gorge is too deep and too wide. To each now comes the moment of truth: "Is this *my* world or is it *our* world?"

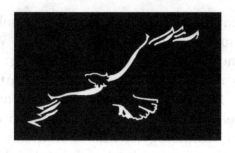

Vol. IV, No. 9, September 1966

Blessed are they who ascend unto a mountain's

height to see the sunrise, for they shall

know creation.

(Golden Scripts, Chapter 52)

Utopia, Really?

UTOPIA runs the risk of becoming an over-used word these days. With the rapid approach of a cybernetic society, the possibility of a life free from want is almost within human grasp. To many, the realization of a life free from want means that Utopia, the perfect society, must inevitably and quickly follow. To such shallow optimists, man lives by bread alone. Given the bread, his troubles are over.

While cybernation unquestionably is going to move us a monumental step forward into a new era, Utopia seems quite likely to be a considerable way up the road ahead. If man does not live by bread alone, what else must he seek?

The questions, which the far seeing is asking, now are *not:* How can we feed the starving multitudes? And, What shall we do to implement diminishing resources,

229

and how many new jobs will the new technology create? These questions have been answered now. We have the technical know-how to feed the starving multitudes. We have learned how to tap the almost limitless gifts of the universe for resources and energy not dreamed of a few short years ago. We are learning to our dismay that the new technology, while it creates new types of jobs, actually is pushing human beings right out of the wage earning business altogether. Not immediately, but eventually. The more technology today, the less jobs next week.

The questions which the far seeing are asking now are: How are we going to free this productive potential so that all men may benefit, and not just those who can pay? And, Who will be in control of these vast resources and this limitless energy up the years beyond? and, What are we going to do with all this beautiful leisure time unfolding before us as machines do the labor, provided there is some kind of purchasing power with which to buy?

As soon as human ingenuity comes up with the answers to these questions (as it unquestionably will), then, say the optimists, Utopia will have arrived, Heaven will have descended to earth, and we may all drown happily if silkily in a sea of milk and honey.

Unfortunately, before we can even give proper attention to the questions, we have some preliminary bouts to battle. We are in a state of transition.

One analogy to our present position is offered by bio-chemist John Rader Platt in a news book, *The Step to Man* (John Wiley, $5.95). He compares civilization's situation with the progress of a supersonic plane on the verge of breaking the sound barrier, on the edge of a pressure wave that creates abnormal turbulence. If we can get through the next few years safely, we shall pass into a much calmer period, where "exponential change gives way to a steady-state condition."

In a much more ancient analogy, we are undergoing the birth pangs of a New Age. It is not an easy birth. Three things militate strongly against it: War, Apathy, and Shortsightedness.

Not only is war battering our tottering economy even further out of whack, but there is increasing, horrifying risk of its involving the entire globe in a last flash of cosmic fury marking the end of the human experiment. A cessation of active hostility is imperative. The peace-seekers of the earth wherever they may be must speak forth with a voice loud enough to be heard above the din of battle. The United States should be doing all in its very considerable power to root out and eradicate the causes of aggression and violence in the world, and not be further aggravating them. May God send us leaders who understand this vital necessity!

Apathy is the legacy of a materialistic society which measures its wealth in dollars and cents and worships bigness as the ultimate status symbol. The apathy of the poor to whom "welfare" has become a way of life, the apathy of the wealthy who refuse to see their human brethren standing outside in the cold and the dark, the apathy of the average, middle-class American who has so many problems himself he refuses to get involved in the next fellow's. This refusal to recognize mutual responsibility, to be concerned, to feel the sharp prick of personal indignation as public wrong, is a serious obstacle to our safe entrance into the New Age.

Shortsightedness, our third problem, is largely due to our collective national horror at anything, which remotely hints as planning. Planning has come to be looked on as a threat to our freedom, our independence and our general welfare. Why this national blind spot? A little study makes it plain. Those who run the Establishments, which run the nation, are involved in a desperate struggle to preserve the status quo.

Any long range planning by the people, of the people and for the people would beyond all doubt lead to changes in the status quo. That such opposition stems from shortsightedness more than greed or malice is shown by the fact that anyone aware of the impact of modern technology knows that changes will have to come regardless if the wheels of the economy are to keep turning, and the runners of the Establishments would be helping themselves by the use of knowledgeable action instead of resentful reaction. To avoid the possible economic convulsions, we all must recognize the imperative need for change. If there are not men of sufficient vision and acumen in office today, let us be about the business of electing them.

Supposing we do solve these enormous problems of War, Apathy and Shortsightedness? Suppose we do work out a more equitable system of distribution for our newly acquired abundance? Suppose new leaders do turn our faces upward toward the promise of a new and better day? Shall that be Utopia?

Hardly, Abundance will not make Utopia, nor will leisure time. Abundance and leisure may prove to be as much of a curse as scarcity and common drudgery ever were, if careful thought is not applied to the problem. Man may wallow mindlessly in his machine-controlled wealth, tossing away his precious hours of life with careless abandon in frivolous or destructive pursuits if he is not prepared to make the transition.

Education at all levels becomes the Number One need. Purposeful participation in the planning of their own futures together becomes the natural goal of all citizens.

Utopia will still continue to be the ideal state toward which man yearns and strives, but there will be this difference between yesterday and tomorrow: He will be a long step farther on the road if he is prepared to recognize, not that his problems have been removed, but that they have altered and lifted to a higher dimension, one more worthy of human destiny.

The primary aim of man up to this point in history has been to survive. In the New Age upon us, the primary aim of man will be to contemplate what the primary aim of man may be. In short, we are leaving an age of physical toil and hardship and entering into an era primarily of mental employment. Free from the duress of hunger or other economic dependency man may choose to what degree and in what manner he wishes to employ the brain with which he has been blessed. Material things, because of their eventual abundance, will cease to attract as the primary goal, and for the first time, man will be free to choose what he wishes to do with the life that is his to live. . . .

It will not yet be Utopia, but it will be a welcome change for the better.

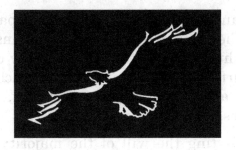

Vol. IV, No. 10, October 1966

Shout it to the housetops: The Son of Man cometh unto every human heart that listeneth for His utterance!

(Golden Scripts, Chapter 54)

Brotherhood of Man

THE FIRST lesson of mankind is to achieve a reverence for life itself. Only as mankind recognizes that each and every life has an inherent right to full existence, to be terminated only by natural causes, can there be any solid premise upon which to work out mutual responsibilities and benefits.

The right to life itself is inherent and irrevocable. No man, no group, no nation or set of nations, can play God and destroy a human being. Whereas it is readily conceded that no one person can have the power to annihilate all of mankind, so it must be equally understood that neither can all of mankind have the power to destroy one solitary person. The principle underlying both is the same.

Fundamental in everyone's thinking must be the bedrock premise that every human being, however humble or thwarted, has a potential capacity to act rationally and altruistically. Such capacity is the essence of the "breath of life" that is intrinsic in every person. It thus becomes the responsibility of society to awaken, nurture, instruct and inspire each person so all natural attributes, however dormant, might find fullest expression.

Society, reflecting the will of the majority, can place limitations and impose just penalties for misconduct but that same society possesses no power to destroy life. There can be no man-assumed power to destroy, that which has the potential both to mend its ways and to excel in later performance.

In any society premised on this understanding there could be no justification for capital punishment *within* nations, nor for wars *between* nations. It is this same understanding that would be intolerant of all forms of violence and every threat to life, whether it be the outward attack or the enforced lack of food and medication.

When all of mankind recognizes and has faith in the inherent good of man, at least in the inherent good of man, the most powerful motivation in the universe can find expression. This is the love motivation. It is the force that spontaneously moves every individual to serve others. It is the force that strives to better one's brother's conduct so any grounds for condemnation are non-existent.

How could stigma be attached to any person when society itself has failed to assist him in putting his best foot forward? How can any person be condemned if there is understanding of the causes of his momentary misconduct or inadequacy of responsibility? How can stigma, penalty or ostracism help the person who needs the most help and care by his fellowmen?

The cornerstone of a rational society must be that every person is of equal importance and every person is susceptible to improvement. But it is not only the improvement of the individual that is the end result. The over-all health and safety of the whole society is improved. It is out of this over-all optimum functioning of the society that the optimum performance of each and every individual is realized.

Lose yourself in others and you shall truly find yourself!

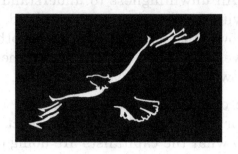

Vol. IV, No. 11, November 1966

We who uphold the world would have it known that

Love is eternally manifesting in lilies as well as

Mountains, in those who do sweep as in those

Who rule empires.

(*Golden Scripts,* Chapter 54)

Realities

THE REAL stumbling block to confronting and solving the problems of this nation is that there are three major realities respecting this nation. There is the kind of socio-economic-political system that people *think* we live under, there is the kind of system that we *do* live under, and there is the kind of system that we *could* live under. Aquila has advanced the thinking that not until a majority encompasses all of these realities will there be sufficient understanding by which to effect social change that is sound and lasting.

A parallel picture can be drawn in reference to the international scene, and we can at least broadly develop the understanding that must prevail if there is to be peace and cooperation among nations. One thing is certain: An unwillingness to understand each other makes inevitable the doom of mankind. Absolute distrust, allowing for no toleration of the other nation's reality, leaves only the frantic and insane pursuit of still more powerful death-dealing weapons.

Irrespective of our reality as to what the communists are doing or intend to do, and irrespective of their reality as to what the capitalists are doing or intend to do, and irrespective of the realities of all other countries as to what both the capitalists and communists are doing or intend to do, there can be only *one reality* that *all* nations subscribe to relating to a Third World War. It is inescapably this: If a nuclear war should be unleashed, there will be no victors. A blackened planet would be mute testimony to an order of creation had *lost* all reverence for life itself and who had blinded themselves to the innate and *unique* capability of man to negotiate differences.

When we think of our own nation as possessing the most powerful nuclear arsenal in the world, we should be foremost in accepting and implementing the foregoing reality. If our adherence to this reality were genuine, we would recognize that every soldier put in battle, every plane that drops napalm bombs, every act and deed that escalates war is a step toward death, not freedom. Even if we were not gambling with the obliteration of mankind, who delegated to any leadership the right to play God and dictate the maiming or killing of one solitary human being? Is it a political right to refrain from applying "Thou shalt not kill" to whomever one feels is expendable, or is of a different color, or whom one dislikes? Ponder on this question and listen to the answer of your conscience.

240

It is within the framework of the above over-riding reality that we have to give thought to the fact that there are three realities to be considered in the international picture as there are in the national picture. First, there is the reality of how "bad" the people are who live under communist governments *as told* by the capitalist power structures, and, equally, how "bad" the people are who live under capitalist governments *as told* by the communist rulers. It is in this reality that we find all the false propaganda directed for the express purpose of maximizing hate and resentment, distorting the minds of tens of millions that there is justification in killing each other. They are unaware that mob psychology and mass murder are being employed having little to do with freedom or justice but having much to do with political and economic stratagems.

The second reality is the grasping that the vast majority of people, of whatever skin color, of whatever momentary ideological persuasion, of whatever country, are struggling, feeling, aspiring human beings very much like each other. They harbor no natural hate for other human beings but have an inner yearning to enjoy a good life for themselves and especially for their children.

The heartaches of the vast majority of human beings on one side of the globe are the heartaches of those on the opposite side. And so it is with their joys, their hopes and the fulfillment of their aspirations. What demonic tragedy that people as people can be pitted against each other in the hell of war when their needs, their yearnings, and their goals are mutual!

241

The third reality is obviously the kind of world that is possible. It is the kind of world that was envisioned by the Prince of Peace when He commanded us to do unto others, as we would wish others to do unto us. It was a plea that recognized the importance of the lowliest among men and underscored that the highest reward came from being of service to others.

Recognizing all propaganda for exactly what it is, facing up to the right of *all* men everywhere for peace and a more rewarding existence, and accepting the fact that this is now possible, these are the guidelines that can and must chart the course to a true Parliament of Man and final acceptance of co-operative, co-existence by all nations.

Whether in the national or the international scene true reality must spring from a clear conscience. Let it be your master in all conclusions. One with God is indeed a majority!

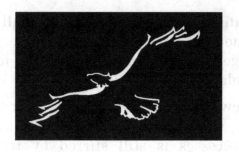

Vol. IV, No. 12, December 1966

Arise then, and worship! Be not as flocks of linnets

twittering in a sage tree. Be as the mighty ocean

in tumultuous rejoicings, that the stars sing

at your Manifest Destinies!

(Golden Scripts, Chapter 56)

The New Reformation

ON A BUSY corner in our little Indiana city, a drive-in branch bank has recently been built, very conveniently for downtown customers. It occupies the corner where formerly the First Methodist Church stood. The church has been moved to the northern outskirts of town, accessible only by car unless you don't mind hiking a mile or so in your Sunday clothes.

The bank has a sign. It consists of a tall, strong post, near the top of which is affixed a heavy crossbar bearing the name of the bank. This crossbar whirls slowly but incessantly, like a spinning crucifix above the scurrying Christmas shoppers.

A curious thing seems to have taken place. We are told that the Man whose birthday we are about to commemorate took up a scourge of small cords and drove the moneychangers from the temple. Today the moneychangers seem to have driven the temple from the marketplace!

Has a new religion supplanted the old? Not individually, we believe. The single human heart in its innermost recesses is still stirred by the Christian message of love, charity, and faith in things unseen. But collectively, it is a different matter.

Consider. A thousand years ago there was but one church in the Western world. It was the Christian church and all followers of the Son of Man belonged to it. Converts were made singly or in batches, sometimes by the countryful, if the ruler thereof was persuaded to follow the Cross. Torture and the stake punished heretics and apostasies. Saints were made by martyrdom and non-believers consigned to ever-lasting fire. The Pope's spiritual power was unquestioned and one opposed it only at the risk of one's eternal soul.

Building on the ruins of a great temporal institution, the Roman Empire, the church had slowly organized itself into an equally great institution, so powerful that it created the atmosphere in which all life was lived. It was accepted with as little question as the air one breathed, it shaped the thinking of both believers and non-believers from the moment of birth till the last rites were administered.

This is not to disparage the good that it did. Such humanitarian work done, such learning as was preserved through the Dark Ages, such creative thinking as was developed from the fall of the Empire onward for a nearly a thousand years owed existence

244

largely to the church or to the more enlightened ones who practiced under its auspices.

What preserved the church was the *enthusiasm* of its supporters, in the root sense of the word. That is, the spirit that possessed them was one devoted to the glorification of God. The cathedral builders, the artists and artisans, poets and writers, almost all creative thinking in medieval times went to this end. It does not matter that their interpretations would not agree with ours, that their views seem to us narrow and sometimes exceedingly dull. The point is that there was a universal preoccupation with Holy Church.

But as an institution the church had wandered far from the simple, austere and profound teachings of the Galilean. It had forgotten His advice to the rich, young ruler, and to Mary Magdelene and to those who taunted her. It had indeed become an institution of unprecedented power, and was therefore heir to the corruptive influences that absolute power brings.

Except for notable exceptions, the popes, cardinals and bishops who governed so-called Christian thought, waxed fat, with their thumbs and fingers in every lucrative political pie a-baking across Europe. Then, almost 500 years ago, one Martin Luther hammered his 95 theses to the church door at Wittenberg and waited for the thunder to crash around his ears. Martin Luther was by no means the only man whose conscience impelled him to question the conduct of the church as it then operated, but the world was ready for an idea whose time had come, and Luther gets the credit.

It is reported that Luther did not intend to lead a faction away from the church. It was only his desire to remedy the evils that time and the schemes of wily and ambitious men had permitted to creep into church operation and administration. But it happened.

The last half of the Fifteenth Century must have been much like the last half of the Twentieth as revolutionary developments broke old patterns and set up new. The invention of moving type, the discovery of the New World and then the breakup of the universal church must surely have filled the hearts of men with confusion, doubt, alarm and excitement, even as men are confused, alarmed and excited today.

The Catholic Church did mend its ways to a great extent eventually, but it was never to be the same again. Somewhere back in the centuries, the dynamic altruism of Jesus the Christ was lost by the wayside, except in individual cases, and the new Protestantism as an institution did nothing to revive it.

Indeed, a strange set of circumstances occurred almost simultaneously that set the pattern for a new universal institution to capture the hearts of men much as the medieval church had done.

Large numbers of Jews, commercialist and financiers by nature, were driven out of southern Europe and took refuge in the Netherlands and the northern countries just as Protestantism was beginning to get under way. John Calvin is credited with first preaching the relaxation of the centuries-old, Christian ban on the taking of interest. These conditions taken together with the Protestant emphasis on work and thrift (with the accumulation of worldly wealth as a natural proof of such dedication) created an atmosphere in which Money and the pursuit thereof became respectable.

With the conquest of the New World beginning, Western civilization was off on its squander bust of colonialism, commercialism, capitalism, and eventually industrialism and imperialism. The building of a modern Golden Calf had begun. The new God, the new enthusiasm, was Money, with the profit-system as its credo and the industrialist-bankers as its high priests.

Preaching against Mammon has been a busy if unprofitable calling for thousands of years, yet never before have so many peoples of the world been forced to bend their knees before so materialistic a "god" as in this day.

We think of ourselves as enlightened. We pride ourselves on our scientific outlook, on our broad-mindedness, on our lack of superstition, yet so subtly and so slowly has this image of a pseudo-deity crept up on us that most of us don't realize how much we give him of ourselves, how quietly but wholeheartedly we worship him, and how much of our lives are controlled by his high priests. The institution of "profit making" has taken us over as completely and utterly as the church of the Dark Ages.

However, on this Christmas Day of 1966 there are areas of great hope. We live in another day of revolutionary development. Once again the corruption of the leading institution is being questioned. We are ripe for a new Reformation. Not just of the church this time, but of our whole socio-economic pattern founded on the profit system.

By Reformation we do not mean take-over. Just as the medieval church rallied against the invading Moslem, so the Western world rallies against the threat of Communism. The Moslem did not overcome the church, but it fell apart through its own internal weakness. It had become Form without Spirit when Luther called it to an accounting.

The dynamic altruism of Jesus is Spirit without form, the only force strong enough to overcome the bastions of Mammon!

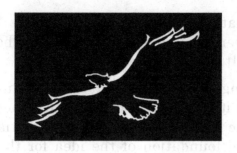

Vol. V, No. 1, January 1967

Take Substance and pull it apart and ye have Energy;

take Energy and pull it apart and ye have Ether; take

Ether and pull it apart and ye have Love; take Love

and pull it apart and ye have Thought; take

Thought and pull it apart and ye have God.

(Golden Scripts, Chapter 57)

A Design for All

PART OF the confusion about, and not a little of the opposition to, the idea of a Co-operative Commonwealth stems from a misconception of what the basic aim of such an economic system may be.

It is very frankly designed for the benefit of *all* people, not simply a favorite few. It is designed to permit *all* people to grow and develop physically, mentally and spiritually to the fullest extent of their God-given potential. Strangely, this seems to be the harder nut to crack, and yet the premise of "all for one and one for all" is fundamental to the whole idea.

"It's agin' nature," says the traditionalist. "No system has ever been devised which worked to the benefit of *all* people. It can't be done."

Paraphrasing Shaw's comment on Christianity, "How do we know it won't work till we try it sometime?" It is the dynamic altruism of the basic Christian message which is the foundation of the idea for the Corporate Commonwealth, and not only is it long overdue for trying, but it is fast becoming apparent that only dynamic altruism can form the basis of a workable system in the cybernetic age we are entering.

The traditionalist who looks backward instead of forward finds it hard if not impossible to accept that man's technology and science has within the past handful of years moved him into a new age, the era of cybernation, which itself is going to put a brand new light on every undertaking to which man turns his hand from here on out. The reasoning that "it's never been done before" is not good enough now.

The self-styled conservative who still views cybernation as a sort of advanced industrialism and thus subject to the rules of the "free market" and "free enterprise" system sees in the Corporate Commonwealth idea a real threat to the "competitive" system which he erroneously considers to be the source of the nation's fantastic wealth. He joins with his spiritual brothers on the political right to inveigh against the corporate commonwealth as "welfare statism," "creator of dronery, "mobocracy." The fact of the matter is he fears the loss of his own power, or if he has no power, he fears the loss of the chance to gain power. "It's a tough world," he says. "It's a jungle, but everyone has the same chance, and if I'm smart enough and tough

250

enough, I'll make mine just as much as the next fellow."

He fails to see that the jungle exists because every man in it is cutting and slashing and biting and gouging as he is because that's the way everybody's been taught to act. Those are the rules by which everybody has to play to win. If you don't play the game that way, you don't succeed.

A Corporate Commonwealth suggests a change in the rules of play by which he could achieve even greater success without all the gouging, slashing, cutting and biting, and without one fellow's gain being another fellow's loss. To the person whose atavistic appetite for combat is not sufficiently assuaged, we would suggest that he take it out in sports, or, better still, join in fighting man's common enemies of disease and hunger and war. That's where the clean battle is to be fought.

Not being willing to admit to his fear for loss of power, he turns instead in fear and trembling for his less hardy brothers, not as successful or potentially as successful as he. "It will make drones of 'em. They'll be worthless weight that we hardworking people will have to drag along with us."

It doesn't seem to occur to him that he's dragging a terrible weight right now in disease and crime and poverty, all aspects of the real welfare that he already lives under. He grouses and growls about the dangers to a society where "everybody is a ward of the state" but he offers no alternative to paying increased taxes to keep up a society where a large proportion *are* wards of the state.

What this person is unable to see is that people are motivated to improve themselves *if given an opportunity to do so.* What logic is there in condemning a person for being ill-mannered if he hasn't been given the chance to become educated? What reasoning supports condemning a person for being apathetic and slovenly if society doesn't afford him equal opportunity to take the raw stock of nature and refine them into usable goods for himself and his family?

This is the kind of thinking that has no real faith in the inherent good of man and fails to recognize that potential capability resides in every human being to better himself. The whole idea of a Corporate Commonwealth is to create a framework within which no one is ward of the state, but within which every person has true independence by reason of his inherent and earned equity in the nation's ability to produce everything to abundance.

Then there are those who shout, "Mobocracy!" In a modern, computerized, technological world, they still retain remnants of *ancient regime* philosophy. "The mob doesn't have the brains to run its own business. The world should be run by us, the aristocrats." What they really mean is that "we, the holders of power in the industrial, political, religious and military establishments, do not want that power taken away and laid on the shoulders of the sovereign people." Of course, their reference to the people is the "hoi polloi" and the "illiterate and indiscriminate" masses. Loss of power. Ay, there's the rub!

No one willingly wants to give up power. However, the overwhelming evidence is that power corrupts and history reveals that both criminality and corruption

252

have been more prevalent in the rulers than in those ruled. Of course, the first line of defense of the powerful is the deceptive propaganda that majority rule is mob rule. It is sheer camouflage to cover up the fact that a corrupt leadership may so bamboozle, propagandize and mislead a people that an entire nation may be led unwittingly toward destruction, but an informed people, voting in their own self-interest, will display rationality and justice, for the very reason that all desire equal treatment before the law and will vote no privilege to anyone.

The Corporate Commonwealth is based on the full dispersal of power, placing the final decision on all major legislation and policy in the hands of the people. Putting such power back in the hands of the people does not in any way preclude the election of the wisest minds to office for the purpose of debating and recommending legislation. Indeed, under the Corporate Commonwealth, the wisest could be elected without, as now, dependence on personal wealth, on personal connections, on fortuitous birth. They would not, moreover, be beholden to lobbyists and other pressure groups because undercover or indirect financial gain would be impossible. Corruption in office would be eliminated.

Lastly, we can hear the anguished cry, "But democracy is so inefficient!" Is it?" In the first place, under the Corporate Commonwealth, useless bureaucracy based on patronage, full of its red tape and duplications, would be eliminated. Most of the bookkeeping, record keeping and accounting hitherto done by human beings reduced almost to automatons will, in the cybernetic era, be done by machines, which are almost human.

But exactly what is efficiency? A truly efficient system would be one not efficient for its own sake but one that best served human beings. A truly efficient system would be one in which human beings commanded the greatest freedom to follows their highest aims, unrestricted by artificial economic or financial duress, political overlordship, and a pseudo-culture shaped by worship of the Almighty Dollar. Today's highly touted efficiency could never pass the test!

We believe that government and a society is in actual practice "of the people, for the people, and by the people," politically, economically, and spiritually, which means an increasingly educated and informed people, will produce a government and a society of better citizens, and therefore a better nation. If the most powerful nation on earth were a better nation, it follows that the world would be a better world.

A participating electorate will be a more and more responsible electorate as the full scope or their individual and combined power comes alive to them.

At that moment, and not before, this nation will begin to rise to the ideals it now earnestly professes!

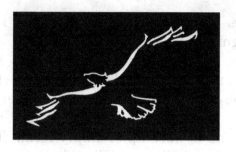

Vol. V, No. 2, February 1967

Now I tell them all together: Strengthen

Yourselves in stamina to inherit!

(Golden Scripts, Chapter 61)

Permanent Moratorium

AS THIS ISSUE was being readied for the press, a second truce was being observed, at least in expression, by both sides to the Vietnam War. This time it was the Vietnamese "Tet," the lunar New Year, which occasioned the cessation of hostilities. Our observance was a reciprocation to an earlier observance of a cease-fire during our Christmas. The hypocrisy embodied in both gestures is sickening.

No one questions that any termination, however, momentary, of the fighting is an act of humaneness. Nevertheless, in the larger framework of mankind's trying to work out its destiny, such fleeting moratorium on slaughter is nothing but a sacrilegious flouting of the Christian admonition, "Thou shalt not kill." In the context of the future, it is blasphemous and an insult to any claim of spirituality.

What defies the most elementary logic is that if a holiday signifying peace and goodwill to men is sufficient to lay down arms, then how much more significant and meaningful to lay down those same arms for the whole year in genuine adherence to the teachings that gave rise to the holiday in the first place. The one is worship of empty form. The other is predicated on principle., The former is simply to profess a principle while the latter is to practice it.

To hold that it is contrary to our conscience to slay human beings on one particular day, or a number of days, but otherwise quite permissible to destroy one's fellowman with the most brutal weapons is sheer expediency and a display of dishonesty. Only a guilt-complex can reconcile such duality, As the mightiest nation in the world, with no physical threat to our security from a nation as small as Vietnam, any claim to mortality in waging that war is untenable.

Is not the same circumstance prevalent in the current controversy over whether or not we should approach the Russians with an agreement under which neither country would construct an anti-missile defense system? The reasoning advanced is that if we were to construct such a defense it would cost the nation 30-40 billions of dollars and presumably it would cost the Russians the same astronomical amount. Therefore, both countries should see the saving to each other by such an agreement.

Doesn't it seem strange that if there could be mutual agreement on refraining from erecting anti-missile defenses, there could not be mutual agreement on complete disarmament? Certainly it would seem logical that if there could be agreement on a mutual economy of dollars, then there could be agreement on a mutual economy of human lives, especially when it could prevent the annihilation of mankind.

Unfortunately, power structures, whether communistic or capitalistic, don't function logically. While manipulated economies might not be able to withstand the strain of an additional multi-billion-dollar expenditure, the horrifying expenditure of a hundred million lives is accepted as expendable. It is such illogic or insanity that shapes the thinking of those who have been corrupted by the megalomania of power.

There can be no salvation of mankind until the people themselves arise from their apathy and commence calling the shots. It is their resources, their fortunes and their lives that are at stake. Throughout the nation must be engendered a true reverence for life, at least for innocent women and children, and such reverence for life must be bolstered by a realistic understanding that even those with whom we differ are not converted to our thinking by burying them beneath the flaming rubble of their homes.

Aquila has pleaded, and will unequivocally continue to plead, that a nation's foreign policy can never exceed one whit in integrity or honesty its domestic policy. The father who drinks to excess, who is indifferent to the pollution of his own home by neglect of a family furnace, who permits his children to go hungry or cold while he gambles away his earnings, and who displays cruelty and violence to his own family, is going to comport himself just as irresponsibly if he suddenly replaced the breadwinner in the adjoining household.

This does not mean that the mistreated wife and children are likewise incapable of honesty and

257

compassion. In fact, their sensitivity to inequity and brutality is usually heightened. It is this circumstance that explains why soldiers and the common run of citizens perform acts of heroism and sacrifice during war. Such humanitarianism, however, is equated too often with the honor and justice of the war policy itself. The two couldn't be further apart or more irreconcilable.

The breadwinner of a good home will always be a good neighbor. So it is with nations in all their relations with other nations. A nation rampant with crime and violence at home, that is in the throes of ethical breakdown within its own national household, will by sheer momentum carry such moral weakness into its policy and dealings with other nations. Any basic attempt to change our international conduct without first changing our national conduct is to misdirect our efforts to effects and not causes.

In the interim, while we set our house in order, let us welcome any cessation to the insanity of killing but let us not be misled by such momentary halt to brutality. The taking of human life, or the not taking of human life, can never be morally justified by certain dates on a calendar. The right to life is an endowment of the Creator and not to be destroyed by the whim of political strategists.

Only a permanent moratorium on all killing can measure up to that endowment!

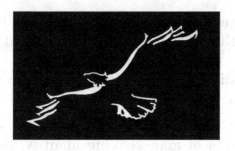

Vol. V, No. 3, March 1967

Love saith: Be created! But Spirit entereth

In and accomplisheth the art.

(Golden Scripts, Chapter 68)

Greater Love . . .

"WHAT the world needs now is love, sweet love . . ." are the words of a current popular song. Several million people will have sung it, hummed it, whistled it, before it fades as an identifiable tune from the dismal Niagara of sound that pours out of our radios daily. Do these people know what they are really singing about?

"Love" is a word that has grown smaller than ourselves by definition. Like Humpty Dumpty in *Alice in Wonderland,* we make words mean exactly what we want them to, no more, no less, and too often the profounder potentials of the terms are overlooked. Superficiality supplants all deeper meanings.

It is when we consider man in his three major relationships that we can truly consider with depth this question of love. The first relationship that man confronts is with himself. The second is with his fellows. The third is with the universe in which he finds himself. They are all interrelated and interdependent. For our definition, it is the essence, the binding quality, and the motivating force of all three that describes, "love."

In man's first relationship, with himself, we confront the whole area of man seeking identity, individuality, an expression of his own particular innate capabilities and talents. He is seeking recognition that he is as important as any other human being and that he is an integral part of all that surrounds him. Fulfillment of this relationship can only be satisfied by constructive creativity, a true love of achievement.

It is in man's second relationship, that with his fellow human beings, that we confront all the meaningless shadings and substitutes for what love truly is. It is here we have subordinated love to mean, "to *like* someone or something" with all the sugary, sweet, sentimental, oftentimes sickening affections that immature minds can contrive. It is here that "loving thy neighbor as thyself" is something to be often professed but rarely practiced.

Love in man's second relationship can only be fulfilled by Reciprocity. It's the implementation of the Golden Rule so that the creativity and identity of each and every human being finds fullest expression. In terms of economics, politics and all forms of social structure, it means that Justice must prevail in all human relationships. It means the recognition that this is an impartial Universe in which the resources and energies of Nature are an endowment to every human being on this planet and must be equally accessible for the use of all people. It means the recognition that accumulated knowledge and science are a heritage of all the people and cannot be so controlled as to restrain man instead of liberating him.

The true love is the motivating force that makes it possible to "love thine enemies." Such displayed compassion arises from the understanding that each and every human being, irrespective of momentary misconduct, has an innate capability for improvement. No one has the right to play God and destroy life which if given that extra chance could mend its ways. There can be no condemnation where there is true understanding.

Increasing disorders, violence, murder, devastation, perhaps complete annihilation of mankind, marks a society and a world that have removed themselves from the influence of the love force. Neither peace nor justice can become realities unless and until man commences to treat his brother in the way he in turn wants to be treated. Such brotherhood of man covers the whole spectrum of human relationships from the smallest hamlet to a world society of all nations.

The third relationship of man is his relationship with the whole Universe. While it embodies the first and second, it is distinctive unto itself. It is man's constant and eternal pursuit of knowledge in order that he can find peace of mind and spiritual ballast. Through understanding himself, his relationships with others, and the laws that govern the Universe, man finds true harmony in all existence. He feels at home and enjoys a true sense of belonging.

Jesus said, "Love thy Lord God, and thy neighbor as thyself." It is in the context of the foregoing that this expression takes on true meaning. Love is the dynamic, constructive motivating force of the Universe itself. It is not important whether we call it Love or whether we identify it as God, the Absolute, Nature, Universal Power or the Causeless Cause. All such terms identify the same constructive and orderly power of the Universe.

It is the power that commands genuine respect and affection between individuals, that motivates justice in all dealings amongst men, that keeps the stars in their courses, that bring the seasons around in majestic sequence eon unto eon, that causes the seed hidden in the warm, dark earth to sprout and send forth leaves, that inspires the heart and hand of a St. Francis, a Michelangelo or a Frank Lloyd Wright, that calls men and women to work and sacrifice and die for the benefit of others instead of themselves.

Yes, "what the world needs now is love . . . " But, it must be a true and profound recognition by man of his own place and importance in a vast and growing Universe, of the tremendous power he has within his grasp to use constructively for the enlargement of human compassion, for the growth of spiritual awareness, for the construction of an enlightened and humane and orderly society eventually over the whole globe!

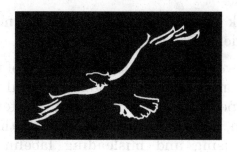

Vol. V, No. 4, April 1967

Say it unto the nations that a goodly time cometh

when man shall love his neighbor and

Fear becomes as naught.

(*Golden Scripts,* Chapter 71)

Woman Power

THE AUTHOR of a new book on women blandly announces on a TV interview that she considers 95% of American women happy, well-adjusted, normal individuals.

We find ourselves forced to respond, "Dear lady, if such is the case, this nation is in worse shape than we thought!"

Normal we will pass by, who knows what the norm is? Well adjusted, if it means resilient, able to take it, durable, we will grant. But happy? If 95% of the women of this country are happy, they are only half as empathetic and observant as we think they are, and at least twice as stupid.

How many women in this country are happy in the face of the cost of living, increasing taxes and their own need to work outside the home in order to meet present and future demands on the family purse?

How many women are happy in the face of the current problems concerning education, hospital costs and facilities, pollution of air and water, built-in obsolescence, food and drug regulation or the lack of it, false advertising and misleading labeling, highway slaughter and the growing tension between the races? If they are not remotely concerned about one or more of these things, they are either kept under glass or they are certifiable. If they may not recognize these problems as national, common to us all, but if they are breathing, moving, anywhere-near-normal women, they are unhappy and concerned to the same degree that such problems impinge on their families, their homes and life itself.

How many women are happy about the state of the world finds itself in up here in the late Sixties? Women may feel helpless, frustrated, impotent to do anything about it (mistakenly, we think) but they are beyond question concerned.

Not a normal woman in this or any other country wants to see her son sucked into the red maw of war, with every high hope she's held for him, every sacrifice she's gladly made for him, all the bright faith she holds for his future, suddenly imperiled or destroyed by a faceless and soulless brutality called war.

It is difficult enough for a woman who considers the war justified, who uncomplainingly accepts the ancient decree that "man must fight and woman must weep." It becomes intolerable for a woman who not only does not believe this war justified, but who realizes that war in this day and age is a brutal, outmoded and insane method of conducting world's affairs.

Jeannette Rankin, the first woman ever elected to the U. S. Congress, now retired and in her 80's, was recently interviewed in Florida. She was asked about her votes against U. S. entry into both World I and II. She did not believe, she said clearly and firmly, that the first vote cast by woman in the U. S. Congress should be in favor of war, nor could she go back on her principles regardless of public pressure in December of 1941. "Stupid" and "ineffective" were the words she used to describe war's futility. You cannot change men's thinking by force, she pointed out. There are better ways to settle our differences.

That it is still a man's world is a meaningless generality, except in so far as women permit it. Many women feel incompetent to deal with public affairs, an attitude which is simply a hangover from long centuries of being considered merely a piece of man's household property. It has been only a handful of years out of history in which women have been publicly admitted to have souls! It is a world in which men and women must equally use their talents to preserve all that is beneficial to the human race, and root out all that is destructive and suicidal.

If it be true that women are by nature better conservers than men (not meaning "conservatives" in the political sense) and if they are less given to false pride and face-saving when it comes to preserving what they hold dear, then in this nation's hour of need, as it struggles with the birth pangs of a New Age, women must assert themselves, as women. Not as pseudo-men.

Women are the bearers of life, the preservers of life, and the first teachers of the human spirit when it enters mortality. We strongly suspect that the rebellious attitude of many of today's young people is to a large extent a reflection of the rebellion of their mothers against the injustices and inequities of today's world. Iceberg-like, this influence may be two-thirds submerged, unrecognized even by the mothers themselves. But all sound psychologists accept the old Arabian proverb, "As the twig is bent, so shall the tree grow."

Similarly, vandalism and other forms of delinquency may also be attributed in large part to the frustration women experience in trying to raise their children in a society whose rank materialism and jungle law conflict sharply with the ethical idealism they have tried to teach in the home.

"Never underestimate the power of a woman," says a well-known ad. No one underestimates the power of a woman but the woman herself. If she ever decides to join with her sisters across the world to end this foolish insanity of war, to demand integrity and honesty in public affairs and in business, to make a concerted effort to see that the children of the world, *her* children, get a fair shake in life and their rightful equity in the gifts the Creator has made freely available to all, we could have a New dispensation overnight.

It may come to that!

266

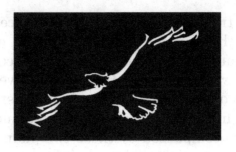

Vol. V, No. 5, May 1967

Disseminate always the bright rays of Truth; subject

always to learnings of wisdom, that by the powers

of your logic ye may see that they are Truth

(*Golden Scripts,* Chapter 77)

Who Shall It Profit?

TWO THOUSAND years ago, a Great Teacher appeared on this earth. Dressed in the simplest of garments, he trod from community to community addressing all those who would listen to His preachments. He displayed no flamboyancy of oratory nor did He comport Himself as a demagogue seeking office. There were no frantic exhortations to "seek and destroy" the enemy, or beseechments to build bigger and better weapons to annihilate those with whom there was disagreement. His was a mission of love, an appeal to the hearts and the minds of men that the brotherhood of man was attainable if mutual respect underscored all human relationships.

And what did such mutual respect embody?" Just two simple, but profound, precepts: 1) Love thy God with all thy might, and 2) Treat all others the way that you want to be treated. In two short sentences had been enunciated the cardinal guidelines for all constructive and interrelated human conduct. The scope of their application was limitless. How people lived together, the fairness of the social structure and institutions set up, and the integrity of government that supervised all laws, were encompassed by these two plain and simple precepts.

This presentation is not meant to be a sermon. We do not intend to preach in favor of any particular religion. We are appealing here only to basic common sense. The world, and particularly our own nation, is in the throes of such aimless confusion and apathy, such vicious antagonism and violence, that failure to reverse the suicidal course we are pursuing can only end in mankind's destruction.

Only a soul-searching affirmation of true values can restore ballast to our thinking and provide rational direction to a world engulfed in violence and wanton waste of energies. There must come into play a resurgence of reason, justice, probity, and a reverence for all life.

This, however, can only be engendered by an unshakeable belief in the basic goodness of man himself and in the acceptance that we inhabit a good and purposeful Universe. This is the message that the Man of Galilee tried so hard to impart to all of mankind.

What did He mean by, "Love thy God with all thy might"? Was He asking us to love some sublimated Moses perched atop some celestial pedestal who ultimately would pass judgment on the fallibilities of his own creations"? This is the interpretation that has been given to us by little minds. Is it not fairer to conclude that Jesus was pleading for man to have love and reverence for *all* creation? The beseechment to "love with all thy might" implies a full encompassment of all that surrounds man in countless forms of living and inorganic structure. More than that, it implies an impartial universe within which each human life has equal opportunity to shape its destiny and its well being. What other justification would there be for "God" to merit all-out love of every one of His creations?

In more practical terms, we are simply recognizing the fact that this planet that we occupy, so abundant in resources and levels of energy, is the heritage of every human being born upon it. It is man who has departmentalized it and through greed and deceit fashioned a world of "haves" and "have-nots." It is man who has set up the rules, which have subjugated and impoverished tens of millions while the shrewd and cunning feasted at banquets. It has been man in his obsession for the spoils of war that has pitted one mass of innocent people against another so that economic or political advantage can accrue to the tyrannical.

The point is that there is nothing inherently wrong, or bad, with God's creation. This is a lush and reasonably stable planet upon which to work out the abundant life for all the human beings who inhabit it. For this we should be grateful. The whole problem develops because as yet we haven't learned to live together recognizing the right of every human being to life itself and to equal opportunity to enhance that life. This carries us to the second precept that Jesus emphasized.

"Treat others the way you want to be treated," is the most fundamental premise that should underlie all

269

behavior, all man-made law, all social structures and government itself in any form. This precept is the functional basis of all *natural rights* that have been championed up the centuries. When we have crystal-clear in our minds that we not only live on an impartial planet but that every solitary human being is endowed with the same and equal natural rights, we have true perspective by which to indict the injustices of the present and to provide rational direction to working out all problems. More importantly, such perspective by the individual gives him revitalized incentive in striving for that better and safer society.

So, let us first imbed in our constant thinking that the true rights of human beings are not the laws which man codifies but the unwritten rules, which are inherent in the scheme of life itself. No person comes into life with more rights than any other person nor does he come into life with fewer rights. Is it difficult to grasp that if each person treated all other persons exactly as he wanted to be treated, "equal justice under the law" would have automatic reality?

What person exists who wants to be cheated of his labor, who wants to be physically or mentally injured, or who wants to be denied a role of participation in life that fulfills his needs and constructive urges? Isn't it obvious that the only need for rules is simply that there are those who aren't willing to treat others the way that they themselves want to be treated?

Right here we have the key to all organized society. Men get together and decide on rules that will *prevent* injustice to any of their group. In other words, such organized society has no power to create rights. Such rights have always existed. Every human being is born with them. The constitutions or governments of society are needed instruments only for the purpose of insuring the natural rights of all participant or members.

IN a more tangible and realistic sense the two basic precepts that Jesus emphasized can be directly related to every human being's right to *equal access to Nature's bounty* and every human being's right to *equal opportunity to be a participant in all life.* In both cases it should be noted that it is human beings as living, breathing, aspiring entities that are paramount. Everything else is secondary. Everything else is subordinate.

It is when we now come to trace developing religion and government that we get the full impact of what has happened. Gradually, subtly, almost imperceptibly, the pristine precepts of Jesus have been distorted to the point that life itself has become the slave of all that which is material. In both religion and government, we have come to worship property in stead of God, and to enhance material things instead of human beings.

Both the life and teachings of Jesus dealt with compassionate concern for men, women, and children, especially the sick and the wayward, those who most needed a helping hand. He himself had no possessions and, further, he admonished the rich that they had as much chance to enter the kingdom of Heaven as a camel passing through a needle's eye. Contrast this with the development of institutionalized religion which has as its main claim to identity, not "fruits by which ye shall know them." But by bigger and more elaborate structure, with softest seats reserved for those able to pay the largest tithes. Where in the

271

whole of it can one find the precept of "treating others the way you want to be treated"?

When the Founding Fathers set up this nation, they were imbued with the true precepts of Jesus in the ringing words of the Declaration of Independence: "We hold these truths to be self-evident: That all men are created equal; that they are endowed by their Creator with certain inalienable rights; that among these are life, liberty and the pursuit of happiness; that, to secure these rights, governments are instituted among men deriving their just powers from the consent of the governed. . . "

The early history of the nation reveals many of the most brilliant forefathers had serious misgivings as to whether the government, set up primarily to insure human rights, might not be adequate to ward off the dictates of property. They did not live long enough to see that their misgivings were indeed well founded. From a government and a society based on human rights has developed a society dominated by property. Artificial entities of industrial monopolies, financial monopolies and political hierarchies have absolutely and despotically taken over the nation. Before the rights of such super-power-structures, the inherent rights of human beings fade into insignificance. Man has become slave to things, the victim of his own science.

Human beings, suppressed, abusively restrained in their natural urges or enslaved, will rebel. A society precluding man's sensible inclination to treat others the way he wants to be treated is a society which historically has degenerated to one of ethical break-down and the eruptions of violence. This is what is happening to our nation today. The inherent human rights have been made subservient to the unjust rights of property.

Wars violate human rights most flagrantly. Through involuntary servitude, human beings are sent to preserve and defend the "rights of property" through mass killing. No act of man is so in violation of Jesus' precepts as the act of taking the lives of others. Any claim to morality and spirituality in the killing of other human beings is spurious and devoid of rationality. Treating others the way you want to be treated, and loving the Creator with all your might, have in war been denied all validity and all opportunity to function.

Yes, there is a need for the Man of Galilee to speak once again to the hearts of humankind on this planet. And as of old, his question to all men would be the same: "What profiteth it to a man if he gain the whole world and lose his own soul?"

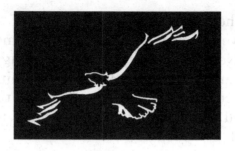

Vol. V, No. 6, June 1967

Stand ye as a rock and know my procedures; stand

ye as Vikings and let the gales lash you.

(Golden Scripts, Chapter 78)

Old Glory

JUNE 14 was Flag Day. In this month, the United States Congress fumbled around and finally got a bill passed imposing certain penalties for desecrating the Stars and Stripes.

Honorable gentlemen, it is meaningless. Those who love the flag and what it stands for are not going to desecrate it knowingly under any circumstances. Those to whom it means nothing are not going to change their minds because there is now a law that says your must respect it or suffer the consequences.

The author of **No More Hunger** used to tell of a certain day when he stood in the bitter cold near a street corner halfway across the world, a lifetime ago. The city was Vladivostok and the time was the fall of 1918. The strains of a Sousa March reached his ears and around the corner came a company of American doughboys with Old Glory waving over their heads.

Instantly, he said, such a torrent of unexpected emotion swept over him as he had not believed possible. Never had he realized so poignantly how much the mere sight of the flag meant to him. He stood on the street corner, bareheaded in the Russian autumn, and could not swallow the lump that swelled in his throat.

Many a traveler in a far and exotic land reports a similar experience. Learned gentlemen in the halls of Congress, you cannot legislate that feeling. You can neither quell it nor create it. It is there or it is not there, because the emotion is a reflection of what the flag symbolizes to each individual.

To those who know there country's face, it symbolizes a vast and varied and beautiful land, full of mountains, deserts, and green woodland, quick-rushing streams and lush meadows of waving grass or golden grain. Silver skyscrapers, fantastic bridges, Cape Cod cottages and white church spires. Ribbons of road that run endlessly into sunset and star-filled night.

To those who know the nation's origin, it symbolizes a new dispensation, the birth of a new kind of freedom, a government formed by the people and for the people. It symbolizes those who have caught the vision up the years and tried to keep her on the course.

To older Americans, it symbolizes the homely and familiar things that are stable and sure, Fourth of July picnics, the schoolroom, the cop on the corner, the Capitol dome.

Yes, the American Flag symbolizes all that is wholesome, and idealistic, and brave, and all that connotes the freedom and progress embodied in the nation's entire history. But this is only half of the picture. We too readily forget that our flag is not an entity unto itself. It can only reflect everything the nation has been and everything it will be. It is the totality of the nation. It *is* the nation.

It is in this context that we should recognize the littleness of the minds who can only see desecration of the flag in terms of the momentary act of rashness and distemper, but are themselves weak of voice in indicting the policies and conduct of the nation itself that have made the Stars and Stripes a despised symbol abroad and an indifferent symbol here at home.

The real desecrators of the flag are not the maverick schoolteacher and protest-marcher, but rather those who have corralled the wealth of the nation and usurped the rights of the people so as to make institutions the master of man instead of his servant.

The real desecrators of the flag are those who have plastered the dollar sign all over Old Glory so that "life, liberty and pursuit of happiness" has lost all meaning to tens of millions of human beings destitute and hungry.

No, learned gentlemen in the halls of Congress, you cannot legislate love for Old Glory. The integrity and sanctity of the flag will never exceed by one whit the integrity and sanctity of the nation over which it flies.

The flag will never fly freer than the freedom of the citizens who salute it!

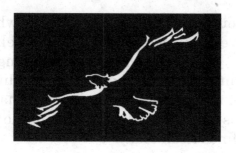

Vol. V, No. 7 & 8, July-August, 1967

Makers of calamities are never prophets: behold it is

the law that no true prophet fortelleth destruction!

(Golden Scripts, Chapter 83)

The Thread

ONE OF the most appealing of Greek myths tells of how Theseus slew the Minotaur. The hero, Theseus, came to the kingdom of Crete for the purpose of disposing of the dread, bull-like monster who was confined in the Labyrinth. It seems that slaying the Minotaur was no more hazardous than getting back out of the Labyrinth after the deed had been done. But the king's daughter, Ariadne, having discovered much charm in Theseus, provided him with a thread which he tied at the entrance to the Labyrinth, and which, after the battle provided him with safe conduct to her waiting arms.

This myth may well be applied to the world's current troubles. The labyrinth is the whole maze of propaganda, equivocation, fabrication, fact and fancy made possible by the world's advanced technology in communication. The monster to be incapacitated is the source, or sources, of untruth and deceit who thrive on the ignorance of the people. As in the Greek myth, how can one find the continuing strand leading out of the entanglement? What can be a single guiding principle which common humanity can take in its hand to guide it by the most direct route out of the perilous situation in which it finds itself today"

The name we would give to such a thread is *equal justice.* Justice for human beings. Justice for people as people. The right of the people themselves to shape their lives and destiny.

Instinctively, every man's hand reaches out for this very thread, well knowing deep down that only through justice for each can justice ever be achieved for all. But many are the deflections, the obstructions, the subtle persuasions that keep his hand from finding the thread.

Confusion in the world today is not caused by the events themselves, but by the explanations and interpretations by those who control the channels of information and propaganda. These are the ones who have made human beings subordinate to institutions and seats of power and who are frantically endeavoring to preserve a tottering status quo because they fight for their own survival only and not for all the people. From a position of prostituted power, they are not disseminators of information but molders of opinion.

The average American searching anxiously for stability, security and peace, finds the pressures insurmountable that deflect his thinking from the principle of equal justice. Unable to reach as far as the principle, he becomes entrapped in meaningless ideology or succumbs to whatever organization he accepts as reflecting his own thinking. Thus he becomes a "true believer," blindly following someone else's ideas because it saves him the effort of doing his own evaluating.

The tragedy is, of course, the resulting confusions in the mind of such a person who has put his faith, not in the basic principle of justice for all human beings, but in the persuasions either of those in power or those trying to get into power, without bothering to make the effort at evaluating the motives behind either, or, more importantly, the truth itself.

Thus the tragedy in Vietnam, where blind opposition to Russia and China in the cold war blinds us also to the just claims of the Vietnamese for "self-determination."

Thus our tragedy in the Middle East, where blind sympathy for persecuted Jews also blinds us to the just claims of the Arabs against the arrogant designs of the Zionists.

Thus our tragedy in city slums, where our blind opposition to broken-down tenements and idleness blinds us as well to the just claims of the poor and the jobless who turn in desperation to crime and violence.

In both our national and international considerations and concerns, we don't reach down to human beings as human beings. Our attention is focused on governments, on ideologies, on institutions, on laws, on commitments so intently that we fail to relate our concern to the people whose struggles and aspirations are primary. As a result, expediency and cruelty have supplanted honesty and compassion. We have blindly followed the dictates of usurpers of power instead of checking with our own consciences and trying to set a just course for mankind to follow.

The technology revolution in all its forms has made the world too small and too dangerous for injustice to flourish as of yore. The voiceless and the oppressed have become self-aware. More than that, they are daring to assert their basic rights as human beings. Nothing less than justice will be acceptable. We only pray that the obdurance of the status quo'ers does not provoke the annihilation of the human race before that justice begins to approach reality.

Neither Communism nor Capitalism are instruments of justice. Both have accentuated more than lessened man's inhumanity to man. New answers, fresh outlooks are needed. Change is inevitable. Man's own brainpower has wrought the potential for a New Age. An aroused human conscience will welcome it.

"It rains alike on the just and the unjust fellow," says the old rhyme. "But mostly on the just because the unjust has the just's umbrella."

For the survival of the human race, and for its very real enhancement, that umbrella must be raised over all mankind. And the sooner we realize this fact, the sooner we shall be on the way not only for a better life for the disadvantaged, but for every human being on this planet.

282

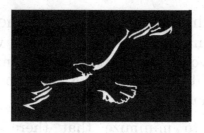

Vol. V, No. 9, September 1967

All things beautiful accrue to us, all things real become

our heritage; all things noble ennoble us.

(Golden Scripts, Chapter 19)

The Corporate Structure

THERE is nothing more intriguing to those promoting for the goals of a Corporate Commonwealth than the ironical circumstance that the vehicle called the "corporation" which has permitted the few to corral the real wealth of the nation is the same vehicle which when employed by all the people will return to them their rightful ownership.

In short, the corporate pattern which, misused, made possible concentrated ownership can, rightly used, return rightful ownership back to the people.

Quite obviously, there is nothing inherently wrong with the structure called a corporation. Like fire, or for that matter, nuclear energy, it is only a question of how it is directed and for what purpose.

Another circumstance equally intriguing is that the corporate structure is very American. Thus, when it is advanced as a solution to our national ills, there can be no cries of "socialism" or "communism." Of course, those who place material values above human values will hurl such empty epithets in the beginning. However, their groundless accusations will be short-lived. Their voices will become increasingly weaker as an enlightened citizenry make their sovereign voices increasingly louder.

This is not to minimize that there is much de-conditioning that must be done before a Corporate Commonwealth receives full acceptance and endorsement. There is need of much education.

If there is one initial barrier in the average person's thinking that stands out above all others in accepting the idea of a nationally incorporated economy, it is the feature that it necessitates *planning*. Is it possible to envision trying to operate General Motors without planning far into the future? It is too ridiculous to mention. Planning is accepted as sensible application of knowledge to performing any task. However, the moment one suggests the equally reasonable application of planning for conducting the nation's production and distribution, it becomes taboo, irrelevant, regimentation and downright subversive.

How has such inconsistency crept into the average person's thinking? Why does he see red, communist-tinged "red," the moment one suggests that the nation's economy is serious askew and there must be national planning to solve intolerable suffering and inequities?

Two reactions immediately are apparent. One has to do with "free enterprise" which is equated with freedom. And the other has to do with the fear of a national bureaucracy dictating the movement of every citizen. Both are understandable reactions, but are no cause for concern respecting an incorporated economy.

284

A Corporate Commonwealth economic framework not only gives true reality and enhancement to the premise of "free enterprise" but would allow no room for the whole gamut of nonproducing bureaucrats. In its simplest terms a Corporate Commonwealth is an economic arrangement by which the sovereign people themselves *direct* and *coordinate* all the nation's resources, raw stock, tools and technological know-how so that *all* the people can enjoy the maximum good life commensurate with utilization of our *full* productive potential. It is nothing more nor nothing less.

There is nothing profound or technical about either words "free" or "enterprise." One simply means without restraint and the other means doing something. When we are considering an incorporated economy, we are underscoring the lifting of all restraints so that the nation can do all those things that need to be done, and can be done. In this sense we not only advocate but make possible an economy of "free enterprise."

What the majority of people must realize is the fact that, outside of the earliest history of this nation, there has never truly been an economy of free enterprise. Private capitalism, coupled with private banking has simply employed this idealistic phrase to cover up the compounding restraints it has imposed on the economy. All the gimmicks of *unearned profit*, exorbitant interest, rent and arbitrary price-fixing have been nothing but camouflaged *theft*.

They have been the means by which the vast majority could be systematically short-suited of their rightful purchasing power and equity, and the greedy and power-hungry could pyramid their ownership of the nation's resources and productive machinery.

Only those who do not want to face reality are unable to see that the inevitable result of current trends is a monopolized economy *by* the few and *for* the few, which will drive out of existence any semblance of "free enterprise." What chance has the millions of workers when they can be replaced with machines? What chance has the small farmer or small manufacturer competing with corporate entities employing the most modern technology and enjoying privileged legislation? What chance has the small retailer endeavoring to compete with giant corporate super-markets?

The tens of millions of workers, consumers and taxpayers in the nation have become the robot slaves of an economic and social system that has thrived on disadvantaging the people. It is a system of creating the vacuums into which bureaucracy, welfarism and indebtedness move to make up for the system's inefficiencies.

It is a system of Twentieth Century feudalism more reprehensible than medieval feudalism, for the serfs of that distant day knew they were slaves and today the people are unaware of their slavery.

Today th e people endure suffering when all the time they have the power in their own hands to terminate that needless suffering. The people themselves are their own worst enemies. They could be secure, they could be prosperous, and above all they could be free if they would comprehend that all the major problems are man-made and as such they can all be eliminated by man-made solutions.

Once the people give serious consideration to their own well being, and recognize their own inherent power to effect every change that will improve their lot, they will see the practical wisdom of adopting a Corporate Commonwealth.

If the corporate structure has been proper and good for the few in our society, isn't this a pretty good recommendation that it would be *proper and good for the entire citizenry?*

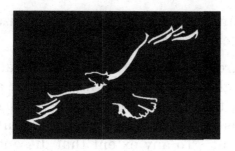

Vol. V, No. 10, October 1967

He who performeth the goodly deed is the anointed;

he who giveth the cup of cold water when the

throat is parched receiveth his accolade

within the Walls of Splendor.

-(*Golden Scripts,* Chapter 88)

A Higher Law

IF THERE IS one singular development throughout this land of ours that shakes the pillars of our society, it is the whole spectrum of protest and rebellion. For the first time in this Twentieth Century, large segments of the nation are openly defying established government. Young men and women, members of the clergy, professors of high learning, and professional men of all sciences are publicly stating their position of choosing jail cells rather than obeying the "law" or policies of their government.

Irrespective of any person's sympathy, either for or against the protesters, the harsh reality must be faced that the nation is in the throes of anarchistic rebellion. Certainly it behooves rational men to exercise the utmost insight in weighing all factors that bear on the instability and insecurity that characterize the times through which we are passing.

The first cardinal premise that must be adhered to is that the "right of dissent" is inherent in any governmental structure brought into being by the will of the people. This is the essence of the democratic principle in government. To any extent that dissent, protest or opposition can be stifled, to that extent despotism has supplanted popular government.

Of course, few Americans, including those in government, would dispute the foregoing premise of democratic government. In fact, the current Administration through all its spokesmen gives lip service to the recognition that dissenters should have full opportunity to communicate and thereby change public policy. The inescapable fact, however, is that a circumstance has come about in the nation where the *opportunity* to change public policy through *legitimate* channels is being denied the people. Thus, open defiance of those constituting government.

This brings us to the second cardinal premise that must be recognized. There is a "right to dissent" inherent in life itself that exceeds all man-made laws and governments. This is an appeal to one's own conscience respecting morality and justice. In the terms of such writers as John Locke, whose writings were the basis of the immortal Declaration of Independence, man retains at all times an "appeal to Nature" as superseding all mortal law that he is called upon to obey

Obviously, as expressed by our Founding Fathers when they refused to obey the constituted power of King George the Third, disobedience to existing authority

290

should not be carried out "for light or transient causes." Nor should it be undertaken until every existing procedural avenue has been belabored and exhausted.

The question that presents itself is whether or not, at this moment in the history of the nation, authority has become so prostituted and the abuses and oppression of citizens and groups so intolerable as to warrant open defiance of those who constitute government.

Two distinct areas, in the main, can be identified in which rebellion has erupted. The first is the whole circumstance within which tens of millions of the nation's citizens are denied any participating opportunity to enjoy their nation's ability to produce everything to abundance but must instead accept enforced poverty.

The second is the circumstance of war within which a citizen can be compelled against his will to support and give his life in the involuntary killing of other human beings against whom he has no grievance.

Both of these areas involve questions of life and death. They involve moral values that transcend the rules and laws of property and commerce and institutions. They involve man's confrontation with himself, squaring his convictions and actions with his own conscience.

It is not difficult to see that "civil disobedience" in either area is a judgment as no man can, in the final analysis, respond to another's conscience. Likewise, no man can pay the penalty for the other person whose conscience compels him to violate a man-made law or governmental dictation.

Aquila can see no constructiveness in any approach that tries either by legislation or force of government to stop rebellion in a society without any steps being taken to eliminate the causes, which justify that rebellion. There is neither honesty nor compassion displayed by a society that, on the one hand, takes no realistic steps to liberate tens of millions from the caged ghettoes of this nation and then on the other, condemns them for trying to break the bonds of unbearable imprisonment.

There is equal dishonesty and lack of compassion in a society that conscripts the nation's best manhood to be maimed or killed in brutal war that the power structures at home may enjoy increased economic and political power, and, on the other hand, condemn both draftee and adult who want no part of such murderous subterfuge.

Across the nation larger and larger numbers are openly rebelling against a military-industrial-political complex that has made the love of power and profit greater than the love of man himself. The minds and hearts and souls of America are in revolt against that which measure achievement in the quantity *of products* and not in the *quality of human beings.* No society can endure without rebellion when the profit and success of the few are achieved by the insufferable agony and loss of the majority.

While Aquila deplores all forms of violence and irrational acts by those who protest either social injustice or needless war, it at the same time deplores more strongly the violence and irrational acts of those wielding abnormal economic and political power whose outrages against humanity outweigh a billion fold that of the protesters. Even more deplorable is the parallel that the protesters are rebelling openly against observable injustice while the profiteers and politically despotic commit their violence in the name of the false emblems of "free enterprise" and "world peace."

What the nation needs to be shown are the alternatives to the whole structure of economics and politics, which spawns violence and corruption. Until these alternatives are endorsed neither justice nor peace can be the achievements of our society or that of the world.

Aquila has been set up expressly for the purpose of showing the nation that there is a socio-economic-political framework available for its embracement that would leave no room for the disadvantaging of any citizen, and would erase all motivations for, and gain from, unnecessary wars.

Aquilas's urgent appeal to all those in rebellion is to acquaint themselves with the idea of a *Corporate Commonwealth* that all energies would be constructively channeled *for* something instead of negatively *against* something.

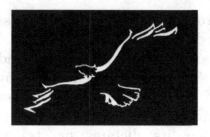

Vol. V, No. 11, November 1967

All things taken together comprise the eternal,

even our solicitude one for another.

(Golden Scripts, Chapter 86)

"We the People!"

DURING the political witch-hunts of World War II, two FBI men knocked on the door of the home of a sweet little old lady living in Kansas. "We are the government!" they introduced themselves, in tones calculated to overawe.

"Well," responded the sweet little lady thoughtfully, "you are mistaken, *I am the government! You are my servants.* What did you want to see me about?"

It is not important here to relate that the FBI agents were following orders out of the Justice Department in Washington to interrogate good, law-abiding citizens whose only "lawlessness" was that they were reading literature not approved by the incumbent Administration. What is important is that the little old lady not only understood the subordinate relationship of government to the sovereign people but she had the intestinal fortitude to express such understanding to those engaged in usurpation.

The deepest-rooted causes of the sickness that afflicts our nation today is that most citizens look on their government as something separate and apart from themselves. They cynically accept "government" as some sort of political Moloch, designed to operate consistently to their detriment, and they feel helpless to check either its dictates or its encroachments. Consequently, those who do run the nation politically find no obstruction in fulfilling their own despotic roles while they sell out the nation to the military-industrial-financial complex which underwrites their elections.

Belatedly, the citizens of this nation must awaken to the realization that in the United States of ours, the *supreme* and *absolute* power rests with the people. This was the enunciated intent of the Declaration of Independence. It is the expressed premise and essence of the Constitution. Those who don't realize the import of this fact should dust off their copies of the Constitution and start reading its Preamble. There they will find these words: *"We the people* of the United States, in order to form a more perfect union, establish justice . . . and secure the blessings of liberty to ourselves and our posterity, do ordain and establish this Constitution for the United States of America."

The importance, and inescapable, fact is that the framers of the Constitution recognized that *the only basic purpose of government is to insure the inherent rights of every individual.* The founding fathers, besides being steeped in the philosophy of John Locke, knew from their own exacting experience that true government is only that which is always accountable to the will of the people. Perhaps Thomas Jefferson best expressed this belief when he stated:

> I know of no safe depository of the ultimate powers of society but the people themselves, and if we think them not enlightened enough to exercise their control with a wholesome discretion, the remedy is not to take it from them but to inform their discretion by education.

However, for a people to recognize that they possess both the constitutional and inherent power to shape their lives and destiny is not sufficient. They must understand how they have progressively lost economic sovereignty over their natural resources, their productive assets, and their issuance of money so that they have become the political slaves of those who control and exploit them economically.

Political freedom without economic freedom is impossible. Since the dawn of history those who have controlled the means of production have simultaneously controlled politically those dependent on such means for their livelihood. It doesn't matter whether you are speaking of the feudal fiefs of Europe or the oligarchic monopolies of the present.

A free society is one in which the democratic principle is inherent in the lives of the people, both economically and politically.

Secondly, the people must recognize the sham of political parties and the farce of trying to run their government without removing both the spoils of office and the tyranny of office from the whole political machinery of government. A people who are to fulfill their role of being truly sovereign must be disposed to consider political reform that is long overdue.

Such reform must encompass the direct nomination of candidates by the people without the political screening

297

of the power structures. The power to elect must carry with it the power to recall any elected candidate who fails to carry out his contract with the people. Above all, the sovereign people must assume direct decision-making on all laws and major policy.

These are the political innovations that will realistically make the people sovereign and the arbiters of their own lives.

Only when such innovations are embraced can the people state with honesty and practical reality, *"We are the government!"*

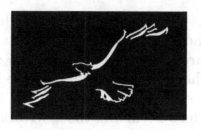

Vol. V, No. 12, December 1967

We are brethren together, plowing the

fertile field of the world.

(Golden Scripts, Chapter 89)

Participation

AT CHRISTMAS, in particular, most people are moved to radiate "good will" to all men. During the balance of the year, it is quite fitting to denounce and indict human conduct. However, this editorial is not timed to evince any special seasonal tolerance for humanity. The purpose of this writing is to highlight an observation respecting inherent motivations that transcend behavior itself.

We want to consider the little-admitted fact that all men are inherently good but that it is the pressures and circumstances largely not of their own making which cause them to act very badly, too often irrationally. We want to recognize the fact that it is the very nature of our whole social system which permits a few to over-participate in our society while at the same time it precludes the majority, especially the very poor, from participating in any meaningful way.

Students of our socio-economic-political system are recognizing that it is the real root cause of human behavior. It makes no difference whether we are considering those occupying the lowest rungs of the social structure, who are victimized and therefore rebel, or whether we are considering the highest rungs, who dictate such victimizing, both segments are corrupted by the system and those within each segment are unable to be their true selves.

Human beings, whether children or adults, display almost identical reactions to the same set of circumstances. Take away a child's toys and refuse to let him join in the games and he will do one of two things. He will either sulk or he'll throw a tantrum. Doesn't the same reaction take place in our adult society? Deny millions of people the opportunity to play meaningful roles, to participate in society's "game of life," and they too will sulk or throw tantrums. We term such sulking indifference and apathy; when in the form of tantrums, it becomes crime, rebellion and violence. However, in the case of both children and adults, the fundamental motivation is that neither has been permitted to be rightful participants.

When we consider the circumstance of over-participation, we again observe the same reactions in both the child and the adult. It doesn't matter whether we are considering the neighborhood "bully" who as owner of bat and ball, or because of physical size, dictates the rules of the game and who shall play, or whether we are considering the minority whom the nation's power structures dictate who shall be destitute and who shall be affluent. In both cases a circumstance exists, a *power* exists, by which the few can over-participate and the majority is forced to under-participate.

The key word that must be emphasized in our whole consideration of participation is *power*. For whether we deal with children and their urge to overly exert the personality in playing games, or whether we deal with the adult society, it is primarily a question of each person's being able to exercise his voice so that his own particular self-interest can be protected and enhanced. It is simply a question of having power to demand one's rightful share and role as every other person.

What must be faced is that from the beginning our socio-economic system has been a self-developing and self-propelling system that has no engineered prescription for the betterment of all men. Instead, the system has allowed for uncontrolled mechanisms by which the majority could be deprived of their rightful equity and participation, which led to bondage and exclusion from the society. Without voice to property, the majority had no means by which to fight back until rebellion was the only alternative to insufferable oppression.

Too many people in this nation are quick to condemn the rebellion that is taking place by indicting the people who have turned to civil disobedience, riots and crime, without recognizing that all of these people are basically good but that man-made circumstances have denied them rightful participation in their own society.

It is a lawless society that breeds lawlessness. If a murderer has you cornered and your life is at stake, the time is past when you can demand that he go with you to the magistrate and be booked for intended homicide. Is starvation in rat-infested ghettos any less murder because the agony of death is prolonged, slower? Or is life any less precious, or less to be protected, because despotic power exists in prostituted government to send your son to die under the camouflaged pretext that he is fighting for his country?

But the pauperized, the bondaged, and the conscripted in needless war are not the only victims of the society. The inescapable observation must be made that it is our system itself that in turn dictates the destructive actions of the minority, who by virtue of their positions in the system, must conform to the motivations of the system.

While the majority have been deprived of their rightful equity and power so that they have not the legal means by which to fight back, at the same time it has been ill-gotten holdings and usurped power which have corrupted the few at the top so they lost both personal integrity and any inclination to change an unjust social system.

An economic-political Frankenstein has cancerously grown to sicken the whole nation. Unarrested, the whole society will become victim to its self-engendered violence and arrogance of misused power. The artificially created disparity of participation must come to an end if the nation is to survive.

A nation serene, stable and safe can only be achieved when the people are ready to adopt a **Corporate Commonwealth.** Its cornerstones are complete dispersal of power and the constant right of every person to be equal participant.

Yes, all people are inherently good. However, there must exist a framework of human relation within which that inherent goodness can find expression. When the social system itself is constructed for the enhancement of all men, then it follows that those within the system have the opportunity to express their natural motivations of love, compassion and respect for each other.

The Brotherhood of Man cannot become a reality until each person has a *chance* of fulfilling his obligation to the Golden Rule!

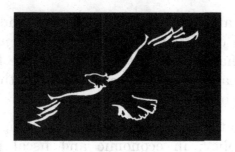

Vol. VI, No. 1, January 1968

Have I not known the vagaries of those who once said:

unto me: Lord, Lord, chose us, for verily we love thee?

(Golden Scripts, Chapter 93)

No Real Obstacles

TWO OBJECTIONS to the Corporate Commonwealth idea most commonly heard 1) "It's too radical," and 2) "It hasn't got a chance against the already established power structures." That these are not valid objections is plain to students of the idea, but since such students are few in number, a capsule of the answers to them may be of help.

First, "It's too radical." The word *radical* for many years has been connected with extreme leftwing activity. Like many another innocent word, it has been invested in the conventional mind with sinister meaning, somehow associated with beards, bombs, and Bolshevism. The true meaning of the word *radical is pertaining to the root.* In this sense, the Corporate Commonwealth idea is radical.

The idea of a Corporate Commonwealth gets down to the real roots of our problems, which lie in an inequitable and unjust social structure, and it presents a clear line of action toward equity and justice It is radical in that it does cut deep, below the fantasy and illusion created and maintained by the constant propaganda of the status-quoers.

This is a nation in deep trouble, in foreign policy, in domestic policy, in economic and fiscal policy. Its people are divided, confused, frustrated, rebellious and angry. All the "bad" things, war, crime, corruption, mental breakdown, are on the increase instead of decrease. Aquila contends that all these difficulties stem from a socio-economic system that glorifies physical force and material wealth, and ignores or ridicules basic human and spiritual values. Correction of our problems will never come by patching up an old and wornout system that patently will not work. It is time we dig down to the very roots of our national and individual thinking to realize that these problems are too radical to be solved by anything less than a radical solution.

Second, "It hasn't got a chance against established power structures." Thirty years ago, when the Corporate Commonwealth idea was first set down in a book, **No More Hunger**, it did not indeed stand a chance against established power structures. Alterations in certain basic conditions were necessary before it stood a ghost of a chance of being accepted as feasible by any sizable segment of the American people. However, in the course of these thirty years not only has technology developed to the point in communications and production at which the nation's economy *can* be operated democratically through a national corporation, but the trend right now is toward one giant monopoly through accelerated mergers.

Secondly, and this is the key to the whole question, while the monopolistic power structures have been gaining their absolute control, the people have been increasingly excluded from the economy. The technological machines do not receive wages, nor are they consumers. A people without purchasing power cannot eat nor enjoy life and thus the onslaught on the overloaded national warehouse to which they do not have access.

Will the power structures relinquish? They have no choice. Their own survival is dependent on major adjustments that will make all citizens owner-participants in the whole economy. Else they shall reap their own physical destruction.

The abuses and misuses of money, with attendant miseries of debt, taxes, bankruptcy and welfare for the individual together with the agglomeration of despotic economic power in pyramiding monopolies are straining every fibre of the social fabric. The unequal distribution of the purchasing power of consumers becomes more and more evident. The creaking machinery of the debt-money system is breaking up. If we are to avoid devastating depression or complete economic collapse, fresh approaches are required.

But the single factor commanding the greatest change in our social philosophy in the last thirty years is the fantastic development of our technology. Automation and cybernation have created as great a revolution in the economic life of the world as, in Alice Hilton's words, the invention of the plow ten thousand years ago. The full impact of this quick evolution has not yet reached the American public. It must be emphasized

307

over and over again until it seeps into the most sluggish consciousness.

General discussion of it has been sidelined as a "hot war" economy and diverted our attention from it. But the shocking fact stands: Machines are rapidly taking over the work man has done since the dawn of time.

We are therefore called upon to consider a monumental decision:

Who is going to control these machines and the vast wealth they make possible?

Shall we become, most of us or our children, mindless, vegetable-like robots, fed, clothed, and sheltered by the Economy of Abundance provided by the Machines and directed by a handful of elite social engineers who will decide "what is best for us," or shall we, as human beings, come finally into our rightful heritage as succinctly put in the slogan of IBM: *Machines should work! Men should think!"*

Are we ready to meet the challenge of a future where man need not toil physically for his sustenance? Are we ready, as mature human beings, to stop the back-breaking, time-consuming, nerve-deadening activity of monotonous physical and repetitious mental labor in order to keep alive, and, instead, to begin the fascinating, expanding, limitless activity of the mind?

So it becomes no longer a question of whether the Corporate Commonwealth idea has the ghost of a chance or not. The CC idea is actually designed to make the economic and social adjustments necessary to conditions that already exist in order that human beings may be free from the economic slavery that not only binds them now but also threatens an even more soulless future. It guarantees the people themselves genuine participation in the political and economic decisions affecting their lives and well being in the Economy of Abundance.

The idea of a Corporate Commonwealth provides the most equitable and practical system for the business of obtaining living under an Economy of Abundance yet devised. It removes painlessly and effectively the threat of dictatorship in any form by guaranteeing every citizen participation in all matters affecting his own welfare. Because it is equitable, it removes the possibility of further settlement of national or international disagreements by force, riot or war.

It is radical, but only in that it deals with root causes of our dilemma.

And it not only stands a chance of adoption. Its provisions have to be adopted if we are to survive!

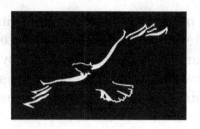

Vol. VI, No. 2, February 1968

Be of good cheer, beloved; your ways are not of

darkness: Ye have opened your eyes and

perceived eternal values.

(Golden Scripts, Chapter 94)

Tragic Stupidity

AQUILA has frequently and unequivocally denounced the Vietnam war as illegal, brutal and demoralizing, both to Vietnam and us.

While we were initially told by the Johnson Administration apologists we were fighting to stop the "aggression" of the Vietcong and the North Vietnamese against the South Vietnamese, it is now emphasized that the basic underlying reason why we must be there and why thousands of American boys must die is actually to stop the spread of Communism across Asia and across the world.

A worse way to accomplish this end couldn't possibly be chosen.

Let us not be misunderstood. Aquila holds no brief for dictatorship in any form. Russian Communism under Josef Stalin was one if the most brutal types the world has ever seen. The editors of *The Eagle's Eye* oppose any system of oligarchic rule in which the individual is made subservient to the enforced dictates of the state. Our only concern is the promotion of a system in which every citizen is a responsible, participating member, the absolute decision-making power resting with the people.

But, even if the world situation were exactly the same as it was thirty years ago, which it is not, or if Communism were exactly the same in practice as it was thirty years ago, we would still be tragically stupid in fighting it by the methods we are using today. We are not defeating Communism by waging war in Vietnam. *We are actually making more Communists by the minute.*

In the days when Russia was the only outright Communist nation, it was ruthlessly ruled by a tight little handful of dedicated revolutionists at the top, bent converting the rest of the planet to their way of thinking by force or subversion. Communism *was* monolithic, international in goal, and Moscow-oriented in its every thought.

What Moscow did not adequately reckon with was the inborn spirit of nationalism that animates the peoples of the world, a clannishness based on language, custom, appearance, tradition or whatever group-similarity may be used as a rallying point, setting it apart from all the rest. Certain Communist ideas of land reform, of lowering the privileged and elevating the under-privileged, of redistributing a nation's wealth among all the people (at least in theory) has great appeal among the lesser developed countries of the earth, particularly those ruinously exploited by imperialistic powers. But national pride is strong in this world, a sense of community among those of like history, tradition and language. Eagerly some of these nations have seized upon certain elements of Communist theory by which the rich and powerful might be humbled and the lowly raised up, but in the ultimate they have refused total allegiance too Moscow.

Thus as Communist ideology has spread throughout Asia and Africa, and parts of Europe, it has undergone alteration, each nation shaping it to its own purpose and situation. The strong centralization has become diluted, phased out, even frankly opposed, as witness Communist China who looks upon Russia as degenerate and decaying, retrogressing from the original Communist line back toward Capitalism.

Comes now the great and all-powerful United States of America, bulwark of the capitalist system, wealthy beyond reason, and takes up the side of French-oriented Saigon against the peasantry of South Vietnam, and the nationalist government of Hanoi. It rains down fire, death and destruction from the skies, destroying Vietnamese economy by the sudden amounts of foreign money, inevitably encouraging the always present, universal potential for corruption, laying waste cities, towns, rice paddies and plantations in the process of "saving" them, uprooting and displacing hundreds of thousands of illiterate and be-wildered peasants from their homes and fields, and by pure force of arms it keeps a government in power that never has had the allegiance of more than a handful of Vietnamese people. This, say the Johnson Administration apologists, is the only way to stop Communism.

Much has been made of the fact by these same apologists that in the current attack by the Vietcong on cities, the populace did not rise up and join openly with the invaders in their endeavors. But it has been pointed out by astute observers, including newsmen on the spot, that the Liberation Front could never have accomplished what it has against the military might of the United States, if there had not been collusion of a sizable nature by the populace, even though they do not openly state their position. How could they possibly do so? The average Vietnamese citizen, peasant or plutocrat, is caught between the devil and the deep blue sea. Either way, he is going to be dealt with summarily. Either way, he is going to lose. Assault from the North and from the Vietcong, aggression from over the sea, it is all one to him, and spells nothing but misery, destruction and death.

Speculation is that more and more of these distraught people see Uncle Ho as their savior, at least, he is one of them.

Sixty-five billions of dollars is the estimate of what the American people have poured into the bottomless pit of the Vietnamese War. A model nation could have built for that amount roads, schools, and hospitals, public benefits beyond number. Modern methods of agriculture could have been introduced, and a technology suitable to the people and the area developed. Illiteracy and disease could have been struck a mortal blow. An ancient and beautiful people, tragically exploited by foreigners for years, could have made a model community for all Asia, gradually, peacefully, and with large and constructive returns in benefits to the whole human race. Communism as such would have faded from the scene.

All the people of the world want a chance to operate on their own, to be fed and clothed and sheltered by their own efforts without interference from faraway "governments" which have come to mean only trouble, misery and death. All men desire to improve their lots in life, and will do so rapidly under the kind of instruction that they can absorb, that demonstrates genuine interest and concern, that respects their own tradition and customs and institutions, changing them by education only and not by force.

This is what the United States should have done when it went into South Vietnam "to fight Communism and stop the aggression."

What if those half a million American boys on the other side of the globe, now engaged in the business of death, had instead been directed and trained in the business of life, in sanitation, in basic laws of health, in the simplest ways of battling illiteracy, in demonstrating rudimentary but improved methods of agriculture and construction in building roads, hospital and schools? Think about it, all ye hawks and beaters of the drums of war! Ask the boy whether they would rather teach and build, or kill! Ask their mothers and wives! Ask the taxpayers of America whether they'd rather put their money into napalm and bombs or into books and plows! What does reason tell you?

The plain fact is, we have not learned to conduct our own society in a constructive way at home. How can we possibly go across the earth and expect to accomplish by persuasion or force what we cannot do ourselves? "Do as I say, not as I do!" remains the poorest method of teaching ever tried.

315

The corollary is, if we do not change our thinking right here in the United States, if we do not begin to use reason instead of force, Communism will grow in its appeal, not just in Asia but at our very own hearth sides.

Injustice seeks balance. Under whatever name it shall be called, we had best find that balance, reasonably equitably and quickly or brute force and anarchy will triumph over us all!

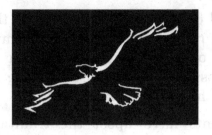

Vol. VI, No. 3, March 1968

Abide ye in me, knowing that all things await

our plannings, infinite in prospect and

beauteous of purpose.

(*Golden Scripts,* Chapter 95)

Upsetting Applecarts

COMES now a presidential election year when in the nature of things perspective becomes warped, focus gets fuzzy and a political landscape, always somewhat distorted, becomes even more so.

The particular year of grace, 1968, everything is even more so to an incalculable degree. As Frank McGee commented in a recent newscast, this year conventional thinking is of no use. So volatile are the elements making up this year's presidential campaigns that no traditional rules, customs or estimates can provide prognostications that have validity. Anything may happen, and a good deal unquestionably will.

Such uncertainty, such unpredictability, such non-conformity to the good, old-fashioned rules of the game must strike fear to the heart of the old-line politicians, and such fear must be reflected as disquiet to a greater or less degree in the minds of the unthinking who have always relied on the professionals to do their thinking for them. More and more people are coming to realize the necessity of doing their own thinking for a change, and the prospect must be unnerving, not to say appalling, to the professionals.

Three elements have upset the traditional political applecart in this nation, in our opinion. The first is the awful gravity of the issues. The Vietnam War is not "just another war." It is on the way to escalating into World War III and global destruction. Poverty, racism and crime are on the way to tearing apart the fabric of our society. These are life-and-death problems, not to be dealt with by conventional "campaign oratory."

Before the national conventions role around, other politicians may, we hope, be moved to demonstrate the rare courage and true patriotism of Senator Mark Hatfield of Oregon who has quite plainly stated that so serious are the issues confronting the nation and the world that if it is necessary to cross party lines for the sake of supporting the best qualified candidate, he is prepared to do so. For him, he said, the safety of the nation comes before the party.

The second upsetting element is the inescapable influence of TV. Beyond any would-be censorship and controlled propaganda, beyond editorial distortion by network policy or advertising pressures, the power of TV to make almost every home in the nation more aware, more conscious of, more disturbed about national issues and problems than ever before cannot be denied. In contrast to newspapers, magazines and even radio, television involves the most casual viewer in spite of himself in the troubles afflicting all of us so that his thinking must to some extent be influenced, perhaps even galvanized for the first time into taking a position on matters with which he has never before identified himself.

The third element upsetting the traditional applecart is the emergence of the power of young people. Over the past decade, the power of young people has been praised, decried, regretted, feared, reacted to in countless ways. Much has been made of the fact that half the population is now 25 years old or less. Twelve million new voters have emerged in the last four years to make themselves heard through the ballot box. A great portion of these new young voters don't like the way things are one little bit, and are resolved to do whatever they can to change it.

This is the bright hope, the breath of spring, the tired, old world sadly needs. Most of these young people (not just here but across the world) have lost respect for traditional concepts. With a vision enlarged by wider education and by the involvement TV demands, this new young breed look upon the mess the world is in, see no reason why it should continue this way, and for their own survival are dedicating themselves to upgrading it. Methods, approaches, attitudes vary widely among them, because all manner of people are young, but there is one resounding chord of agreement that binds them together into a commanding force and a power to be reckoned with. They want a better world to live in and they believer it is possible to make it so.

John Kennedy was attuned to this chord and young people responded. By association and by his own appeal, Bobby Kennedy also is attuned. It is to be expected that young people of all conditions and persuasions will rally to his banner. What is more surprising and significant is that the low-key, quiet professional approach of Senator Eugene McCarthy has also called forth the enthusiastic response of young people. It demonstrates very clearly that young people are concerned as much with the issues as with the personality.

That is what is marvelous about the future. Whether they be hairy or shorn, whether they take their styles from Carnaby Street, Himalayan gurus, or off an Iowa farm, whether they strum guitars, carry placards, or bury their noses in books, they are a new breed, the like of which the world has not seen before.

It is useless to say, "Oh, they'll settle down. We were wild, too, when we were young," because the inescapable fact is with us that *the world is not the same as when we were young.* These kids know that, even if some of their elders haven't absorbed it yet.

They know that the atom bomb has made war a matter of survival or extinction. They know that automation and cybernation are revolutionizing our concepts of work and leisure and employment and purchasing power. They know the world is no longer the plaything of the "superior" white race, that people of color are refusing to be dominated any longer, and that peace with justice for all must be constructed.

They know the world is one little backyard planet in which man has to learn to get along with his fellows or there just won't be any more planet to get along in. This knowledge, this uncluttered acceptance of reality is what makes this new young generation different.

They are dedicating themselves to a world without war.

They are dedicating themselves to a world of justice for all people.

They are dedicating themselves to a world in which the individual may find purpose and growth for himself, on his own terms, according to his own abilities, talents and personal predilections.

Older toes are being stepped on. Older ideas are being scoffed at with impartial glee. Unquestionably it is painful. Unquestionably, the good old traditional baby is sometimes thrown out with the bad old traditional bath water. Unquestionably, it is distressing to have our own fears scorned and our own motives scrutinized, if we are "over thirty."

But these young people search for Integrity. They search for Reality. They search for Truth. In the process, what is sound will endure, and what is false will crumble away as it well should. These are tomorrow's leaders and the prospect is good.

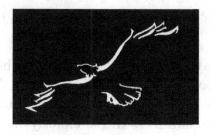

Vol. VI, NO. 4, April 1968

Beauty is a product of knowledge, wedded to

Wisdom through human perception.

(*Golden Scripts,* Chapter 96)

The Generation Gap

THE LEAST understood and the widest-spread process of polarization now going on in this sadly divided nation is the one called the Generation Gap.

The commonest complaints among the older generation: "What's gotten into these kids?" "I can't even talk too my son (or daughter) any more!" "What are they teaching them these days that they turn out so recalcitrant or rebellious? It surely isn't anything they're getting at home!"

Commonest complaints among the youngsters: "My parents are just absolutely out of it!" "They mean well but that just isn't enough." "Why on earth should we follow their advice when you look at the mess they've gotten us into?"

The common problem, of course, is lack of communication. They cannot talk together because they do not talk the same language. They use the same words, but with utterly different meanings. It is a matter of background, as if they came from completely different countries.

Those who say, "Oh kids are always the same. We were wild, too, when we were young. They'll settle down," are as much out of it as the smug parent who brags that his children think exactly as he does, and they'd just better not try thinking any different!

Kids are different from what their parents were at their age, different by astronomical measure. There are those who say that a different breed of child is being born these days, but this esoteric consideration is by no means necessary in explanation. Indeed those who say so may be quite unaware of the most relevant and significant fact: *The world is completely different from what it was in the days of their youth, even as short a time as thirty years ago.*

Of course there is more of everything: more people, more communication, more knowledge, more technology, but persons of forty to fifty (the common age to be coping with children of college age, or late teens) are inclined to think of new developments on a purely quantitative level. On the simple bases of there being more of everything, the problem appears to them as merely trying to cope with the increase.

Some jet plane passengers can remember one-horse power as the only way to get to town, in a buggy jolting along a shady gravel road. Many a grey-haired but dynamic executive dealing with a battery of push-buttons for inter-coms, telephones, dictating machines and PA systems can remember the little thrill of anticipation when the right ring came up on the party line! There are even dwellers in split-levels who remember washing lamp chimneys. (It wasn't a matter of poverty; the REA just hadn't gotten out that far yet). Most fifty-year-olds can remember the first time they ever heard a radio, either by earphone or a morning-glory horn. They can remember when an airplane passing overhead was worth remembering to tell the folks about when they got home.

This background has roots laid in a slower-paced, seemingly more stable, predictable world, the one that existed before World War II. Time was when one remembered back to real stability before World War I, so they tell us. Like almost everything else, it seems to be a relative matter.

But there can be no denial of the fact that there is a qualitative difference between the world before Hiroshima and the world after Hiroshima. It must be remembered that all babies born after 1945 have lived under the ghastly mushroom shadow, hearing talk since they were old enough to understand words of how the planet could suddenly cease to exist. For them there is no security, not even in memory.

For them the world is a tiny place, made so by jet planes, by communication satellites, by orbiting, man-propelled rockets, most especially by television. To them, television is not just another dimension added to their knowledge of the world as it is to older folk who have already gained their knowledge through reading. Television involves you in the here-and-now.

World-famed personalities become as familiar to a television viewer as members of his own family, sometimes more so. World leaders, national and international events, crises and tragedies, cultural milestones are no longer dependent on the imagination of a reader or the skill of a writer to glow with life or

325

die aborning. Through the TV screen you are *there*, if you wish to be. This is quite different qualitatively from any individual's view of the world even thirty years ago.

The whole concept of "work," of getting a job, has undergone a revolution in the past decade. Young people at both ends of the economic scale are aware that "getting a job" cannot be the sole end and purpose of life. College students know from studying the facts that automation, cybernation is undermining the whole traditional idea of planning one's life. They know that there are not enough jobs to go around even now, and that jobs are going to decrease instead of increase. The unfortunate have learned this hard fact by bitter experience. Both know that human beings must eat, must have shelter and clothes.

Both know that economic readjustments are inevitable in our society if it is to continue, and there is neither time nor excuse for hidebound thinking. Unemployment, in fact, is not just a temporary, passing thing to be coped with by government handout until the economy picks up once more and absorbs the jobless in another boom. This is a different matter qualifiedly from former days, even of the Great Depression.

All these factors, doomsday weapons, instant communication almost everywhere on the planet, revolutionary concepts of "work," explosions both in knowledge and people, constitute our young people's world, and it utterly lacks any memory of "good, old days" that might be returned to if things would only quiet down once more. Young people know that things are never going to be the same again. Revolutionary ferment is in the air, quite possibly much as it was during the Renaissance, which marked a similar though not so drastic a turning point in world history. Economics, politics, religion, education, in all these areas, the old rules are being tossed away as useless, old anchors no longer hold.

Because young people are after all as varied as their parents, they are reacting to this new environment in as many varied ways. There are always those who take life as it comes, doing what "authority" tells them, and leaving the thinking up to others.

Then there are those who have decided that there is little use in trying to change the old world as it stands. They are not concerned with making the effort. They are the "drop-outs" from society. They may join the "hippies" seeking Nirvana in unusual and sometimes destructive ways. Or they may look for companions in intentional communities who likewise feel alienated from the current stream of materialistic, success-intoxicated, status-seeking, middle-class Americans.

They may turn in disgust, resentment, frustration or pure inability to envision any other course to crime, rioting, vandalism, looting, any kind of violence in a blind effort to "get even" with a society that refuses to acknowledge their existence.

Insofar as they are able, all of these young people have resigned from the human race. They are not lost. Most will be responsive to a constructive idea that has any promise of success.

There are a good many others who are actively pursuing more idealistic goals. They are embarking on crusades to improve the world as best they may. Sometimes their crusades may appear ridiculous, unrealistic, perhaps shocking or unworthy. Sometimes their crusades are difficult, demanding and dangerous. Frequently they are required to stand up against the scorn and the sneers of their fellows, of their parents, of persons in "authority." Often they have risked life and limb and freedom to stand up for what they believed was right.

With Henry David Thoreau, one of their dearest idols, "they listen to a different drum."

The whole point being that a different drum is now beating, and it behooves all of us to listen to it. It is beating a roll on the other side of the Generation Gap and when older ears pick up the rhythm, the gap will begin to close!

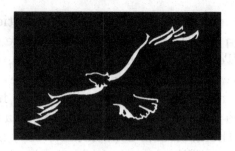

Vol. VI, No. 5, May 1968

"Every life, no matter how humble, no matter how

tragic, no matter how broken and thwarted

hath a meaning and an inner glory

and is precious in My sight."

(*Golden Scripts,* Chapter 7)

Right to Be Different

ONCE AGAIN, because it can't be emphasized too often, we take up the cudgels in behalf of the right to be different, the right to be an individual.

Americans have always taken pride in being the chief defenders of this theme, but of late years we are becoming its most ardent antagonists.

Harry Overstreet has given the high-sounding name of "empathetic provincialism" to a widespread malady which has always afflicted the human race, but which is only now reaching a stage of crisis. By it, we believe is meant the tendency to protect and defend only what one is familiar with. Strangeness, differentness, are by such definition unacceptable and wrong, and not to be allowed.

The Jews have long enjoyed the reputation of being God's chosen people. Having a good share of the force of the Old Testament behind their claim, it has been accepted by many non-Jews, with some remarkable interpretations. Many other non-Jews have fought such an idea aggressively to the point of asserting the claim for themselves, consciously, or more often, unconsciously, "Black power," "white supremacy," "yellow peril", all which are variations on the same theme. All are examples of "empathetic provincialism" in one form or another.

The fact is the world has gotten too small in the last couple of decades for any such pushiness of self-proclaimed superiority by class or group.

The great lesson, which must be learned in the next decade if civilization is to survive, is the true meaning of *individualism.*

All of us human beings are willy-nilly in this mortal experience together. All must learn to abide by some agreed-upon rules permitting us to get along with each other somehow. Otherwise, we face such violence and destruction as will sooner or later descend to anarchy and annihilation.

There is no question but that the white race has been more aggressive, more ambitious, and more clever in its self-aggrandizement. To this point in time, it has dominated any scene where the visible action is.

As colonialism vanishes from the globe, as non-white races make their bid for equal attention in the arena of world affairs, the white world's definition of "civilization of "civilization and "progress" is being seriously questioned. Advanced technology cannot be equated with advanced spirituality. As Eric Fromm has said, we are the Twentieth Century technologically but are still moving in the Stone Age spiritually.

We are learning the bitter lesson that we cannot equate technological development, material wealth, social status and the possession of countless gadgets with spiritual wisdom. Wars, riots, violence, mental and physical breakdown, the perils of upsetting natural balances, the upsurge of resentment and hate between classes, nations and races indicate that we have as yet learned little in answer to the great question now demanding response: "How do men learn to get along with each other so all may survive?"

We come back to the matter of individuality and America's unique role in its development. The United States has always clung happily to the myth of being a melting pot of the nations. That it has, in a sense, derived strength, resilience and self-reliance from blending of nationalities cannot be denied. However, in a large sense, the myth is false because it is not a universal melting pot as implied. The descendants of white Europeans alone dominate all American power structures. The Establishments of this nation, that is, those who hold and wield the power of government, who control the great monopolies that constitute our economic life, who set our cultural standards are predominantly white. Millions of our native-born citizens, whose family trees may have been for generations rooted in American soil, Indians, Negroes, those of Mexican or Oriental ancestry, are never credited with having any part whatsoever in our national heritage or our published history except as quaint or picturesque footnotes.

That day is over as non-white races here and across the earth begin to demand recognition and respect simply as human beings. Some white Americans, lost in a provincialism that may be fatal, want to blame the challenge to white domination on Communist subversion. Only communism, they argue, would arouse the Negro out of "his place," causing him to disrupt the status quo with his looting and burning. They fail to observe that this is an era of ferment unparalled in history, and that if we, all of us members of the race called human, are to survive it, we shall have had to recognize one great principle: Each human being will have to be taken at the value of what he alone as an individual contributes to society, regardless of his skin color, religion, social or economic position.

Individuality, the right and the basic need to be different, will have to be honored if we are to save ourselves from dictatorship, mass conformity, or domination by eternally warring factions.

The United States, long priding itself on being a melting pot can indeed, because of its widely diverse roots, demonstrate the solution to the greatest problem now afflicting the globe. It can, if enough of its citizens so choose, not only accept but encourage the infinite diversity of its people, and from this diversity draw unheard of strength spiritually and in wisdom.

The new "one-world" philosophy thus becomes not a leveling process wherein all difference are erased, all individuality forced to conform, but simply the basic acceptance that all human beings are different, have the right to be different, and *can* be different, provided that a majority of those human beings agree to accept each other on individual merit alone, agreeing to help the less fortunately endowed to better themselves and also agreeing to restrain the more aggressive from illegal usurpation of power.

Such respect for differenceness, for individuality, not only is part and parcel of the true heritage of America, but is in fullest accord with the deepest urges of the human heart in its search for identity. It is the preservation of such differences that colors and enriches human experience, expanding, the consciousness and the mind. The United States of America, drawing its composite culture from the many diverse cultures of the earth, can serve as a model, if it so wills, for the fullest, most colorful, most exciting form of mortal existence yet to be lived.

We are still a long way from such an agreed-upon goal, but if this world is to be kept intact, if its inhabitants are to flourish and grow, we shall have to accept nothing less!

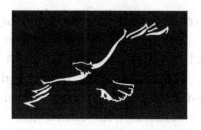

Vol. VI, No. 6, June 1968

Beauty is the Divine Ideal in process of revealment

through spirirtual perception

(Golden Scripts, Chapter 96)

Welcoming Change

THERE SEEMS to be, in all the full Niagara of self-reproach, recrimination, and honest soul-searching which has followed the two assassination straining our recent history, a shying away from any consideration of real and meaningful change which would remove the root causes of the violence we so earnestly deplore.

The good citizens of San Francisco are asked to turn in their guns voluntarily. The brutality on TV screens is excoriated. The President of the United States begs us, "for God's sake, to cast out our violence from our hearts." But all exhortations end up with the affirmation that "our institutions" must be preserved. It is as though all public concerns in the nation were organized exactly as they should be, perfect and whole and sacred, and it is only ungrateful and troublesome citizens who keep rocking the boat, not only dangerously but unnecessarily.

It is in the nature of elected leadership to avoid all notion of change. Every Congressman and appointed

335

official is naturally interested in keeping his job. The simplest way followed by most is to exhort their electorates and the general public with the tried and true old clichés, pointing with pride and viewing with alarm, but most carefully avoiding all contact with lean and hungry Cassiuses who think too much, because such men are patently dangerous to the jobs of office-holders.

Change is the bugbear of the ruling body of any state, never to be sought voluntarily, always to be approached with quick objection and dragging heels, then, when avoidable, to be pummeled, devitalized and whittled into shapeless molds. "Our institutions must be preserved," at whatever cost to the people.

Aquila has no desire to seek change for its own sake. Life is too complex and too dangerous in these combustible days to tip over apple carts just to see the apples roll. What disturbs Aquila is the failure of leadership generally even to recognize change that has already happened, let alone what impends, with consequence failure to recommend the necessary new directions in which we must move in order to cope with these changes successfully, indeed to survive.

The greatest legacy of the Kennedy brothers is that in daring publicly to recognize and welcome change, they gave others the courage also to recognize it, coupled with the faith that the unknown future was just as likely to be beneficial as disastrous, if we applied ourselves constructively to it. However, even they were practical politicians enough to realize that to be elected they had to promote change always "within the framework of our institutions."

336

Aquila is not running for office. Neither is a member of the Old Left, the New Right, nor the Middle-of-the-Road, where someone has pointed out that the yellow stripe is found. Aquila therefore feels quite free to ask, "What are these institutions that must be so zealously guarded? Our political system with its electoral abuses, its patronage, lobbying and corruption? The military-industrial complex that is endeavoring frantically to keep us eternally geared to a war economy just short of going up in the mushroom cloud?

A social system which contains 30 million poor people and, according to one of Robert Kennedy's last statements, a billionaire who paid only $500 in income tax, or which provides its full share of the world's reserve of 30,000 pounds of TNT for every man, woman and child on earth, as Norman Cousins points out, without a compensating reserve for each of 30,000 pounds in food, medicine, clothes or books?

A private banking system that has led us into public debt approaching 3 trillion dollars and a private debt of over 900 billion dollars? Our great universities, which tremble on the brink of anarchy and dissolution? Our school systems, or our hospitals, or our penal institutions which are understaffed, underhoused, underequipped, underfinanced and underconsidered at all times?

Our fantastically wealthy and powerful corporations where the action truly is, at the expense of every farmer, small businessman, taxpayer and consumer in the country? Are these among the institutions to be preserved intact and unmodified?"

Aquila suggest that as a people we begin to develop the wisdom to differentiate between our ideals and our institutions, and that we begin to develop the courage to insist that our leadership do the same. The sooner we recognize that most of our "institutions" have either become crystallized by the timid, albeit stubborn, defenders of the status quo, or have been taken over by unscrupulous self-seekers or have grown so enormous as to have lost all touch with the individual human beings which they are supposed to serve, the sooner we will be in a better position to give them all a careful re-appraisal and where needed, a thorough overhaul. It is not our institutions, which need preserving so much as our people, and the hour is late.

As long as the preservation of institutions is put ahead of the preservation of people, we may expect that violence will continue in our nation till all institutions are indeed destroyed and our society along with them.

However, before that time comes, Aquila dares to believe that a leader or a group of leaders will stand forth in the nation and declare themselves *for* the people, *all* the people simply as human beings, all possessed of the same basic hopes and desires, the same basic needs and satisfactions. These leaders will suggest how new institutions may be built, based on cooperation instead of competition, on justice and equity instead of privilege and power, on abundance instead of scarcity, on peace instead of war, on respect for life instead of brutality and violence. They will begin to give us new direction and new purpose.

In a climate of unified purpose, clear direction, and high resolve, our passion for old and worn-out institutions will fade away before our enthusiasm for better ones to take their place.

It will not be easy. More assassins' bullets may fly, more buildings burn, more innocent victims suffer loss of life and property as the status-quoers fight to a last ditch before the gates opening on a new age.

The degree to which disruption and bloodshed may be avoided in making necessary social change is directly related to the speed at which the citizens can be *enlightened* about the underlying causes of all our dilemmas and as to what constructive *alternatives* exist that can and must be embraced.

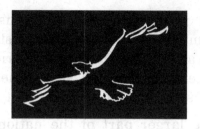

Vol. VI, No. 7 & 8, July & August 1968

Beauty is God expressing Himself to matter,

by and to your spiritual consciousness.

(Golden Scripts, Chapter 96)

How to Answer

SOME MONTHS ago a song was given much radio and TV time that was called *Who Will Answer?* The song highlighted most graphically individual cases of distress and portrayed the insanity of a people unprotestingly marching to mass annihilation through nuclear war. But it wasn't the anguish of the individual nor the wiping out of mankind in one blinding flash of destruction that lingered in one's consciousness after, long after, the singer finished.

The real emotional wallop in the song was simply the plea, "Who will answer?" It was a direct challenge to the individual's own conscience.

It is too much of a generalization to state that the majority of the people have so drifted into apathy and indifference that they have become immune to both suffering and danger. For one thing there is increasing evidence that more and more people, both young and "over thirty," are involving themselves in grappling with the nation's most serious problems. Realistic

341

analysis even recognizes that all forms of rebellion, however we might be superficially disturbed by the hippies, the draft-card burners and the rioters, must be identified as responses to the sham, the needless war and the oppression throughout our society.

Right now the larger part of the nation is aware, at least statistically, of the suffering and injustices endured by tens of millions of its citizens. But this is just the first step. There has to be empathetic sensitivity. As Michael Harrington stated in his book *The Other America,* people have to become "angered" over the brutal condition of millions being forced to live in squalor and isolated from the rest of society.

Harrington was simply emphasizing that one has to *feel* the predicament of those in the ghettos, the Appalachias and the Indian reservations of the nation and react as if one were one of the victims.

There is an Indian saying that goes, "Don't judge an Indian until you have walked four moons in his moccasins." How applicable this admonition is in considering the plights of all fellow human beings!

Recognition of the problem and then sensitivity to the problem are the first steps. But this is only half the picture. For example, a person might happen along a highway just as a car loaded with passengers plunges over a railing into the water. No matter how much he recognizes the nature of the situation, no matter how much he shares the grave feelings of those trapped in the car, if he cannot swim he is unequipped to give assistance.

He cannot *answer* because he does not know *how* to answer.

342

The same is true in regard to all distresses whether we are dealing with individuals, with our own nation, or with the world. People have to be equipped with workable solutions. Nations have to be equipped with workable solutions. The vital question, therefore, is not so much who will answer but how to answer.

The corollary, of course, is that there will be neither lack of courage nor a lack of direct involvement when people recognize the "how" of solving their problems.

It is most encouraging to us that more and more people are directing their attention to the underlying causes of the problems instead of just dealing with symptoms. That they are rising above centuries of racial prejudice. Above all, they are recognizing that all people are inherently good but that bad systems corrupt all people irrespective of their station in the society.

We at Aquila know that at last there is real hope for the nation. That hope is based on the fact that there is increased concentration on the *how to answer*. Out of this concerted thinking will be presented the kind of an America in which every person is a winner and there are no losers.

A constructive force for change is building in America, which cannot be deterred. The rallying point of that force is the love of man and not his hatred!

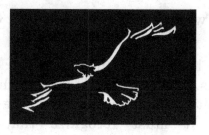

Vol. VI, No. 9, September 1968

So be it, beloved . . . Courage is your watchword! . . .

Stamina is your shibboleth! . . . Action is

your tocsin!

(*Golden Scripts,* Chapter 98)

Imperatives

ONE NEED, above all else, up here in the closing years of the Sixties, is for a new breed of leadership. The nation is on half a dozen collision courses and is headed for breakdown and collapse unless new courses are charted. A new sense of direction, bolstered by tangible goals, is the urgency of the moment.

The gaps between the rich and the poor, the young and the old, the blacks and the whites, the government and the governed, the revolutionaries and the status-quo'ers, have grown so deep that something dynamic in the way of leadership is imperative to dissolve the fear, hate and bitterness that increases hourly between each group, to turn the energies each group wastes in fighting the other into constructive channels where all may benefit.

It is a truism to say that leadership must have dedication, vision and courage. The important thing is dedication to what? Vision to see what? Courage to do what?

The needed leadership must first be dedicated to human beings. It must be leadership that recognizes that all rights are inherent with the birth of an individual. It must recognize that institutions, technology and tools have no purpose in themselves except as they improve people. It must recognize that governments are expressly for the purpose of insuring that inherent rights are protected equally for each and every citizen, irrespective of race or national origin.

The needed leadership must have the vision to encompass the kind of abundant life this nation could enjoy if its productive potential could be employed constructively. Simultaneously, it must have the vision to see where the bottlenecks and restraints exist in the socio-economic system preventing the full utilization of the nation's resources and ingenuity in creating a wholesome, prosperous and safe life for the entire citizenry.

However, it must be a vision that goes beyond our own borders, that focuses on all of humanity. In the pocket-handkerchief world created by modern technology, there is no room for narrow chauvinism or egotistical flag-waving. For the United States to be considered the most powerful country on earth means equally that she must carry the responsibility for sane and wise and altruistic action. Our thinking must be reversed from "What is best for America is best for the world," to "What is best for the world is best for America."

Without detracting in the slightest from America's heritage, or her ideals, or her own national sovereignty, it is possible to think of her as one among many other nations, each having it own sovereign identity.

It is further possible to envision a cooperative world where peace is a reality because there is a mutuality of understanding and respect among all races. It is the *human* race itself, which now stands on the brink of possible destruction, not just a nation or a people. It is the safety, security and happiness of a whole world to which we must raise our sights, and any leadership that hopes to succeed in saving this nation must be so globally dedicated.

But dedication and vision are not sufficient in themselves. They must be coupled with courage. For all the dedication, and all the vision, in the world have little meaning if they are not put into action. Men are political slaves who either in ignorance or in fear dare not seek and achieve that change which will improve the well being of themselves and their fellowmen. Courageous leadership can be neither deterred nor stilled until justice has both substance and universality.

John Kennedy gave us a glimpse of what such leadership might be. It was only a glimpse and no one can say whether or not his leadership might have held up to the enormous pressures to which it would have been subjected. His own death may indeed demonstrate how great those pressures are. What is important here and now is how the people responded to it. It was like a new day dawning. But it did not fully dawn and black night closed in again. The real dawn will yet come.

The American people are ready for new and inspired and courageous leadership into that new day. A really new day. Not a warmed-over, rehashed, patched-up re-working of an outmoded system.

They need to be led from a senseless and extremely dangerous wrangling over where to place the blame for the past mistakes into a viable, cooperative, dynamic new approach to the business of living, in which every citizen by right of birth becomes a willing and energetic participant as he comes to understand how the welfare of all are inextricably intertwined.

We shall seek out and encourage that new brand of leadership in the troubled days ahead and we shall do all within our power to let that leadership be heard!

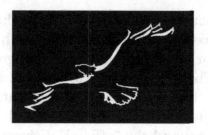

Vol. VI, No. 10, October 1968

Event succeedeth event, always with change, but

out of the stillness cometh a whisper: The Voice

of Change Is the voice of the Eternal; let him

heed it who Would run his course!

(*Golden Scripts,* Chapter 100)

On With the New

THE HISTORY of mankind is one long search for Truth. The efforts men have spent in this search are almost equally by their efforts to cover it up. Almost, but not quite, Thus do we make progress through the ages. Thus have we continued to exist. If the search for truth had not been at least one degree more successful than the effort to cover it up, we would long since have perished from the earth.

Periodically, history seems to be convulsed by years of disturbance, revolution and disbelief. Odd as it may be, these uncomfortable years are more likely to be the honest years, and the years of man's greatest advance, just as civilization seems most apt to come apart at the seems.

Mankind seems able to contain itself with a degree of stability (it is a process of crystallizing, really). For periods of about four hundred years when it goes off again into a century that boils over with heresies and revolutions, eras of fundamental change in attitudes and mores. The last previous one would have been the beginning of the Protestant movement, which very closely coincided with the technological breakthrough of movable type, and the "official" discovery of the New World. A very exciting century to have lived in, from 1450 to 1550, and very like our own.

We are going through another such convulsion now from 1950 to 2050. The woods are full of heretics, disbelievers, troublemakers, and upsetters of the status quo. All are carefully built-up institutions and mores which have been developing and then crystallizing since 1500 are now up for question again. The winds of change have once more begun to blow a gale. We cannot allow ourselves to be too astonished, nor too outraged. Only thus do we advance. How great is our depth of vision to see and understand how basic are these changes?

Traditional war becomes impossible with the advent of the doom machines. We shall have to figure out how to live at peace or not at all.

Traditional politics are about to be shaken up as our bluff is being called on the nature of democracy. We shall have now to make it real and workable, painful as this may be to the present monopolists of power.

Traditional economics is about to be stood on its head as our time-hallowed concepts of the relationship between labor and its reward are tossed overboard by the advent of automation-cybernation. We are going to have to find and adopt a more workable ethic than the one we call "Protestant."

350

Traditional concepts of education, that is the young learning from their elders, are blowing up in our faces because the young all to frequently know more about what is going on than their well-meaning but hide-bound elders. Old and young will have *to learn* to learn together.

Traditional concepts of religion are shattering before the onslaught of iconoclasts who cannot in honesty accept the mythology and dogma of the ancient church. Religion is not dying. It simply needs re-stating in fresh terms of logic and integrity.

And out of this turmoil are born brand new approaches to the whole business of living.

As old facts are reassembled in a new way, as new facts are uncovered at an unbelievable geometric rate, old concepts and old explanations crumble. If any of us knew all the answers, we should probably no longer be on earth, because the business of life seems to be the digging out of those answers. Human beings, limited by the three dimensions of mortal experience, are capable of absorbing only so much at a time.

One of life's most profound lessons is contained in John Godfrey Saxe's poem about the blind men of Hindustan who tried to discover what the elephant was. For each it differed from the description of his fellows, according to his own experience. Thus truth comes to each of us in different ways, each of us perceiving it as best we may, but only in fragments. Difficulty arises, of course, when each of us insists we have found the whole answer, the absolute truth.

Bearing this in mind, it is well not to become too alarmed with the disordered state of today's world.

Barring some insane gesture of defiance that blows us all to Kingdom Come, we shall find ourselves presently on the other side of the stormy period with enhanced perceptics of what life may be all about, what our purposes on this small mudball may be, a little nearer to seeing and understanding the great, shadowy outline of the elephant that constitutes our Absolute.

For those who want to seek truth for its own sake, who really want to know, who welcome the chance to analyze and learn and make sense of this apparently crazy business of living, this is a period of challenge and growth and freedom of opportunity which it may be counted a privilege to be a part of.

Now is the time for commitment, for involvement, for participating as never before, and we should call ourselves lucky to be living at this moment!

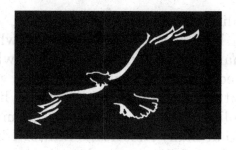

Vol. VI, No. 11, November 1968

Horns blow! Music riseth! The hearts of the

Faithful burst with rejoicings!

(Golden Scripts, Chapter 102)

A Question of Who Plans

THE LEAD editorial in a recent issue of *The Indianapolis Star* is entitled "Collective America." It provides the background for us to counteract some of the more insidious attacks on all who promote any form of incorporation of the nation's economy. While the *Star* is ultra-rightist, thus viewing with contempt anyone questioning the infallibility of private capitalism, the points it raises are characteristic of many defenders of the status quo in our society.

It is not surprising to find in the initial paragraph of the editorial the insinuation that all engaged in promoting any idea of coordinating national production are to be found in "the new left, the old left and a legion of large but uncertain numbers of socialism." To make sure the reader doesn't fail to paint all such advocates of social reform as being "communistic," a paragraph follows that ties in all their thinking with that of Karl Marx and Nicolai Lenin.

353

To the enlightened, the foregoing is, of course, stereotyped handling of any and all who advance economic change whereby the people, the whole people, would be economically sovereign and would have absolute control in shaping their economic lives, as well as their political lives. However, it must not be discounted that many Americans fall for editorials like that of the *Star,* failing to realize that the prejudiced and untrue presentation is deliberately calculated to distract the reader from considering those steps which would lead to his true freedom and prosperity.

Having disposed of all proponents of a "planned economy" as bad, yes, very bad, the editorial now proceeds to use the oldest subtlety in the books for discrediting opposition. It is the trick of accusing the opposed point of view with being guilty of the very thing that the accuser is actually guilty of. Only the unwary and the uninformed are obviously taken in by this type of persuasion.

First, we are told that if American production were to be done in "one huge, coordinated operation," it would mean "the death of the free market and freedom of choice for the consumer." The absurdity of this charge is evident by the fact that the "free market" has already been destroyed long since by monopoly in every field of production in this nation. With less than 200 giant monopolies and conglomerates controlling, owning and directing two-thirds of the nation's entire productive potential, and the pace of concentration accelerating, any contention that we now have equal competition in a free market indicates a lack of even elementary observation.

354

As to "freedom of choice," it hardly deserves mention. The consumers in this nation buy what the monopolies put on the market. They not only pay for all the obsolescence built into the products but they pay the administered prices that provide for an estimated 80% of the monopolies expansion.

Secondly, we are informed by the editorial that under a planned economy, criticism "must be eliminated, for any serious negative comment or criticism would undermine the authority of the planners and thus endanger the entire system." This accusation of no criticism is as asinine as that of destroying an "open market" that has already been destroyed. The very nature of monopoly is to remove itself above criticism. It is monopoly, not only economic but political and financial, throughout our whole society that has created an environment within which it is quite acceptable to agree but quite out of order to disagree.

In closing, the editorial raises what they must consider their most devastating argument. It states: "Now the question arises who will select the planners? They will necessarily have to be superior men of extremely high intelligence, morality, judgment, integrity, honor, foresight and general competence. It is our honest and studied opinion that those who advocate a planned economy can visualize only themselves as having sufficient brains, mettle and character to fill such sensitive and all-powerful roles."

Since the editorial has already characterized all such advocates in one lump as "leftists" and subscribers to "isms" foreign to America, the reader should conclude, of course, that both the ides for, and promoters of, any nationally incorporated economy should be thrown in the nearest ashcan.

The whole fallacy and weakness of the editorial can be challenged very simply: If it is quite proper and constructive in principle for monopolistic corporations, performing in both volume and power as "governments" within out society, to plan production down to the smallest detail in the interests of only a few, why is it then wrong or un-American for the entire sovereign people to use the same principle of incorporation to coordinate the nation's resources, tools and know-how to produce the necessities and comforts for the majority? Of course, the answer must unreservedly be, it is not.

In fairness to the editorial, it must be noted that it centered its thinking on Big Government doing the planning and coordinating. Perhaps wittingly or unwittingly, it didn't want to give recognition to the basic feature of a Corporate Commonwealth which provides for, not State planning, but a sovereign people, as voting and dividend-receiving stockholders, democratically owning and directing their own nation's economy. We, too, are opposed to over-lording government. The ironical fact is, however, that it is monopolists, owning and directing the nation's military-industrial complex that at present dictates the major policies on all levels of government.

Free enterprise, open market, free choice and all other identifications of a free society can only be achieved when all restraints can be removed from utilization of the nation's full productive potential and all production is geared to the good life of all and not for increasing profits and control for the few.

Increasing rebellion is fomenting throughout the nation. Only if the power structures show a tangible disposition to accept major social and economic reform can safety and justice become actualities in the nation.

No, the monopolists of the society have no objection to planning *per se*. They are only opposed to persons other than themselves doing the planning and coordinating!

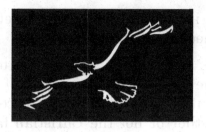

Vol. VI. No. 12, December 1968

I tell you of truths that make for your heads a resting

place upon the bosom of the infinite; I tell you of

truths to come as a blessing to your hearts,

redeeming your sacrifice in flesh.

(*Golden Scripts,* Chapter 103)

A Relevant Religion

AT THIS one period of the year when all Christians come closest together in acknowledging their faith, it is not uplifting to consider that the essential meaning and teaching of Jesus' life is completely subordinated to the glorification of the Manger Story.

This is understandable. The Babe in the Manger does not represent a threat either in conscience or a way of life. Almost everyone is in favor of babies, and the Christmas Story, beginning so inauspiciously and ending so gloriously, must have universal appeal to all struggling humanity that seeks deliverance from its own problem.

Strange, is it not, that the rest of the year Christians can be divided so sharply in their belief and faith? Or, perhaps what is strange is that so much of His message yet remains after almost two millennia of translation, interpolation, interpretation, misinterpretation, rationalizing and theological wrangling!

We are come, here in the late 1960s, to a very real dividing of the ways in interpretation of His message, as the institutionalized church is discovering to its dismay. Whether or not the Christian faith is to mix itself deeper and deeper into the hurly-burly of the world, or whether it is to withdraw itself more and more, becomes a question upon which the Christian church of all denominations may tear itself asunder.

The more responsible young people upon whom will devolve the running of this planet as their elders retire from it are less fragmented over the question than those elders themselves are at present.

Many of them have simply foresworn their allegiance to any kind of formal religion. They are, however, dedicating their lives to a service that emulates Jesus' teaching much more closely than their church-going parents ever undertook.

"Woe unto ye, Scribes and Pharisees, hypocrites" they cry, as they take up the scourge of small cords to drive the money-changers from the Temple. They have, in the words of a later poet, "sounded forth the trumpet that shall never call retreat. They are sifting out the hearts of men before the Judgment Seat." This is a crucial moment, for these young people are set upon an irreversible path.

They have not really foresworn religion at all if we take the definition offered by Bishop Crowther: "Man's entire view of his transcendental self." What they *have* foresworn is the dogma, ritual and crystallized theology of organized churchianity, which they see as meaningless and irrelevant to the demands of our times.

There are many other people (not all of them) who have not left the church, but who see the need for a changed emphasis in its message, and in its meaning. These are they who find inspiration and constructive food for thought in a new and amorphous movement known at the "Underground Church." Without formal organization or hierarchy, without defined doctrine except the Eleventh Commandment, many ministers and priests are beginning to associate themselves with it. Its chief concern is to make religion relevant and useful in the solving of war, racism, poverty, alienation and ignorance.

The shadow of Jesus stands tall over this group, not as a deliverer to the dubious joys of a sugar-candy heaven, and certainly not as scapegoat for the sins and inhumanities of centuries of human ignorance and error, but instead as teacher and as social reformer, as champion of justice, and as upsetter of crystallized and dehumanized institutions.

Jesus, even in Scripture, was after all a revolutionary figure, a consorter with publicans and sinners, an unorthodox healer, a champion of the outcast, of the poor, underprivileged and downtrodden, an opposer of the Establishments of His day, whether Jewish or Roman, and an advocate of conscience above mortal law.

Should He suddenly reappear on earth again in mortal form, without question He would be rejected by the Establishment of our own day.

This is one of the keys to the conflict. Establishments are solidified, codified, systematic, crystallized, dehumanized, carefully structured organizations, deliberately concentrated amalgamations of power whose wielders conserve but do not create. However, it seems to be the nature and perhaps the sole purpose of mankind to create on all levels, to grow and expand indivdually and collectively in this mortal arena. Thus when the power of conservation attempts to outweigh the power to create, oppression results. And after oppression, revolution, as the creative power refuses to be held back in an impossible status quo.

Jesus, whether in the reality of myth or in very literal terms, was an upsetter of existing institutions, and a troublemaker, a disturber of public order. In his tradition, if not always of it, came Martin Luther, Rousseau, Tom Paine, Gandhi and Martin Luther King, bringing not peace, in life's most difficult paradox, but a sword.

"King deserved what he got!" exclaimed a young man of our acquaintance. "Trouble and riot followed him wherever he went." So this young man two thousand years ago would have shouted for the release of Barabbas instead of that "maker of seditions."

"I tremble," said Thomas Jefferson, "when I reflect that God is just."

Have we learned anything at all in twenty centuries? We are racing at breakneck speed toward the unknown answer!

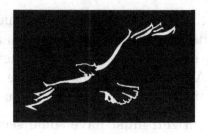

Vol. VII, No. 2, February 1969

What went ye forth to seek, the avenues of goodly hopes,

or the roads of circumscription that make you to

know no resting place that hath luxury in it

while there are trudgers in hot sunshine?

(*Golden Scripts,* Chapter 105)

An Eye to the Future

LIFE, IDEALLY, should be so ordered that all of us receive justice, not just legal justice, but political and economic justice as well. There will be no law and order in this land or anywhere on this planet very soon if such justice is not achieved.

Each individual must have a meaningful stake in this nation, a reason for caring, for making the effort. He must feel identified with it, to feel sorrow at its troubles and joy at its progress. He must feel that *his* work and *his* effort was toward goals that identify him with his counry, and with him.

Somehow, pride and pleasure in being an American should flow within him naturally, not because it is a rich, proud and powerful country, but simply because he loves it, and has reason to love it. Individuals from time to time feel such an emotion now, but it is not a national spirit. It has not been so for many years. Of late, Americans, many of them, have been ashamed of their country, or have resented it, or they have begun to ignore it. An *esprit de corps* must be re-awakened, and it can be, if the goals are clearly defined.

Ideally, every citizen must have some security, enough to prevent panic or apathy or despair. We are a very long way from solving all of our problems, but we are in a position for the first time in human history to meet the demands of our citizens for the necessities of life. In other words, the great benefit of our technology is the potential for the creation of an economy of abundance instead of the economy of scarcity, which has kept man struggling for survival since the dawn of time.

Thus it is possible for man to have now at least sufficient security to be sure of not starving to death, or freezing to death, or wandering homeless and hungry. There is no need for anyone in our technically advanced civilization to be subjected to a fear, a deprivation that corrodes his spirit, and leads him either into hopeless apathy or desperate violence.

This is the most exciting thing in the world when you stop to think about it. Mankind has turned its greatest corner since its advent on this planet. Its main pre-occupation no longer needs to be physical survival. IBM has hit the keynote: "Machines should work. Men should think." However, adjustments in purchasing power and distribution must be made before such benefits will accrue properly to all persons.

Ideally, life should provide every human with a chance to grow, physically, mentally and spiritually at his own pace to the fullest extent of his own capacity. This means that education should not only be available for as long and as intensively as any individual may want, but it must also be made inviting, and desirable, so that it will entice all people to make the growth and flowering of their minds a delightful and invigorating and continuing experience throughout their lives.

And lastly, life should be so ordered that every individual has the chance to earn the enjoyment of the good things that large numbers of Americans only dream about now. Good homes, travel, recreation, and some, at least, of those things deemed luxuries that only a few enjoy today, largely by the accident of fortunate birth.

Life today does not provide any of these basic necessities to a large segment of the American people. Cultural deprivation is a growing disease in the nation which will take years to remedy, but which we must undertake if we are to continue to exist, let alone grow.

We are, day unto day, with the merging of one great corporation after another into larger and larger units, approaching the Great Corporation status. It becomes a question as to owns the stock in this Great Corporation. Under present trends, fewer and fewer person are coming to own and control the stock. The laws of the Jungle, dog-eat-dog, maintain and to the most powerful and the least scrupulous go the rewards.

This trend must be reversed before the resentments and the needs of more and more alienated Americans become so strong that we are plunged into chaos, bloody civil war and anarchy.

For self-preservation, as well as a matter of simple justice and common sense, the adjustments will have to be made and eventually all Americans will come to their rightful heritage of all the wealth bestowed on this land by the Creator, and all the technological know-how and all the blood, sweat and tears poured into it by all our ancestors back through the centuries. God built no fences around His bounty to us. Neither does man simply by inheritance or guild have the right to deny any of his fellows the opportunity to enjoy the fruits the labors of all our ancestors who together built this land into what it is today.

Congress will either permit the necessary reforms, both in its own rules and in the laws of the land, to be made or it will be destroyed in the holocaust that burns all our institution and traditions to cinder and ash. The warning is clear. The changes that make for the new era are on their way and no amount of obstruction or repression will hold them back. Like the oak seedling dropped in the cranny of the boulder which eventually splits it in two, so the power of growth will not be held back.

Are the old gentlemen who rule the Congress with an iron hand prepared to accept change? If they are not, let us prepare to send men to represent us who do understand what is happening in the world and who will know how to help us look after our best interests through the period of change.

There are those who are going to object and obstruct, to fight tooth and claw against any change at all. In addition to the opposition of the defenders of the status quo who fear change for its own sake, there will be opposition from those whose livelihood comes now from inherited and unearned wealth. The thought that they might be called upon to earn their right to luxury will not be welcome.

Scheming stockholders who *control* the giant corporate conglomerates (not the many individuals who hold a handful of shares) will not willingly give up their power.

The manipulators of money, those who make fabulous livings from the control of money and credit and from lending it out as interest-bearing debt, will not be eager to give up their parasitical livelihood. The corporate managers, the established politicians, the players with power for its own sake will not welcome the sound of a whistle that calls their last play.

These are desperate times, and we shall have to recognize that our help will not come from those now in positions of power. One thing alone can save the nation and its people. One force alone holds power equal to the present power of money and position. This is the power of the people themselves. Across the length and breadth of this land, the sleeping giant which is the power of the people must be awakened and put to work to clear away the injustices and the obstructions that plague us.

To every American citizen who desires to live in freedom and in peace, who wants even to survive on the good green earth, the call must go out, not to rise in anger and revenge, but to stand up and be counted as a searcher for simple justice.

We need not concern ourselves with trying to place blame. Time is too short to fritter it away in such useless wrangling. It is the system that is at fault and no one of us can be sure how we ourselves would act if the mantle of great and undeserved power hung from our own shoulders. The only safe solution is the dispersal of that mantle of power across the whole body politic, permitting the checks and balances to act in favor of all as they should, and not in the favor of a fortunate few.

Many years ago, Victor Hugo said, "No army can withstand the power of an idea whose time has come!" The time for the idea of true justice has arrived. Black and white, the poor and the rich, Jew and Gentile, the young and the old, conservative and liberal, all can stand together and demand an end to the great game of power-grabbing that has been going on unchecked for generations.

All can stand together as individual citizens to demand their rights to life, liberty and a chance at the pursuit of happiness that can be ours in the days of great promise that lie ahead!

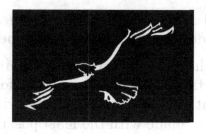

Vol. VII, No. 3, March 1969

We give strong embrace to the cohorts of justice; we

open our hearts to the goodly intent and perceive

when the righteous would call us unto phalanx.

(Golden Scripts, Chapter 107)

Nowhere To Go But Up!

THE REASON for Aquila's existence is to advance and promote the idea of a Corporate, Cooperative Commonwealth as outlined in the book **No More Hunger.** The theme of this book is that the pattern of the corporate structure, which has been so successful for the few, should be adapted and extended for the benefit of the entire body of citizens. We grant that this is a radical idea, but we consider the problems facing this nation and the world to be of a most radical nature, and only radical solutions will serve.

It is our studied opinion that if the idea of some sort of Cooperative Commonwealth is not adopted, then sooner or later vast catastrophes will descend upon the nations of the earth, brought about purely and simply by human beings themselves because, due to greed, ignorance, apathy or pure laziness, they were unwilling to make changes and adjustments in their own attitudes and behavior that their own cleverness in technological development has deemed inevitable.

In short, if the human race is not going to commit physical, mental or spiritual suicide, it follows that we must be about the business of discovering how these changes may be made with the least possible stress and strain.

Disaster is not far off. The Age of Anxiety has moved inevitably forward into the Age of Protest. Few inhabitants of this small planet are satisfied with the Way Things Are. If they are not protesting war, poverty, taxes, censorship, bureaucracy, regimentation, communism, capitalism, atheism, orthodoxy, injustice, moral decay or a score of other blights, they are busy protesting the protestors.

Wars, riots, crime, vandalism, bigotry, materialism, all destructive of what are considered moral virtues, are on the increase all over the world. Traditional bulwarks of ethical behavior and thought are deteriorating; ancient codes and mores are melting away. Few constructive goals of sufficiently wide appeal are being offered to hold civilization back from a long, downward slide into oblivion.

Aquila offers the Cooperative Commonwealth idea and invites challenge to its feasibility and high purpose. If a better, more far-reaching, and equitable solution exists for man's economic and sociological problems, we would be glad to hear of it, and we would be happy to dedicate ourselves to its promotion instead. So far, a better idea has not been brought to our attention.

We cannot go back, as so many of our older, more conservative citizens would like to do, to a stabler and less confusing age. The poor, the Negroes, the young people of the nation are not to be pushed back into the box and the lid put on again. The nature of warfare in the atomic age now makes it impossible to stir unified patriotic fervor at the wave of a flag.

American prosperity becomes a hollow mockery to the thousands living in Appalachia and rural Mississippi and the ghettoes of every city in the nation. The old slogans and the old symbols and the old clichés have lost their power to sway and unify. We cannot go back.

We cannot escape, as the "hippies" half-heartedly hope to do, or as the many well-meaning founders of "intentional communities" hope. The "system" will not permit individual escape. Any individual or group of individuals who reject today's materialism and conformity is doomed by the inevitable encroachment of, and absorption into, the large community. Such individual or small-group rejection of today's society also of necessity must reject the potential benefits of that society in advanced technology and the possibility of abundance that such technology offers. This is going backward with a vengeance!

If we cannot go backward and we cannot escape, we have no choice but to go forward into an unknown future, which holds both promise and peril. We can have no sure chart of that future, except the new and startling awareness that the future *can* be shaped by ourselves, depending on how we decide to think and act and *be*. The world is suddenly too small for anyone to rock the boat for his own selfish purposes.

Such would-be rockers must have it brought home to them that they not only endanger others, they invite annihilation on their own heads. The world has

371

awakened to a new self-consciousness, and never again can man go seeking his own fortune without considering whom he is thereby disadvantaging.

The disadvantaged may now see and resent and wrest back with violence and a shattering vengeance. The ancient code of many faiths, which we call the Golden Rule, becomes now not just an empty and often-mouthed aphorism, but a stern and binding guide to self-preservation.

The old ideologies are out of date. The rugged individulism of capitalism has now become a mad-dog-eat-dog race to ruin, with power resting in the hands of the hardiest and the most ruthless few. The statism of communism weakens in the face of human individuality demanding recognition, and as the machine supplants the workers of the world. The iron hand of Communist dictatorship cannot survive as a monolith among the varied cultures of the world. We have need of new goals, new visions and new ideals.

Human beings for millennia have sought ways to escape the drudgery of hard labor. They have at last, through the development of their own technology succeeded in finding that escape. Human beings have sought for centuries to gain, each man for himself and his family, more than a mere subsistence. Again, man's own ingenuity has, through technology, opened the way to provide far more than the bare necessities for every human being.

Above all, human beings have always sought ways in which each might make his mark in the world as his talents and ability permitted. This desire has not yet been fulfilled, indeed, its frustration lies at the root of most of our troubles. With a new approach to the economic structure, with the assumption by each individual of his rightful equity both in Nature's bounty and in government's power, with the incentive of added gains for constructive contribution to his own society, a solution to this problem can be reached as well.

The moment a sufficient number of us decide to take for our slogan, "cooperation" instead of "competition," when our leaders decide to use the power of moral suasion instead of brute force, when each of us begins, one by one, to lift our heads and to walk as human and civilized beings instead of brute savages or beasts of burden, at that moment we shall have turned the corner into a New Order on earth.

We may be thankful that we yet have our choosings, but the time is growing short. We shall not have a second chance on this earth!

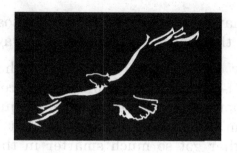

Vol.VII, No. 5, April 1969

Thence cometh Matter, that Spirit doth manifest verily

through Love to get that which is of substance.

(Golden Scripts, Chapter 109)

"Are you with it?"

EVER SINCE the days when Adam and Eve won one and lost one, people have never found the job of being parent easy.

A few years ago, it was popular to quote a certain letter from a parent to a son upbraiding the younger generation for its wildness, lack of respect, and assorted other shortcomings, then reveal that the letter had been written a couple of thousand years ago. It was supposed to prove that every generation has had its trouble with the one preceding and the one following, but it didn't mean anything in the long haul because they'd all come out right in the end. You don't hear that quoted so much today. Instead you hear about the Generation Gap as a growing gulf, which begins to appear unbridgeable.

Parents as a species can take quite a lot. They can endure defiance, disobedience, childish stupidity, wildness and many another lapse from sober and mature behavior, passing it off as wild oats that all youngsters, themselves included, have always sown.

What really distresses parents most in these perilous days is steel-eyed and uncompromising scorn. This is an adult emotion to which there is no adequate answer. Mark Twain's comment that he couldn't understand how his father got so much smarter in the first year Twain was away from home doesn't seem to have application today. A child goes to college for a year and comes back with the attitude at worst that his parents are driveling idiots. At best, he treats them with the good-humored tolerance accorded small children. "You just aren't with it Pop!" he'll say.

A parent already sore beset by problems his child knows little about (he thinks) concerning inflation, increase taxes and prices, bureaucracy, deteriorating labor relations, crime in the streets, fair employment practices, finds this Olympian view of the world frustrating. "I'm paying enough for that child's education," he storms. "I'd have given my eye teeth for his chances. And this is the thanks I get!

So the generation gap widens another quarter-inch.

Most parents are too close to their own problems to have that Olympian view. They are too tightly enmeshed in coping with the ever-increasing demands of the system ever to be able to stand off and ask, "Does it have to be this way?"

The college student, cut loose in the world of ideas, with everything to gain and nothing to lose, has had the opportunity to look at the whole business of Twentieth Century living objectively and he doesn't like what he sees. The father, in the thick of it, has his hands full just trying to keep afloat. The son, not yet committed to the battle, has in this generation been able to encompass a broader view, which causes him to reject the necessity of any such commitment.

Born in the shadow of the Bomb, his whole standard of values is affected by it. Born into a technological age of computers and systems engineering, of exploding population on a shrinking planet, he is without memory of the "stable" world in which his parents anchor their childhood.

Growing up in a highly mobile, uprooted, kaleidoscopic society, one child may come face to face with vital questions of race and poverty and injustice that never even touched his parent's lives, or else, if he is a part of that submerged and silent portion, he has suddenly perceived cracks in the suffocating upper crust that give him promise of light and air. Either way, things for both these young persons will never be the same again.

On top of all, they are not only expected but forced (at risk of dire penalty) to wage a war and risk their lives for the preservation of a set of values which from their unhampered view make no sense whatsoever.

Parents unfortunately are frequently moved to *demand* the respect needed to keep things manageable and in line. They forget that respect and love are never given on demand. They are commanded, by example, by *being*. The individual parent may behave in such way that he does command that respect and that love himself, but his leaders are letting him down in commanding that respect from the young for the society as a whole.

Witness insanity: Vice President Agnew in a recent speech saying, "It's the peaceniks in this country who cause the enemy to think our nation is divided."

Witness incitation to violence: Eric Holler, the highly touted citizen-philosopher, testifying before the Congressional committee investigating campus upset, hysterically shouting that "school administrators have been too soft. They should have shot those students who invaded their offices."

Witness hypocrisy: Mr. Justice Fortas, in the week prior to resigning from the Supreme Court, piously intoning, "How wrong they are, how wrong they are, these students who violate the law."

Witness an incredible inversion of priorities: A government spending two-thirds of its astronomical income on war-oriented activity while its total natural environment, its cities and its people are deteriorating at alarming speed out of sheer neglect.

Witness insanity: A government that loudly proclaims its devotion to peace and freedom throughout the world, while it secretly works at developing germs for biological warfare so powerful, so resistant to any form of control or extinction that they actually comprise a new form of Doomsday Weapon.

In their innermost hearts, conscientious parents know that the protests of the kids are fundamentally sound. The world has gotten into bad shape and needs much improvement. But parents, fearful of losing all control, plead, "You're right! We need to have change. But work within the system to improve it."

For all the irrelevant side issues beclouding the situation, this is the heart of the problem of the

Generation Gap. As long as the irresistible force of youth confronts the immovable object of the older generation, we shall have trouble. Somewhere, somehow, there is going to have to be understanding, mutual respect, and confidence established on *both sides* in order to reach a viable solution.

This is what we all will have to work at as if our lives depended on it, for in truth they do!

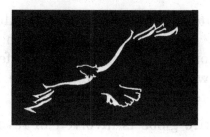

Vol. VII, No. 6, June 1969

Thus do I warn you, thus invite myself,

knowing your love awaitheth me.

(*Golden Scripts,* Chapter 113)

A Bridge to Tomorrow

SURVIVAL has become relevant. The survival of the human race is being threatened more and more seriously with every passing day.

We are, as every thinking person knows, surrounded by an intricate network of social evils and problems, no one of which (excepting only nuclear war) need damage us irretrievably but which together form a rising tide of destruction that will sooner or later overwhelm us if we do not somehow reverse the trend.

Bad as the situation is, however, it is not hopeless. The problems that most seriously threaten us, man himself has wrought. They can be unwrought. They can be unwrought by him, IF. If we understand the problems thoroughly, if we dig far enough down to fundamental causes, and if we can muster the will to undertake the constructive measures that will solve them.

We need a much longer perspective than we are using. We're like the Blind Men of Hindustan, bickering over what constitutes our elephantine difficulties. Each of us may have grasped a facet of truth, but we are inclined to stop there and upbraid our fellows for not seeing it our way. We are going to have to stand back much farther to get the whole picture.

While the entire globe is involved in revolution today, the United States is the real keystone in the arch to a better tomorrow. We have the opportunity to make it a good, sound bridge. If we as a society crumble, there will be no bridge at all, and for us, no tomorrows. Such is the awesome responsibility of holding the greatest reservoir of power on earth!

The United States is unique in the history of man. It is a magnificent, if inadvertent, experiment in human relationships. Made up of all races, all creeds, all cultures, all historical backgrounds, it forms the ideal arena to discover if such diverse collection of human beings as we are can develop a satisfactory working relationship among ourselves. If we can, there is no reason why the rest of the world cannot do the same.

That is why the trend toward polarization in this country is the gravest existing threat to survival. Even as among nations across the world, our own society is curdling into resentful, suspicious, hate-riddled segments, confronting each other eyeball to eyeball, ready to spring at each other's throats at the drop of anyone's hat.

As long as each segment is concerned only with the suppression of its opposite number, we shall never be able to make headway against the real causes of our serious problems. We shall never be able to grasp the constructive alternatives, which would make for the good life for each and every segment of the society.

382

The polarization which exists, and which continues to intensify, cannot be dissipated until every segment of our society, and this includes those who wield abnormal power, get their sights set on common goals that rise above prejudice, partisanship and privilege. Whatg must be faced is that there can be no survival for any segment of society, except in the framework of survival for all segments.

Even more assuredly, there cannot be a just, safe and meaningful life for anyone without a mutuality of goals that excludes no one from the abundant life that is now technologically possible.

There is no difficulty in engineering a socio-economic-political society in which the nation can utilize its resources and technology to build, to manufacture and to supply to a surfeit all material goods and services. Nor is there any problem in identifying the barriers existing in our current way of doing things that preclude the full utilization of our productive capacity for the benefit of all the people.

The problem is one of persuading people to make the transition from the old to the new. The national enigma is how to induce people to cross the bridge to a better tomorrow that already potentially is in existence.

Right now the nation is meandering aimlessly in the face of its dilemma. It is tired of its problems and wishes they would go away, but yet it refuses to root out the evils, which are really causing the problems. It deals with the victims of society without considering with any depth the underlying causes, which continually produce new victims. Of course, all such approaches of trying to put new wine in old bottles is due to the fact that the sovereign people have unwittingly left the well-being and the destiny of their nation to the politicians who are but fronts for the power structures.

The bridge to a better tomorrow cannot be crossed until a majority of the people themselves realistically envisions the constructive and good society that is within their reach.

Already a healthy sprinkling of men and women throughout the land do envision it. The need of the hour is that this small group of people with clear vision and dedicated purpose can erect the road signs on sufficient thoroughfares and crossroads so that the mass of Americans can be re-directed from the chasm toward which they are heading and instead be able to make their way up to the bridge.

There is only one sound Bridge, leading over the chasm of anarchy and destruction to that Better Tomorrow. It is one that is built on pillars of equality of human opportunity, of complete dispersal of power, and of the most efficient utilizing of our full productive capacity, all of which lead toward making possible the maximum expression of each and every human being's creative and altruistic energies!

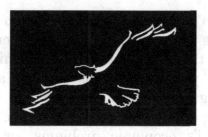

Vol. VII, No. 7 & 8, July & August 1969

I say unto men: Rise up and do honor unto yourselves,

who are gems of light in a diadem of immortality!

(*Golden Scripts,* Chapter 114)

Impact of Television

ONE OF THE most far-reaching developments of this age is television. It has served to lift people out of their provincialism and has humanized all problems. Through all electronic communications, the world has become one big family.

Marshall McLuhan, among others, has focused our attention on the fact that from the time of the caveman, when the whole family was involved, civilization has passed through a continuous development of specialization with less and less communication between groups. With the advent of electronic communication, particularly television, the world has again become one large "caveman society," although much more sophisticated.

Three wide ramifications of television are extremely important in considering social change.

The first we have alluded to in pointing out that the world has been brought into communication with all its parts. All the nations of the world are actors on the same stage. The same, of course, is even more evident respecting the components of our own society. Because of this fact, there is increasing recognition that all problems, all peoples, are inseparable and the well-being of any group, or any individual, is dependent on the well-being of the whole society. Thus, the solving of the individual's economic problems, or a particular group's economic problems, is directly dependent on the proper functioning of the whole economy.

The same is true in respect to crime and the burden of war. Safety of life itself cannot be assured for one, or any group, without its being assured for all members of the society. It has been primarily through television that the interdependence and interrelationship of all peoples have come to be recognized.

A second ramification identifies a perhaps even greater impact that television has had in influencing people's perspective respecting the major problems of the nation. For the first time, the human element has been brought into focus. Up to the time of the advent of television, people were dealt with primarily as statistics. Television added a new dimension. It transformed statistics into human beings.

In the past, one read in the newspaper or heard on the radio that there were so many tens of millions of poor people in the society who lived in substandard houses, didn't have proper food and adequate clothing, and who existed on the meagrest incomes. No one was emotionally moved by the plight of the poor simply because it was not only difficult to translate cold figures into human beings but also because it was easy to erase pure figures from one's mind and thereby shun any responsibility for being concerned about one's fellow humans.

Television altered our whole reaction. It not only translated statistics into human beings but so graphically registered the plight of the poor on our consciousness that their agonies became our agonies. Right into our living rooms were brought the families of the nation's ghettos and the Appalachias. We became witness to their despair, their heartache, the emptiness of their lives. The distended stomachs of little children and the drawn faces of mothers and fathers etched themselves indelibly on our minds.

And war? How easy it was to go along with wars when the suffering, the dead and dying, were only identified as statistics. Like the statistics on the poor, how easily we were able to take in stride that so many thousands had been wounded, so many hundreds had been killed on a certain day, and so many cities has been bombed. It was even easy to accept blindly that all such killing and destruction were for stopping some "monster" or for upholding "democracy" when only statistics were used to appraise the cost of battle.

It has been television that has made the people realize the inhumanity and hell of war. It has been television that has shown us that the young who bleed and die on the side of the "enemy" are no different than the young on our own side. Belatedly, far too late, we are awakening to the realization that even allowing for atrocities the real "monsters" of war are those forces on both sides that can play god and send the young of their nations to kill each other that political and economic advantage might accrue to the predatory few.

Television has humanized the major problems of the nation. However, it has an even greater role to play in the society. This is the third ramification of television, which has yet to come into its own.

This is in the fields of education and government itself. When its full potential is utilized, it will be recognized as one of the most encompassing instruments of our age!

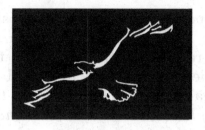

Vol. VII, No. 9, September 1969

I say, dry your tears and look upward into brilliance,

for the beacon hath been lighted; night is only in

earth's valleys!

(*Golden Scripts,* Chapter 117)

For Alternatives

THE chapter "Who Are 'We the People'?" from the book *Twilight of Self-Government"* by Thomas H. Uzzell is concluded in this issue. No subject is more pertinent and vital to a solving of our major problems than the thinking in this chapter. It is only in terms of the people, all the people, exercising absolute sovereignty that social reform can be achieved and it is only in terms of all the people exercising absolute sovereignty that social reform can be sustained.

If there is one inescapable fact it is that those who have usurped the inherent and constitutional power of the people will not on their own volition relinquish that power. They must be compelled to relinquish it. For it is the very nature of power-oriented structures, whether we are considering economic, financial, or political, to always increase their entrenchment in the society, and thus ever increase their dominance over the people.

Therefore, a people who have become slaves of such power groups have no other course in seeking their freedom, and restoration of their power, than to create a force sufficient in strength to exceed that of those wielding illegal power. The questions that arise are simply ones *of how to create that force and what should be the nature of that force.*

It should be apparent that in dealing with these two questions it is imperative that we unequivocally grasp, and make part of our constant thinking, that it is *We the People* who are the absolute arbiters of our lives and our destinies. Constitutions and the governments set up derive all power from the sovereign people. There is no change or reform that cannot be made by the sovereign people!

There are elements throughout our society who see change only in terms of disruption or revolution by force. It is passing no judgment on their reasons for rebellion to recognize that it is futile to believe that the power-structures can be physically unseated when those power-structures have at their command the FBI, the CIA, the Armed Forces, and the direction and control of the law enforcement agencies stretching the length and breadth of the land. While there is some validity in pleading that certain outbursts of rhetoric instill uneasiness in the sanctums of the powerful, such rhetoric at the same time causes polarization resulting in the alienation of many people who otherwise would be sympathetic.

The only force that can effect lasting change in this nation is an enlightened sovereign people who *organize* their demands *for specific alternatives.* An appreciation of what those alternatives should be necessitates first, of course, an understanding of the built-in flaws of our "system" that has resulted in the compounding problems that reflect the nation's dilemma. However, it is the alternatives that constitute the positive program to which the people are rallied.

The immediate need is to reach as many people as possible with the realization that a New Ordering in the affairs of their society is now possible if the sovereign people have the desire and will to bring about true freedom for all, including future generations. Without the conviction that *We the People* have the supreme power in our hands to solve all problems, there can be no steps taken to renovate the society.

Throughout society there is increased anxiety and despair as to the future of the nation. There seems to be no surcease to increasing taxes, increasing debt, increasing crime and all the foreboding threats to an environment that becomes more and more polluted. For the first time, threats to life itself are causing people to begin looking for solutions to the nightmare that day-to-day living has become.

The publication of **Challenge to Crisis** has already stirred much enthusiasm and interest in its presentation of the "Corporate Commonwealth" as the only natural and workable solution to the serious problems of the nation. For the first time, concerned people have come across an *alternative* to our current socio-economic structure which unleashes our full work potential and at the same time removes from society all the corrupting influences of power by making the people, every solitary individual, absolutely sovereign in directing, controlling and shaping their society.

391

Sufficient acquaintances with the Corporate Commonwealth idea will create its own demands for adoption.
There is no power that can equal the power of the
people when they are moved into concerted action.
When they can be *for* something that guarantees a
better life right here on earth!

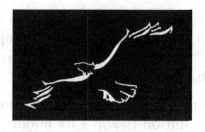

Vol. VII, No. 10, October 1969

What ever hath been said, hath been said in God's truth; ye do have goodly missions, each one of you in spirit.

(Golden Scripts, Chapter 118)

What We Seek

IN THESE TIMES of much distress and anxiety, of increasing insecurity by the threats to life posed by chemical, biological and nuclear weapons, of increasing pollution of water, land and air, and of increasing burdens by the whole spectrum of taxation, crime, indebtedness, and inflation, there isn't an American who is not seeking a more stable, secure and safe society, and world. It is only a question of not knowing the *what* and *how* of achieving them.

Ninety-nine percent of the difficulty at solving our problems is due to the fact that from the cradle to the grave, people have been conditioned to believe that the only economic system that is "American" and which is conducive to "freedom" and "liberty" is one in which the strong have the right to overpower the weak, and the cunning have license to outsmart the unwary and the innocent. Belatedly, clear-thinking people are recognizing that however our economic system is sugar-coated and overlaid with such beguiling slogans as "free enter-prise," "rugged individualism" and the "open market of competition," we have been operating actually according to the Law of the Jungle.

The first recognition that people must make is that the inability of the nation to solve its major problems, and eliminate the threats to life that exist, is that the work potential of the nation has become lodged in the hands of less than 200 monopolistic financial and industrial giants which have no motivation to improve the lot of human beings. This concentrate control of the nation's producing assets came about because the whole thrust of the economic system was simply for the ever-increasing power and profits of artificial entities. In short, we have blindly accepted a "system" that by its nature brutally excludes people from the work potential of the nation to the exact degree that it lodges that work potential in the hands of fewer and fewer conglomerates of power.

To assess the real dilemma of the nation is to recognize that a work potential, manpower, natural resources, productive machinery and technological know-how, exists which could solve every major problem that afflicts the people and their nation. The tragedy of our times is that all the while have so many *unmet needs,* at the same time we have *unused capability* that could easily fulfill all the requirements of a healthy and just society.

The whole idea of a Corporate Commonwealth is the unleashing of the nation's work potential to do the things that could and should be done. It is the setting up of a framework of producing and distributing goods and services in order that every solitary human being

394

is an actual participant in the economy instead of being excluded out of it. It is so conducting the business of the nation, through valid purchasing power in the hands of every person, that all the scourges of indebtedness, fictitious capital, confiscatory taxes and ruinous interest will be eliminated from the whole economic picture.

The idea of a Corporate Commonwealth is simply using a pattern of business that has been so successful for the few and making it successful for all. Instead of having *private* capitalism, or, for that matter *state* capitalism as in communistic and socialistic countries, we would have *public* capitalism. In short, it is incorporating the nation's entire productive capacity and making every newborn a common and preferred stockholder in the entire national productive plant.

Those who have read *Challenge to Crisis* can get the full impact of the fact the current owners and controllers of the nation's assets and patented technology are not valid owners. Such ownership and control came about because the whole economic-financial history of the nation has been the progressive deprivation of the people of their rightful equity and purchasing power.

The ironical development is that an unworkable "system" is grinding toward total disaster for both the profiteers and the victims. Adjustments are in everyone's interest!

Along with economic sovereignty must come political sovereignty of the people. The price the people have paid in waste of both resources and lives by turning over their absolute power to others has been far too costly to tolerate further. Concentrated political power encourages all forms of criminality and corruption.

There must be complete dispersal of power by restoring to the people absolute sovereignty in directing and controlling their government. This can only be achieved by the elimination of political machines, by the exercise of direct choice and recall of all office-holders, and by the final vote of the people on all major policy and legislation before it becomes the policy and law of the land.

To seek anything less than true economic and political sovereignty for all the people is to gamble with our very survival!